How to Do Everything
with Google Tools

About the Author

Donna L. Baker is a seasoned graphic designer who has been working on the Internet since the late 1980s. She taught software applications for several years both in a college and online, and has been a full-time author and writer since 2000. Donna has written numerous books on Web and graphic design.

Dozens of tutorials and tips Donna has written are available at Adobe Studios. She also contributes a monthly column to acrobatusers.com. Her web site is www.donnabaker.ca; her blog is www.acrofacts.donnabaker.ca. You can reach her by e-mail at donna.baker@gmail.com.

About the Technical Editor

Bill Bruns is a the Webmaster for the Student Center at Southern Illinois University Carbondale (www.siucstudentcenter.org) and also serves in a volunteer capacity as Chapter Advisor and Webmaster for the Beta Chi Chapter of Tau Kappa Epsilon (www.tkebx.org). For more than 10 years, he has been a technical editor, working on more than 125 books related to the Internet, web servers, HTML and Office applications. In the late 1980s, he first ventured into the hypertext world by creating "Grants in Graduate Study" (GIGS) in Gopherspace for New York University's Tisch School of the Arts. Bill holds bachelor's degrees in Telecommunications and English Literature from Indiana University, and a Master's of Public Administration from New York University. Bill, his wife Debbie, daughter Marlie, son Will, and two bearded dragons live on the edge of the Shawnee National Forest in Carbondale, Illinois. You can reach him at billbruns3@yahoo.com.

How to Do Everything with Google Tools

Donna L. Baker

New York   Chicago   San Francisco   Lisbon
London   Madrid   Mexico City   Milan   New Delhi
San Juan   Seoul   Singapore   Sydney   Toronto

The McGraw·Hill Companies

Library of Congress Cataloging-in-Publication Data

Baker, Donna L., 1955-
  How to do everything with Google tools / Donna L. Baker.
    p. cm.
  ISBN 978-0-07-149626-1 (alk. paper)
  1. Google. 2. Web search engines. I. Title.
TK5105.885.G66B35 2007
025.04—dc22

2007042222

How to Do Everything with Google Tools

2 3 4 5 6 7 8 9 0 CUS CUS 0 9 8

ISBN: 987-0-07-149626-1
MHID: 0-07-149626-2

Sponsoring Editor Megg Morin	**Copy Editor** Julie M. Smith	**Illustration** International Typesetting and Composition
Editorial Supervisor Jody McKenzie	**Proofreader** Nigel Peter O'Brien	**Art Director, Cover** Jeff Weeks
Project Manager Vasundhara Sawhney, International Typesetting and Composition	**Indexer** Broccoli Information Management	**Cover Illustration** Pattie Lee
Acquisitions Coordinator Carly Stapleton	**Production Supervisor** George Anderson	
Technical Editor Bill Bruns	**Composition** International Typesetting and Composition	

This book is dedicated to the millions
of people who have contributed to
the ever-changing world of the Internet.

Contents at a Glance

Contents

Acknowledgments

What fun this book has been to write! Although I am usually enthusiastic about the subjects of my books, Google Tools is one of the most interesting topics I have ever written about, if not one of the most frustrating. It's been interesting, because new features and tools are always being published, and frustrating for the same reason. By the time you read this page, I am sure there will have been several changes to some of the programs, other content has moved from Google Labs and beta products into mainstream tools, and even more products have been introduced.

I want to thank the terrific gang at McGraw-Hill for the opportunity to write this book. My thanks to Megg Morin, who has patiently answered a myriad of questions, laughed at my jokes, and sent me the most beautiful pale green orchids as I recovered from a leg injury. Thanks to Carly Stapleton for keeping track of what I was doing and handling the numbers so competently. Thanks to Bill Bruns for his insightful technical editing, not to mention testing the hundreds of tinyurl links.

Cheers to Google for producing these cool tools that gave this book its substance. It's an amazing organization with amazing products, and it's been terrific to explore the toolbox in such depth.

Thanks to my dear hubby Terry. He gets the long commutes, and I get to watch the wildlife and water from my office on the lakeshore. Thanks to all my girls—Deena and Erin, and my four-legged pals, Daisy and Abby. Finally, as always, thanks to Tom Waits, my ongoing inspiration and muse.

Introduction

Nearly twenty years ago I was introduced to a fascinating new technology that has now become part of our everyday activity. At the time, I thought it was extremely cool to log into a distant server and read stuff. At the time, that stuff came at a hefty price—Internet time was over $2.00 per hour, connection speeds were measured in bauds, and to read the cool stuff required differentiating the Unix code from the content and following lines of text written in yellow as they wrapped against a particularly ugly green background. But it was extremely cool.

The coolness is still there, although it has certainly changed. It has been a pleasure to participate and experience the changes, from the yellow/green to the black text on gray backgrounds in the first Netscape browsers, to using images. And now we have the ability to interact with full-featured web-based applications like Google Docs & Spreadsheets, or downloadable tools that connect with Google servers for further functionality, such as Picasa and Google Earth.

Google Tools

This book is about Google Tools. If you thought Google was just about searches, you are in for an interesting read. Google searches are fundamental to the company, and they do factor into most of their products in one form or another, but there's so much more to learn and explore. I think the folks at Google take much the same approach to problem-solving that I do: If I want to do x, what do I need to have in place? You'll find lots of answers to that question in both the full Google Tools products, as well as myriad others in varying stages of development at Google Labs.

It was difficult to decide what Google Tools to feature in the book, and which to mention in passing. Google Earth, for example, was described in a single chapter, while it could have filled half the book on its own. The approach to including or emphasizing a tool basically rested on whether or not the average small business person would find a practical use for the tool. Not many of us have a great need to explore Mars, and, although the program was featured in a large sidebar, it didn't have the practical use of Google Maps, for example. Maybe in the 2050 edition of the book!

About This Book

To bring important information to your attention, I've included short Notes, Tips, and Cautions throughout the book. Many of the Notes offer online locations where you can find more information about a topic. With a few exceptions, such as www.google.com, the URLs are constructed using tinyurl, a Firefox plug-in that produces a shortened URL pointing to the same page as the long and cryptic URLs that often identify online locations. Each URL is written as **http://tinyurl.com/** with a six-character suffix.

You'll find sidebars in each chapter that come in two variations. Some are How To sidebars, which explain an aspect of a Google feature or tool in depth. For example, "How to: Offer Links with the Link Field," in Chapter 14, describes adding additional code to your blog template for linking between postings in Blogger. Other sidebars answer the question "Did You Know?" by offering information about something associated with the subject at hand, but not required for you to have an understanding of a topic. For example, the Chapter 6 sidebar entitled, "Did You Know: You Can View Color Information on a Graph?" describes how you can graphically view color information from an image in Google's image program, Picasa. You don't need that information in order to edit the file, but the sidebar describes advanced information for those who like to explore the nuances of a program.

Finally, the Spotlight section in the center of this book profiles some of the Google Tools that the average business owner can access to construct and manage an online presence for their business. Hart of Glass custom glassworks is a fictitious business, but there's nothing fictitious about the capabilities of Google Tools to help in bringing your business online.

Enjoy!

Part I

Use Google to Search

How often do you hear someone say that they've "googled" for this term or that term? The term google, used as a verb, is now synonymous with online searching for information, and people now google for information all the time.

In this part, you'll look at the different aspects and elements of the Google Search site that have made the Google name an everyday word and the Google search engine the leader of the pack.

Chapter 1

Search with Google

How to...

- Perform a basic search
- Understand how Google searches for content
- Use search results
- Personalize and focus searches
- Use Google Toolbar for quick searches

As the Internet has evolved, so too has the ability to search for (and find) information on anything from people to products to images.
Google is the undisputed leader in search engines, and lets you find information in all kinds of ways, from general text-based searches to searches based on file type, such as .pdf or .doc files. In this chapter, you'll learn how to perform a search, improve the quality of your *query*, or search terms, and find specific types of content.

You'll see how extra features, such as a personalized search history and Google Toolbar, can add more to your searching accuracy.

Conduct Basic Text Searches

Starting a search is simple. Open the home page at www.google.com, type your search terms in the field, and click Search. In less than a second your results are shown in the browser window (Figure 1-1).

Decipher the Search Results

Of course you already know that clicking a link will open the page showing results. However, not all of us are aware of the different features and bits of information that are shown on the results page like the example in Figure 1-1.

A Checklist of Basic Page Components

Here's a rundown of the basic elements of a search page:

- **Links at the top of the page** These links identify the type of search you are conducting. The default is Web search, but you can also choose Images, Video, News, Maps, and other types of searches.

NOTE *Read about other types of searches later in this chapter and in Chapter 2.*

- **Queries** In the default mode, type in one or more terms, called a query, to use for conducting the search. The next section describes ways to improve the accuracy of your search.

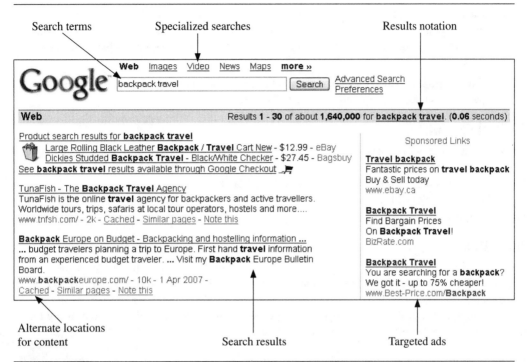

Search terms   Specialized searches   Results notation

Alternate locations
for content   Search results   Targeted ads

FIGURE 1-1 A simple search can produce millions of results.

■ **Summaries** The summary of your results are shown with a colored background at the top of the search results window. You see a list of your search terms, the number of results, and how long it took to conduct the search.

> *Each of your search terms is also a link. Click the link to rerun the search using that term alone. In the example, you could click either backpack or travel to search on that keyword alone.*

TIP

■ **Page Title** This is the name of the page, and is always the first line of the search result. You may see a URL instead of a title if the page doesn't include a title in its HTML code. Also, if a page hasn't been indexed by Google, it may not show the title.

■ **URL for result** This is shown below the text information about the page.

■ **Text for search result** The text below the title is a clip from the result page that contains your keywords. You see the terms in bold on the search result.

■ **Text size** The size of the text for the web page is shown after the site's URL to give you an idea of how long it takes to display the page. The size doesn't include images or other content such as Flash movies or video, which can increase the size dramatically.

- ■ **Cached page**   This is a link to the page as it was last indexed by Google. Once in a while you might find that you can't visit a website for some reason. If that happens when you are checking out search results, click Cached to see the information from the page as a static file.
- ■ **Similar pages**   Click these to extend your search automatically. Google locates similar pages with related information and lists them for you.

Multiple Results

Sometimes a search will generate a number of pages from the same website. If that happens, the most relevant result is listed first and the others are then listed as indented entries, as shown in Figure 1-2, which presents the results for a search for Star Trek.

    If there are many results, you may see a *More results from* link that leads to further results from the same page.

Note This

Some search results (such as the ones shown in Figure 1-1 or 1-2) display another link called *Note This*. This is a feature of Google Notebook, which is a plug-in for your browser that lets you capture bits of information from a web page (such as a URL or image), and saves them for future reference. The Note This link opens Google Notebook for you, in order to add a listing for the search result. Read more about Google Notebook in Chapter 8.

Extra Information at the Click of a Button

Sometimes you might search for information or a location that offers a map along with other search information, such as the map of the Pacific Design Center's location in Los Angeles. You can toggle this map open and closed by clicking the button at the upper left of the map image. Along with this small pop-up map, you are offered links to more mapping features.

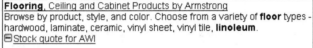

Star Trek
Currently featuring Enterprise, the latest in the **Star Trek** series. Includes news, interviews, cast biographies, episode guides.
www.**startrek**.com/ - 5k - Cached - Similar pages - Note this
    Enterprise - www.startrek.com/startrek/view/series/ENT/
    Star Trek - www.startrek.com/startrek/view/series/TOS/
    The Next Generation - www.startrek.com/startrek/view/series/TNG/
    Movies - www.startrek.com/startrek/view/series/MOV/
    More results from www.startrek.com »

FIGURE 1-2   Multiple results from the same site are listed by relevance.

NOTE   *Read more about using Google Maps in Chapter 3.*

Here's another example. As you can see in Figure 1-3, the act of searching for a flooring product produced a result from a company called Armstrong Flooring. Along with the usual information and link choices, the search return includes an option to check the company's stock.

Flooring, Ceiling and Cabinet Products by Armstrong
Browse by product, style, and color. Choose from a variety of **floor** types - hardwood, laminate, ceramic, vinyl sheet, vinyl tile, **linoleum**.
Stock quote for AWI

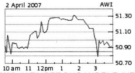

AWI (ARMSTRONG WORLD INDU)
50.90 +0.05 (0.10%) Apr 2 4:00pm ET

Open: 50.95	Volume: 379,400
High: 51.44	Avg Vol: 236,000
Low: 50.76	Mkt Cap: 2.75B

NYSE data delayed by 20 minutes - Disclaimer
Armstrong World Industries, Inc. (AWI) is a producer of flooring products and ceiling systems for use primarily in the construction and renovation of residential, commercial and institutional buildings. Through its United States operations, and United States and international ... More information about AWI »

www.armstrong.com/ - 19k - Cached - Similar pages - Note this
[More results from www.armstrong.com]

FIGURE 1-3   Extra information can include stock quotes.

Ways to Choose Laser-Sharp Search Terms

In Figure 1-1, you'll notice that the results are shown as over 1.6 million, which makes it difficult to find specific details about the subject. Google returns are based on the text terms you enter, called *keywords*.

Keep these tips in mind when creating keywords:

The Keyword Order Is Important   In Figure 1-1, the terms "backpack travel" produce results geared toward backpackers; if the results are switched, the terms "travel backpack" produce results about specific types of backpacks used for traveling. Of course, there is a great deal of overlap as many returns use both terms.

The Search Uses Stemming   Other forms of the word are included in the search using a process called *stemming*. In the example search, the keyword "floor" will also yield results for "flooring," as you see in Figure 1-3.

Specify Exact Terms Using Quotes   It's common to search for a person's name online. If you are looking for a specific name, or another phrase such as a business name, place quotes around the keywords. That way, Google knows to search for the entire phrase. For example, suppose you know a business is named "Something-or-other Backpack Travel". Decrease the number of returns by searching for "backpack travel" in quotes. In my experiment, using the term in quotes returned less than 100,000 results, many of which are companies that use the terms in the right sequence in their names.

TunaFish - The **Backpack Travel** Agency
TunaFish is the online travel agency for backpackers and active travellers.
Worldwide tours, trips, safaris at local tour operators, hostels and more....
www.tnfsh.com/ - 2k - Cached - Similar pages - Note this

The Backpack and Africa Travel Centre
The Backpack and Africa Travel Centre's web page-information for
Africa-you read about us in the Lonely Planet, now book your tours, ...
www.backpackers.co.za/ - 14k - Cached - Similar pages - Note this

Internet Bakpak Travel :: Australia :: **Backpack travel** in Australia
Backpack travel agency for budget travellers. Tours and transports
around Australia. Agence de voyages francophone pour voyageurs à
budget limité.
www.bakpaktravel.com/ - 14k - Cached - Similar pages - Note this

TIP   *If you can't remember how a word is capitalized, don't worry—Google doesn't pay attention to uppercase or lowercase spellings.*

Be Careful Using Multiple Keywords   Using more keywords can help zero in on your search, but may also be too specific and miss the actual content you are looking for. In the backpacker

FIGURE 1-4   Using multiple keywords doesn't necessarily mean precise results.

experiment, a string of terms such as those shown in Figure 1-4 doesn't necessarily show the scope of information in the results that might be expected. The reason? The search is too muddy—I've added too many terms and haven't necessarily organized them correctly.

Leave Out Words   Don't bother using words such as "and", "a", and "the". Google won't search for prepositions and common words due to their widespread popularity and use, which often slows down the search without improving the results. For example "The Backpacker Journal","A Backpacker Journal", and "My Backpacker Journal" will produce a search using the last two words only.

Use Simple Operators to Shape the Returns

The more information Google has about what you are searching for, the better the results are going to be. Sometimes, it's worth the time to both shave down what Google has to search for, and specify precisely what you need in order to receive better results.

> **NOTE**   *For in-depth information on operators and conducting an advanced search, see the section "Focusing a Web Search" later in the chapter.*

Use symbols, known as *operators,* to define what you want or don't want to see in your results. Here are several ways you can zero in on the exact information you need:

Use a Wildcard   If you aren't sure of a portion of a name, but you know it should be included in the search, use the *wildcard* operator (*). Taking an earlier example, looking for a business named "Something-or-other Backpack Travel," the search terms could be phrased as "* Backpack Travel".

Specify What You Don't Want to See   Suppose you want to find out about crystals used for chandeliers. You don't, however, want to view pages of results for eBay offerings and lighting sales sites. Tell Google what terms you do not want to see by prefacing them with a (−). Phrase the search as "chandelier crystals -eBay" to receive results like the example shown here. Be sure to leave a space before the (–) and follow it with the term for exclusion without a space.

Chandelier Parts, Swarovski Prisms, **Chandelier Crystals** ...
Fine **chandelier** parts and replacement **crystal chandelier** parts. We carry the greatest selection of **crystal** prisms, strass **crystal** parts, bulbs, **chandelier** ...
www.**chandelier**parts.com/ - 30k - Cached - Similar pages - Note this

Premium **Chandelier** Prisms
Premium **chandelier** parts and **crystal** prisms for the demanding consumer.
www.**chandelier**parts.com/index.
asp?PageAction=VIEWCATS&Category=23 - 79k -
Cached - Similar pages - Note this
[More results from www.chandelierparts.com]

ROBMAR's **Crystal Chandelier** Parts
Features an array of parts to repair or refurbish chandeliers like **crystals**, prisms, lamps, sockets, and finials.
www.crystal**chandelier**parts.com/index.htm - 6k -
Cached - Similar pages - Note this

TIP   *Phrase the terms in the query according to what you are looking for. As described earlier, the sequence of the terms makes a difference in results: "crystal chandelier" produces much different returns that "chandelier crystal".*

List What Must Be Included   You often want to see a specific term or word in your result. To help Google find the results you want, include (+) in the search. Using the same example, if you are in the chandelier design business, and looking for a wholesale source for your material, try "chandelier crystals -eBay +wholesale" to customize the terms. Be sure to include a space before the (+) term in the search string.

Did you know?

Google Handles Numbers in a Special Way

Google excludes single digits and letters from search queries, since they often slow down the search without improving the results. If your search string includes a number, use (+) before the number. For example, if you are looking for information about Rocky Balboa, searching for "Rocky" will result in many returns related to the movie, but also to mountaineering and bicycling. Typing **Rocky +3** narrows the results to sites and pages about the movie.

You can also enclose the name in quotes like "Rocky 3" to produce the same results.

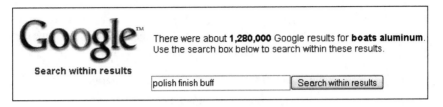

FIGURE 1-5   Use Search within results to focus an existing search.

Search Within Your Results

Once you have a completed a search, you have an option to zoom in further by searching within the results. You can only search within your results one time.

Follow these steps:

1. Type your search terms and click Search.

2. Scroll through your results page to check the quality of information you are likely to find.

3. At the bottom of the page, click Search within results.

4. In the Search within results window, type additional terms. You'll see that the number of results you are searching is also included on the page (Figure 1-5).

5. Click Search within results. In the next page, you'll see that all the terms specified in the original search, and the expanded search, are included in the results.

Web   Results 1 - **10** of about **40,700** for boats aluminum polish finish buff

See It Shine features the ultimate in auto, **boat** and motorcycle ...
Finish First **Polish**. **Aluminum Polish**. Towels & Applicators. Cycle **Polish**
... your towel and gently spread the **polish**...turn towel and lightly **buff**.
WOW! ...
www.seeitshine.com/order.htm - 101k - Cached - Similar pages - Note this

See It Shine features the ultimate in auto, **boat** and motorcycle ...
Lightly wipe the **finish** to spread the **polish** and safely remove bugs, dust
and road film. Turn towel and gently **buff** to a deep, long lasting shine. ...
www.seeitshine.com/whyaceit.htm - 39k -
Cached - Similar pages - Note this
[More results from www.seeitshine.com]

Caswell Inc. - How To **Buff** and **Polish**
Aluminum side covers, not subjected to great heat can be sprayed with
VHT Clear Lacquer. ... Then **buff** the area to **finish**. Bench Mandrel ...
www.caswellplating.com/**buffs**/buffman.htm - 71k -
Cached - Similar pages - Note this

Do You Feel Lucky?

If you are looking for basic information, don't know much about a topic, or are looking for a starting place, don't bother with a full-blown search and making the effort to search through pages of results. Instead, take your first step into a topic using this method:

1. Type the basic term in the search field. For example, type **Parthenon**.

2. Next, click the I'm Feeling Lucky button, as shown here.

3. Read the resulting page. Instead of being shown a list of results, Google opens the website with the most relevant results for your search, as shown in Figure 1-6.

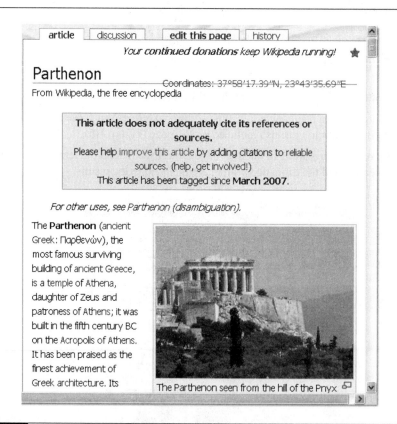

FIGURE 1-6   The website with the highest ranking is opened automatically.

 *To test the feature, type the same search terms and click Search. In the results page, the website that opened in response to I'm Feeling Lucky is listed as the first and most relevant listing.*

How Google Searches

Google searches for information using a specific process. A search follows four steps. The first step is a simple keyword search, as described in the previous section. Once Google has a collection of keyword matches, the results are processed in three additional steps:

1. Rank the page using its content
2. Determine the relevance of the content
3. Display the results in an order determined by using PageRank, a Google technology

Rank a Page Based on Its Content

Google uses web crawlers or search bots to review and index pages for future reference. If you look at the code in a web page you'll find information stored in the `<head>` tag on the page that includes keywords and descriptions written for the page, like the example shown here.

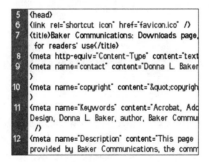

These lines of code containing name/value pairs for information the web page author would like to associate with the page are called *metatags*. The most common metatags that search bots look for are `<keywords>` and `<description>`. As in this example, you see there are also `<contact>` and `<copyright>` metatags.

How Relevant Is the Content?

Google doesn't take the existence of a string of metatags at face value. Although the tags and values are listed in the code, it's more important to determine where and if the keywords are included in the headings on the page, including the `<title>`, `<h1>`, and `<h2>` headings.

Finally, the URL of the page itself is used to define the value of the keyword. A site named www.antiquerosesbysarah.com probably contains more relevant results for a search on the keywords "antique roses" than a page showing a collection of tableware named "Antique Rose" on a site named www.finechina.com.

Set the Order Using PageRank

Google has patented an algorithm for measuring page importance. The PageRank algorithm analyzes the quality and quantity of links that point to a page using a scale from 0 to 10, where 10 is the most relevant.

The PageRank value is based on the number of links that point to a particular page, and considers the PageRank of the linking pages. It is complex, but basically breaks down like this:

- My site is www.dbrosefarm.com, where I grow and sell roses. I have 100 sites that link to my site.
- My competitor has only 30 sites linked to her site at www.antiquerosesbysarah.com.

You may think on the surface that my site is more relevant, but that's not necessarily the case. If 95 of the links to my site lead to link farms, and Sarah's site has 30 sites from real horticultural societies and organizations linked to her site, it's a fair assumption that her information is far more relevant than mine.

How to ...   View a Page's Ranking

If you have Google Toolbar installed you can check a website's PageRank visually. In the example, the PageRank for a help page for the Google Toolbar is shown. As you see, its PageRank is about 4. The PageRank also includes a drop-down menu from which you can choose to view a cached version of the page, similar pages, or track back in your links.

Read about installing and using Google Toolbar in the section "Look to Google Toolbar for Faster Searches" later in the chapter.

Personalize Your Search

Using the default settings for any program, whether on your desktop or online, is fine when you are starting out. However, as your skill and experience develops, you often want to tweak settings here and there to make the program work better for you. Google Search offers a range of preferences and language options you can choose to customize the search experience.

Specify Preferences to Speed Up Searches

To get started, click Preferences located to the right of the search term field on the main Google page (shown in Figure 1-1).

The Google Preferences page contains settings applied globally to all your Google services, as well as those specific to searching. Global preferences include specifying an Interface Language and a Search Language.

By default, the interface is displayed in English, and the Search Language selects "Search for pages written in any language". If you prefer, you can choose a specific language ranging from Arabic to Turkish.

> **TIP** *As you'll discover in the next section, you can translate a page in another language into your language, great for hunting for specialty items like Lamborghinis or high-end home furnishings!*

There are three settings on the window that you can use to speed up your searching (Figure 1-7). Look for these features:

SafeSearch Filtering   Google offers three levels of filtering for explicit sexual content. Choose from strict filtering, which filters out both images and text; moderate filtering, which filters out images (the default), or removing the filters altogether.

SafeSearch Filtering	Google's SafeSearch blocks web pages containing explicit sexual content from appearing in search results. ○ Use strict filtering (Filter both explicit text and explicit images) ◉ Use moderate filtering (Filter explicit images only - default behavior) ○ Do not filter my search results.
Number of Results	Google's default (10 results) provides the fastest results. Display 50 ▾ results per page.
Results Window	☑ Open search results in a new browser window.
Save your preferences when finished and **return to search**.	[Save Preferences]

FIGURE 1-7   Adjust preferences for quicker searches.

Some seemingly innocuous search terms can yield a raft of unnecessary (and unsavory) results. If you remove filters, don't be surprised if searching for a recipe for "hot cross buns" produces dozens or hundreds of unexpected results.

Numbers of Results One page of results shows ten returns by default. Click the Display drop-down arrow and choose another value from 20 to 100 if you routinely check out several pages of results. Choosing a lower number of returns does display the page quicker, but the time it takes to click Next to view the subsequent page of results and reorient your view likely decreases the importance of the faster loading.

Viewing Results Some people like to have several browser windows or tabs open at once, while others find it confusing or overwhelming. If you want to see the page you started from as well as the results, select the "Open search results in a new browser window" check box. The next time you search, the search is shown in one tab, and a selected site in another like you see here.

Once you have made your choices, click Save Preferences; click OK to close the information dialog that specifies that your preferences have been saved, and then return to the Google Search home page.

In order to save preferences, you must have cookies enabled in your browser. Refer to Chapter 8 for information on finding cookie settings.

Work with Multiple Languages for Fuller Results

Many non-English sites around the world that attract an international audience offer choices of language, like the example shown in Figure 1-8.

You are likely to find many more sites without page translations than those with translations. Google offers ways to tap into the concept of a global community and marketplace using the Google Language Tools.

FIGURE 1-8   Some international sites offer multiple versions of their content.

Click Language Tools to the right of the search terms field to display the Google Language Tools page. On this page you can specify particular types of searches, translate content, or view Google in other languages or via your home country's domain.

Search in Specific Locations or Languages

Here's an example search for European wood stoves. Whether you are looking for a company that sells a product in your country, are interested in serving as a distributor, or are yourself a wood stove manufacturer looking for inspiration, try searching in other languages. It's not as overwhelming as it seem.

Follow these steps:

1.   In the Google Language Tools window, click the Search pages written in drop-down arrow and choose an option, such as Danish.

2.   Click the Search pages located in drop-down arrow and choose Denmark.

3.   Type the search terms in the Search for field; as you see in Figure 1-9, the terms include "wood stove manufacturer."

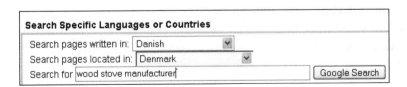

FIGURE 1-9   Search in other countries and other languages for insider info.

4. Click Google Search. The results are shown in a standard Google Search window. As you see here, there is an option to Search Danish pages shown at the top in the search area. Also note that the text from the page is shown in English.

5. Scroll through the list to a likely result and click to view the website.

You see the listings in the search returns page are prefaced by [PDF] as the listed return is a PDF file. Read about using PDF files in Chapter 2.

Translate Content Into Your Language

As mentioned, you might not be fortunate enough to find a site that offers translation in your preferred language. Google offers two companion tools that let you translate a block of text or an entire web page.

Not only can you find information from the source, but occasionally the translations are amusingly incorrect, great for those late-night work sessions.

Translate a Block of Text Copy the text you want to translate and paste it into the Translate text box on the Language Tools page. Click the drop-down arrow and choose a translation mode.

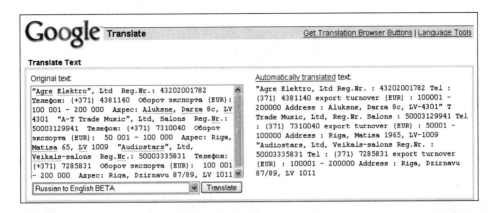

Quickly translate text from one language into another.

Some of the translation tools are final products, such as French to English, while others are still beta tools, such as Russian to English. Click Translate. The text translation is placed to the right of the original text as you see in Figure 1-10.

NOTE   *Click the Automatically translated link to open the translation FAQ at Google.*

Translate an Entire Web Page   Rather than pasting selected text, translate an entire web page at the click of a button. Type the URL for the page into the Translate a web page field, choose the desired language conversion from the drop-down list, and click Translate. The page opens in a browser window with a notation at the top stating the page is a translation. If you move your mouse over translated content, you see the original in a pop-up balloon as you see here.

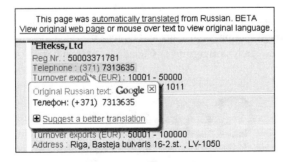

Add a Bookmark   If you regularly need some quick translations, check out the Translation Bar Buttons. Click Get Translation Browser Buttons, shown in Figure 1-10, to open a list of the available translation services. Drag the translation button of your choice to the top of the browser window and drop it on the toolbar area.

FIGURE 1-11   Choose from many languages, including Klingon.

Reset the Google Interface

If you want to use Google in another language, you can specify the settings in the preferences, as discussed earlier in the chapter. If you want to quickly search in another language, select a language from Afrikaans to Zulu from the list on the Language Tools page. There are even languages that aren't spoken in many earthly locations, such as the example shown in Figure 1-11.

NOTE   *Fortunately, not all the content on the Language Tools page is converted to the selected language so you can find your way back from your language experiments.*

Use Google on Your Home Domain

Google search results are listed according to the pattern described in the section "How Google searches." Those not living in the US often have to search within the results to find listings pertaining to their laws, cultures, or shopping restrictions.

Save one step in your search by using Google for your home domain. On the Language Tools window, scroll down to the list of national flags and choose the desired language. If you choose some country's home pages, such as Belgium or Canada, as shown here, you'll also have to select a language.

Focusing a Web Search

Regardless of the type of content you are searching for, there are ways you can focus the search beyond the keyword tailoring described at the beginning of the chapter. For example, most types of searching offer advanced search features. Whether working in an advanced search or a regular search window, use different terms to tell Google how to structure its search and your results.

Configure an Advanced Search

There are more ways to tailor a search using the Advanced Search settings. Click Advanced Search to the right of the search terms field on the main search page to open the window shown in Figure 1-14.

There are three collections of settings, including advanced options, as well as Page-Specific and Topic-Specific searches.

> NOTE   *There are also ways to search for specific topics and subdomains for Google products, such as images and Froogle. Check out how that's done in Chapter 2.*

As you see in Figure 1-12, there are many different options for shaping the search terms. You don't have to use all of them, of course. The example search is a quest for an oriental chest called

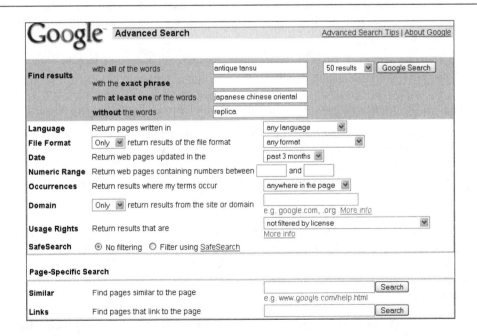

FIGURE 1-12   Configure a search precisely using Advanced Search features.

a *tansu*, which must be an antique. The two required terms are shown in the first field as "antique tansu":

- Rather than scrolling through multiple pages of results, the results field is reset to 50 results, by choosing the number from the drop-down list.

- There is no exact phrase required, so the field is left blank.

- At least one of the words, either "japanese", "chinese", should be included; the antiques originate in Japan, but there are similar Chinese antique wedding chests that I might like, too. The web page author may not know the country of origin, and there may be other appropriate items that originate in India or Northern Africa, so "oriental" is included.

- I'm looking for an antique, so I don't want to see the word "replica" in the results.

- The page can be written in any language as I don't know where the current owner of a piece resides.

- The date is specified as within the past 3 months by choosing the option from the Return web pages updated in the field's drop-down list. Other choices include anytime, with the past 6 months, and within the past year. It's likely easier to find a piece that is still for sale by searching for more recent pages.

- There are no numeric terms required for the search.

- The terms can occur anywhere in the page. If you are looking for a specific element, click the Occurrences drop-down arrow and choose an option such as the title, text, URL, or links to the page.

- If I know the specific domain I want to search, its URL can be entered into the Domain field, such as .net, .org, .biz, .ca, and so on.

- If I know a specific location where I don't want to search, such as eBay, I could select Don't from the Domain drop-down list and type the URL, such as www.ebay.com.

- I don't have to worry about licensing so the Usage Rights don't have to be included; nor am I worried about adult content so the SafeSearch filter isn't required.

NOTE *Read about usage rights, domain searches, and page-specific searches later in this section.*

Once the terms are set, click Google Search to start searching. The returned page is shown in Figure 1-13, and contains several bits of information you won't see in a general search.

In Figure 1-13, you see the selections made in the Advanced Settings window have been carried over into the results page. The specified search terms are highlighted, as in a basic search. You see that:

- The results are shown as Personalized Results in the returns information line above the search results.

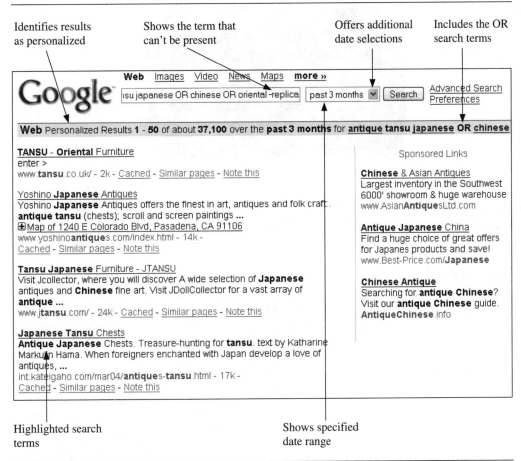

Identifies results as personalized

Shows the term that can't be present

Offers additional date selections

Includes the OR search terms

Highlighted search terms

Shows specified date range

FIGURE 1-13   An advanced search shows additional information on the results page.

- The choices typed in the Find results with at least one of the words box are listed in the search field using the operator "OR".

- The date options are included in the Search results window.

TIP   *If you don't have as many results as you hoped, click the Date drop-down arrow and choose a longer date range.*

Using these parameters, the results are exactly what I am looking for. For example, clicking the first result on the page opens the website shown here. As you can see, it includes all of the search terms (and some very beautiful antiques).

Apply More Advanced Search Features

Not all of the advanced search options are included in the example used in the chapter. Google offers a few more features you can use for building custom searches.

Choose a File Format

You don't have to view results in all file formats. For example, imagine you are looking for a manual for your camera. You can't remember where you found it, but you know it is a PDF file—and that you didn't save a copy. Choose Only from the first File Format drop-down arrow and then the PDF format from the list shown here.

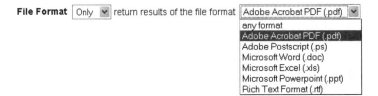

The results only include PDF files, making it much easier to find your file (Figure 1-14). Notice in the search terms at the top of the Google Search home page; the advanced term is written as "filetype:pdf".

TIP   *You can also search for PS, DOC, XLS, PPT, and RTF file formats.*

Select a Usage Type

You can't use everything you find online. The Usage Rights option lets you find content that has been published—whether music, books, movies, images, or educational material— and that you can share or use.

If you want to search for content that you can reproduce in a newsletter, for example, choose an option that allows you to distribute the content. As you see here, there are five different

FIGURE 1-14   Restrict results to a specific file format.

formats, ranging from unfiltered, which is the Google default, to "free to use, share or modify, even commercially" if your newsletter is sold to subscribers.

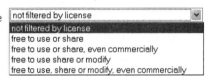

Type Operators in the Search Window

The search parameters that you select in the Advanced Search window can be typed directly into the Google Search field, if you remember the operators.

Include Character Operators in the Search Field

The list of operators described throughout the chapter, as well as others you can also use, are listed here along with examples:

Operator	Results
Include	Type (+) before the term to include in results
Exclude	Type (−) before the term to exclude from results
OR	Type OR in caps between each term in a list, such as *dolphin OR porpoise*
Synonym	Type (~) before the term to find the word and synonyms, such as *patio ~lantern* to return results including lantern, torch, and lights
Separator	Type two terms that you want to be separated by at least one word and include (*) such as *coral * polyp* to find results such as coral button polyp
Numrange	Use the format [#]…[#] to specify values to include in your search results such as *plexiglas sheet $30...50* to find results where sheets of plexiglas ranging in price from $30 to $50 are included in the results

FIGURE 1-15 Start a search by requesting information pertaining to a site.

Specify Text Operators in the Search Field

Some of the Advanced Settings options display text on the search field, such as the previous example showing the filetype:PDF search operator. The operators described in previous sections, as well as other text operators include:

Advanced Operator	Example	Results
date:	date:6	Results are from pages dated within the previous six months
filetype:	filetype:xls	Results are in Microsoft Excel format
info:	info:www.newyork.com	Returns results listing the site and offers options for more information as shown in Figure 1-15
link:	link:www.nasa.gov	Returns pages that link to the NASA site—about 155,000 pages
related:	related:concrete forms	Returns results for stabilizing forms, release agents, and the like
safesearch:	safesearch:hot cross buns	Returns recipes for delicious baked goods and children's nursery rhymes without adult site content
site:	site:www.donnabaker.ca	Returns results from the specified website

Google Can Calculate for You

You don't have to resort to your system calculator or a pen and paper to perform calculations, or other mathematical processes in Google. Instead, type the formula into the search field and click Google Search to use the Google Calculator. The calculation results are shown on the search returns page, as well as a link to search for documents containing the character string.

Arithmetic   Use traditional symbols for performing arithmetic calculations, such as (+), (−), (*), and (/) for addition, subtraction, multiplication, and division respectively. Query a percentage by typing 30% of 425 for example; or define an exponential power by typing 10^3 (10 cubed) for example. By the way, the percentage value is 127.5, and 10^3 is 1000.

Currency Exchange   Using numbers isn't limited to calculations. Instead of hunting down currency exchange programs, simply type the values in the search field as shown in Figure 1-16.

 *Click the link to read about using the currency converter. The rate is general, fine for calculating the cost of purchasing a product in Euros, but not designed for managing your dollar trading account.*

Convert Measurements   Some of the world works in metric, while the rest works in Imperial systems. You can use Google to discover whether a storage cabinet is the right size for your office by entering the conversion values as a search term, like the example shown here.

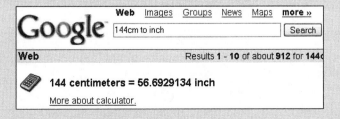

FIGURE 1-16   Calculate currency exchanges in the search window.

Use Google Personalized Search to Store Your Searches

Your browser stores history information, but it is limited in scope and only lists sites you have visited by name for a short period of time. Google offers a service called Search History that keeps track of what you have looked for in the past, lets you bookmark previous searches, and even lets you search your searches!

NOTE   *Find out more about using search histories, such as searching bookmarks, at http://tinyurl.com/22zu4k.*

To use Google Search History, follow these steps:

1. From the Google home page, Click Search History at the top of the browser window to display the Search History login window.

2. Type your password to sign into the Search History with your Google Account. As you see here, you can also select to have the service automatically started on your computer.

3. The Search History opens in a browser window. You see a number of different search types listed at the left of the window, and search locations (Figure 1-17). Toggle search types on or off to condense the page results if you like.

4. To find a particular month's or date's search history click the links on the Search Activity calendar at the right of the window, shown here. The date currently displayed is shown in bold text ("6" in the example). Pause the mouse over a date to display the number of searches conducted on that date.

Here are some features and search options to explore:

Manage Your Search Contents   Click Pause in the column at the left of the window to stop the service from collecting your search history; you have to click Resume to restore the history. Specify sources, such as Sponsored Links or Video to stop by clicking Settings, choose a source and click Remove Items to delete all reference to that source, and click Save Settings. If you want to remove content from the history altogether, click Remove Items to open another view of your search history. Select searches or sites and click Remove to delete them from the history.

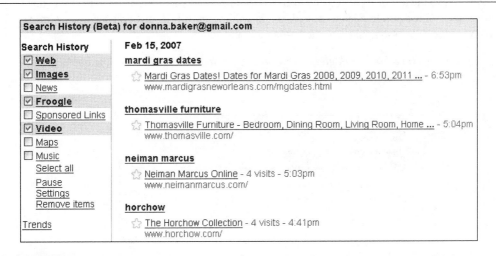

FIGURE 1-17   Find details of past searches in the Search History.

Track Your Trends   You can watch your search activities over time by tracking trends. Click Trends at the left of the Search History window to display your top 10 queries, sites, and clicks displayed by different time frames. Choose from the past 7 days, last 30 days, last year, or from all time. Scroll down the page to show a chart of your activities shown by month, daily as seen here, or hourly.

Interesting Items   Click Interesting Items in the left column of the web page to show generic items that relate to your searches. You see lists of top queries that correlate with your searches as well as a list of pages that correlate with your searches. If you have included other types of content such as video, there are a few videos displayed that match your interests.

Bookmark Listings for Future Reference   What a nifty feature! When you come across a site that is something you're likely to return to in the future, take a few seconds and make it a bookmark. Click the star to the left of the listed site to flag it as a bookmark and add Bookmark Edit and Remove links. Click Edit to open text fields as shown in Figure 1-18 that you use to customize the name of the link, assign labels to the bookmark, and add notes.

NOTE   *You can add a bookmark gadget to your custom home page that lists the bookmarked search items. Check out gadgets in Chapter 8.*

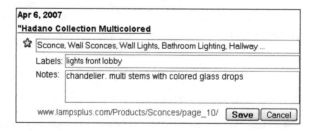

FIGURE 1-18   Assign labels and customize the text for bookmarked items.

Look to Google Toolbar for Faster Searches

Whether your browser of choice is Firefox or Internet Explorer, there's a Google Toolbar plug-in that offers ways to search, communicate, and manage your search efforts. There are many, many features of the toolbar that aren't covered in this book, be sure to check out the toolbar's options and the links below to learn more.

Download Options for Different Browsers

To start, open the Toolbar site at toolbar.google.com. There are download pages for different Toolbar products, including:

- Google Toolbar for Firefox 1.5 and newer at http://tinyurl.com/yuwued
- Google Toolbar for Internet Explorer 7 at http://tinyurl.com/23fnzb
- Google Toolbar for Enterprise (beta) from http://tinyurl.com/saslt

TIP   *You can also find links to Google Toolbar for older versions of Windows from this page.*

Click the download button on the page to have the toolbar automatically download and then follow the prompts during the installation. Once the installation is done, you will see a notification in the browser window, and the toolbar is added to your browser window (Figure 1-19).

NOTE   *There are slight variations between the Internet Explorer and Firefox versions of the toolbar. For example, on IE's toolbar, click Go to initiate a search; on the Firefox toolbar, click Search.*

What's on the Toolbar and Why You Want It

You may think you don't need any of the tools on the Google Toolbar, and of course you can manage without it. But it's interesting that as you learn to use it you are likely to use it more and

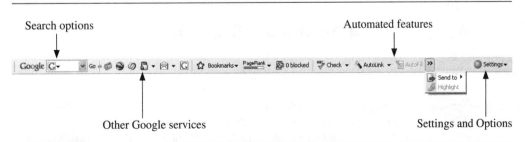

Search options   Automated features

Other Google services   Settings and Options

FIGURE 1-19   Google Toolbar offers many search and browser features.

more, often to the exclusion of more traditional (and lengthy) ways of handling searches and interacting with web pages.

Quicker searches with Google Toolbar

First and foremost, the Google Toolbar offers a shortcut for searching. Drag the vertical bar to the right of the Google label to increase or decrease the width of the search text field. As you type your search terms, a drop-down list opens from the toolbar showing your search history and bookmark listings for the search terms as well as popular Google search suggestions as you see here. The suggested content changes as you continue typing your query. Click Go (IE) or Search (Firefox) to start the search.

Click the Google icon in the search text field to open a list of options for searching Google sites, the current site you are viewing, or those using custom search buttons.

Easy Access to Other Programs and Links

You'll find a number of buttons that automatically display other Google products, such as Gmail or Desktop. Click the Button Gallery drop-down arrow to open a long list of additional programs

How to ...   Use a Shortcut to Open Sites

Part of the Google Toolbar is a feature called Address Bar Browse by Name. If you don't need any prompts for typing search terms as in the toolbar's search area, simply type the site name in the browser bar. You don't need to worry about any of the protocol notations such as www or http. If Google can't find a site with the name you typed, the text is used as search terms and results are shown in a browser window.

you can add to the toolbar, shown here. If you want to remove content, click Manage at the bottom of the menu to open a dialog box that lets you organize your toolbar items.

NOTE *If you use the IE version of the Google Toolbar you also have a control for blocking pop-up ads. Also, a Search Settings Notifier lets you know that the default search values are set to Google. If spyware and other malicious software tries to change default search settings to other sites, this feature displays a notification.*

Automate Actions to Help Find and Distribute Content

One group of tools on the toolbar are used for managing both what you find on a page, and what you do with the page's content. The features are shown in the Firefox toolbar segment (Figure 1-20) and include the following:

Tool	How It's Used
AutoLink	If you find a US location cited in a page and want to know how to get there, click AutoLink to create a link on an online map. AutoLink also works to link package tracking numbers to delivery status, VIN numbers (US) to vehicle history, and ISBN numbers for books to Amazon.com listings
AutoFill	AutoFill completes common Web form fields with a single click. Specify the information to use in the Toolbar Options dialog box (next section).

Send to	Click Send To and choose from Gmail, Blogger, or SMS (from within the US only). The entire page is sent, unless you select a portion of the page before choosing the command. Sending messages from the Google Toolbar is free, but your cell phone system may have fees.
Highlight	Click the Highlight button to automatically identify each instance of a search term in a page
Search terms	Terms from the latest search are shown on the toolbar. Click a term to display search results

Configuring the Toolbar

There are many ways in which you can make the Google Toolbar your own. For example, you can add and remove content, create your own buttons, or choose a different display format.

To display the options and settings, click the Settings button at the far right of the toolbar and choose Options to open the four-tab Google Toolbar Options dialog box.

TIP *If you are signed into your Google Account, the button is green. If it is grayed out, you have to sign into your account to proceed.*

Check out the features you can add to your toolbar in the dialog box. When you have made your choices, click OK to close the dialog box and modify the toolbar. At any time you can click Restore Defaults to return the layout to the toolbar default settings.

Add and Remove Features The Features tab of the dialog box lists some of the main features on the toolbar, ranging from the Search Box to AutoFill. Each offers a link to more information on the feature, as well as a button that opens a settings dialog box for a specific tool, such as the Search Box Settings. Choose which features to include by selecting or deselecting the features' checkboxes.

FIGURE 1-20 Automate your actions from filling in form fields to searching for terms.

Decide Which Buttons to Work With   On the Buttons tab of the dialog box, select and deselect items that you want to show on the toolbar from the options listed in two categories. You can reorder the locations of the Custom buttons on the toolbar by selecting a button and clicking Move Up or Move Down at the right of the dialog box seen here.

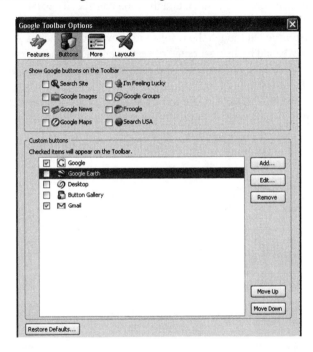

Find Even More Buttons   Some people never have enough buttons! If you are one of them, check the More tab of the dialog box for additional features. Some of the default items such as Send To and Highlight search terms are on this tab of the dialog box.

Configure the Toolbar Layout   Choose one of three common displays for the toolbars on this tab of the dialog box. You can use the default which adds a toolbar to the browser interface. Alternatively, you can replace the search box on the browser with the Google Toolbar search box, or replace the search box with the Google Toolbar search box and hide the other buttons.

NOTE
For the diehard tweaker, click Learn how to make your own custom layout to open a web page explaining the ins and outs of toolbar design. The page is located at http://tinyurl.com/3xgah6.

Summary

This chapter introduced you to the world of Google searches. As you discovered, there is far more to searching than typing a few words and clicking a button. You saw that the order and number of search terms influences the results, and that you can specify what is included or excluded from the results. You learned that Google uses an extremely sophisticated method for deciding what to display, even though the results are shown very quickly. A search can be personalized in many ways, and by using a range of text or character operators you can pinpoint the results even further. For added convenience and access to many tools, add the Google Toolbar to your browser.

In the next chapter, see how to use Google to find specific types of information, such as video and online groups.

Chapter 2

Dig into Power Searches

How to...

- Find images and entertainment files
- Look for groups and online communities
- Access a range of different search types
- Search for scholarly journals and other professional sources
- Shop online using Google Product Search

Remember the set of links for items such as Images and Groups that you found above the search term field on the Google home page? This chapter is about those different types of searches and the realms in which to search.

Search for Images and Entertainment

The Internet—and the world it describes—is a big place. That means there are many ways and forms that you can use to hunt for information. Fortunately, Google offers an array of different types of specialty searches. On the Google home page, you see a number of links for search types; click "more" to show a list of the services you can use (Figure 2-1).

Hunt for Pictures

Images are one of the most common search objects. To help find images, Google offers three ways to search:

- As an accessory to basic web searches
- From the Google Image Search page
- Via advanced settings

Specify a category to search from one of the lists.

Track Down Images from a Regular Text Search

Sometimes, you'll see a page of search results that include some images at the top of the page. There's no mystery: if your search is specific— Google displays the best matches, including those that are visual, as in this example.

> **TIP** *Narrow down the search by including picture or image in the search terms.*

Start from the Image Search Window

Rather than assuming you might find images in a site by searching for the terms, click Images above the search term field on the Google home page to open the Google Images Search window. Type your search terms, and click Search Images to display the results in an array of thumbnails (Figure 2-2).

The images are shown at all sizes by default. If you are looking for a specific size of image, click the Showing drop-down arrow and choose from Small, Medium, or Large images. In Figure 2-2, only the medium-sized images returned as image results for my search terms "presentation folders" are shown.

> **TIP** *There is no advantage to sorting the images by size in the example—it's simply to illustrate the size options.*

If you decide you'd rather find information textually, click "View all web results for presentation folders" to display the regular Google Search results window. On the other hand, if you decided to search visually for presentation folders to get ideas for a work assignment, scroll through the thumbnails and click an image that catches your eye.

You see the image open in another window containing two frames. The thumbnail and details about the image are shown in the upper frame. The source page containing the image is shown in the lower frame.

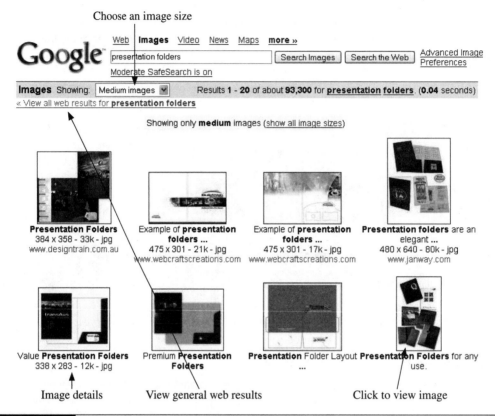

Choose an image size

Image details   View general web results   Click to view image

FIGURE 2-2 Display and choose images from the results page.

From the returns page, you can

■ Click Image Results to backtrack to the search results page.

■ Click the URL for the page shown in the top frame to open the page containing the image.

■ Click Remove Frame at the upper right of the window to display the website containing the image.

Set Custom Image Search Options

Suppose you are looking for inspiration for a logo for your new company, GreenSpace Realty. Use the advanced search features to source specific types or formats of images that will tweak your imagination.

Follow these steps:

1. Click Images on the Google Search home page to specify that images are to be searched.

2. Type the terms in the search field, "green space" in the example, and click Advanced Image Search to open the Advanced Search Settings window.

TIP
You can type the search terms either in the Google Search or the Advanced Search Settings window's field.

3. Specify the terms for the search in the appropriate fields as seen here.

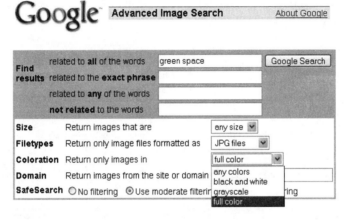

4. Choose a file format from the Filetypes drop-down list. You can select GIF, JPG, or PNG files.

5. Select the color required in the image. Leave the default any colors, or choose grayscale, black and white, or full color.

6. Click Google Search to perform the search.

NOTE
Read about using other advanced settings in the "Focus a Web Search" section in Chapter 1.

Search for Moving Pictures

Bandwidth improvements in the last couple of years have made uploading and downloading video a practical activity. To help you source video of all types, Google offers Video Search.

Although it is still a beta product, Video Search offers a wide range of features and opportunities for you to share and view video in a range of categories and genres from all over the world.

NOTE   *Google Video has policies for U.S. and non-U.S. copyright complaints under the Digital Millennium Copyright Act. Content appearing on Google Video is subject to the act, and processes for writing and filing complaints of copyright infringement are available at www.google.com/video_dmca.html.*

Start from the Home Page

Like other Google services, you need a Google Account to access Google Video. Log into your account and open the Google home page. Click Video from the links above the search term field to display the Google Video beta window (Figure 2-3).

The Google Video home page is the hub of the program. From this interface, you can search for video in a number of formats or genres, scroll through multiple categories of thumbnails, access blogs and top 10 lists, or upload your own video.

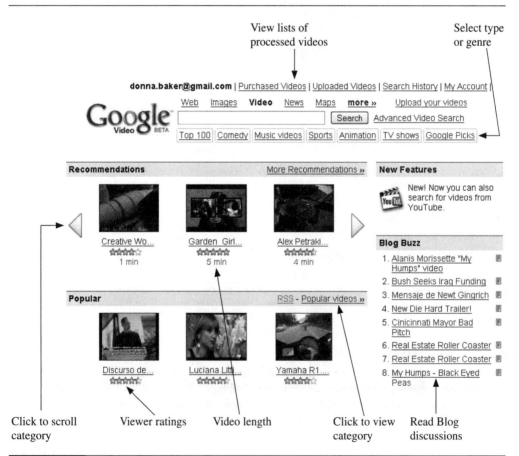

FIGURE 2-3   Search for and view video in Google Video.

If you are in the United States, you can purchase, rent, and download video from Google Video at http://video.google.com.

Search by Category or Type of Video

There are literally thousands of videos available in several categories. For most categories, you can either click the button below the search text field, or type the operator in the search text field as listed here. The Top 100 category doesn't have an operator; so click the button to display the list on the page.

You can also search by title using the operator title: in the search text field, such as title: "November Rain."

Category	Operator
Comedy	genre:comedy
Music videos	type:music_video OR genre:music
Sports	type:sports OR genre:sports
Animation	genre:animation
TV shows	type:tvshow
Google Picks	type:gpick

Read about operators in Chapter 1.

To search for a video, follow these steps:

1. Select a category or type the operator in the text search field.

2. Type additional keywords and operators as necessary to target your search and click Search. Your returns are shown on a results page.

If you have used a combination of operators, such as a genre and a specific search term, the results are listed by genre, followed by a tilde sign (~) and then the search terms, such as **genre:animation ~ traffic**.

3. To further narrow the results, click the duration drop-down arrow and choose a time frame. Choose from short, medium, or long clips.

You can sort the videos as well. Click the Sort drop-down arrow and choose one of relevance, rating, views, date, or title.

4. Scroll through the results to find the video.

Play the Clip

Whether you are browsing, or have searched for a specific video, click the thumbnail or the link in the results page to open the playback window, shown in Figure 2-4.

The playback window offers a number of features for viewing, playing, and downloading.

More Fun with Video

There are many more Google Video features than there is space in this book for a full description. Other service areas and features, along with a URL to find more information, have been discussed below.

Upload Your Video   Google Video offers methods for uploading your own video to watch on Google Video, distribute, and add to your website. View the upload form and instructions at http://tinyurl.com/3cvyfa. For information on how to enter details for your video, see the topics at http://tinyurl.com/2nelea.

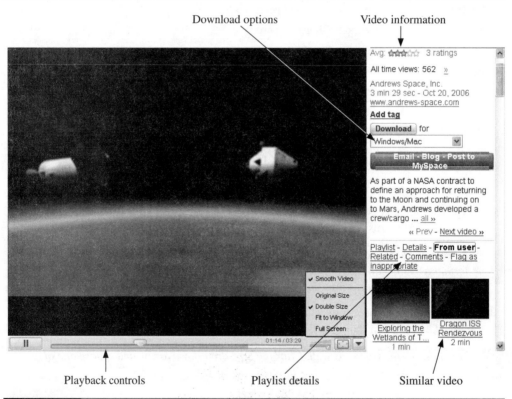

FIGURE 2-4   View and download a video from the playback page.

Subscribe to a Feed   You can access Google Video feeds by subscribing to the links. Click the RSS link shown on the main Google Video page at the top of the listed categories, to be notified when new videos are added to the selected category. Read more at http://tinyurl.com/2rdy9w. Check out Google Reader in Chapter 5 as well.

Download Videos   Many videos can be downloaded to your computer for playback. In addition, you can download the Google Video Player. Video can be downloaded in Windows/Mac or Video iPod/Sony PSP formats. For instructions on downloading, visit http://tinyurl.com/38vzox.

Purchase a Video   In the United States you can purchase videos using your Google Account. Some videos are available in different purchase categories, such as High Quality or Day Pass High Quality. If you buy a copy-protected video, you have to watch it online. Learn more at http://tinyurl.com/2og9s5.

Use Google Video International   Google Video is available in several other countries, including Australia, Canada, France, and the U.K. Scroll to the bottom of the Google Video Search window and click an international link.

Google Video for the Big Guys   If you are a major producer with over 1000 hours of distributed video, you can apply to be included in the Premium Program. Check out the form for submission details at http://tinyurl.com/hj6q4.

How to ...   Be a Good Video Consumer

Google Video isn't equipped with a SafeSearch feature to block material. If you view a video that you think is inappropriate for some viewers, or contains obscene content, click "Flag as Inappropriate" from the links on the page.

In the resulting form, choose one of these options to flag the video:

- pornography or obscenity
- graphic violence
- racially or ethnically hateful content
- other content inappropriate for young viewers

Check Out Different Communities

The Internet isn't a single system. Along with websites for information, providing resources and commerce, there are millions of sites devoted to virtually any topic under the sun, hosted and frequented by groups and communities. To let you search in specific areas of the Internet, such as the Blogosphere, Google offers specialized searches.

Blog Searches

Blogs are an entire web culture in themselves, and an important component in your information gathering arsenal. One of the best places to find what's important about a topic, as well as the best links to other content, is by using a blog search.

To start, either click "More" from the links on the Google Search home page and then choose Blog Search from the list, or add "blogsearch" to the end of the address string for the page. That is, www.google.com/blogsearch.

Type the terms to use for the search and click Search Blogs. If you need to customize the search terms, click Advanced Blog Search and add features to include or exclude as with other forms of searching.

The Blog Search results are shown in the results window, sorted by relevance. If you prefer, sort the results by date using one of the Published options at the left of the results page shown here. You can also subscribe to specific blog feeds on the results window.

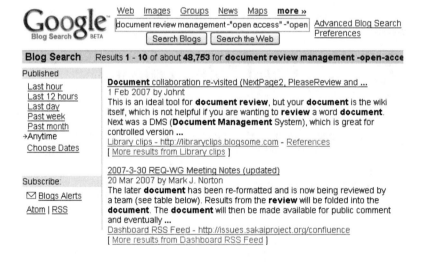

Group Searches

Google Groups is a service that lets you set up, organize, monitor, and administer your own groups and communities. Like blogs, groups offer a wealth of information.

To check out what people are posting to their groups, or to find groups that share your interests, follow these steps:

1. Click Groups from the links above the text entry field on the Google Search home page.

2. Set advanced preferences if you like by clicking the Advanced Preferences link, or type your search terms in the field and click Search.

3. The results are shown listed by relevance (Figure 2-5). Click a link to read the post.

TIP *If you prefer, click Sort by Date at the upper-right corner of the results returns page to show the results chronologically.*

Each Group search result also includes a link to the specific group. Click the Group link to show a listing from the group, including topic summaries and a list of active topics, shown here.

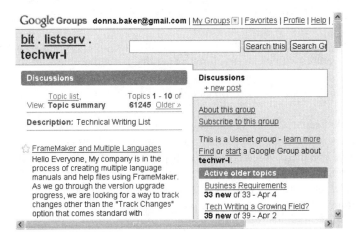

NOTE *Check out Chapter 5 for information on Google Groups*

FIGURE 2-5   Find group posts and check out groups from the results page.

Did you know?

Google Offers Accessible Searches for Visually Impaired Users

As described in Chapter 1, Google uses a series of processes to return the best and most relevant search results. For those who are visually impaired or using assistive devices to browse the Internet, Accessible Search adds a final process to order the documents in terms of their level of accessibility.

NOTE   *The search results aren't filtered by accessible vs. inaccessible status.*

Accessible pages are determined by the HTML code on the page. Google Accessible Search looks for features with clean structures, pages that remain usable with images turned off, a process described as *degrading gracefully*, and pages that are accessible with keyboard navigation. Accessible Search is based on Google Co-op, which uses specialized interests to influence search results.

The Accessible Search window is the same as that for regular searching. It also has an Advanced Search window to choose customization terms as with other Google Search tools.

Once you have completed a search, the results page offers a choice of searching the results using Web Search or Accessible Search to allow for comparison of results. In the Google Accessible Search results window shown here, notice that the page logo has been replaced by text for reading by screen reader programs.

Google Accessible Search

document workflow design   [Search]

⦿ Google Accessible Search ○ Web Search

Results **1 - 50** for **document workflow design**. **(0.15** seconds)

Document Workflow Management Solution|**Workflow** Template **Design**
Document workflow management solution to create, submit, review, approve & distribute any electronic **document** from a web browser.
www.altimate.ca/**workflow_design**er_ds.html - 13k - Cached

Google **Custom Search**

Workflow Design Documentation
By Khy Huang on 12 April 2001. ACS Documentation : **Workflow** :
Workflow Design Documentation. This is the **design document** for the **workflow** package. ...
www.wgbh.org/doc/acs-**workflow/design**.html - 32k - Cached

Workflow Design
Workflow Design. The question arose: how to define a generic **workflow**, ... States are the stages which a '**document**' flows through during a

NOTE   *Read about Google Accessible Search at http://labs.google.com/ accessible/.*

A Quest for All Sorts of Neat Things

You have seen many ways to search for information in this and the previous chapter. There's more! You can find information using numbers, or restrict your search to different entities such as governments and universities.

Track Numbers in Google Search

How often do you have to look for a number? Maybe you have a voice-mail with an area code you don't recognize, or need to track a parcel. Google includes a specialized type of search that looks for numbers according to the pattern typed in the search string.

Look for Area Codes and Packages

To find out where that voice-mail originated, simply type the numbers into the Google home page text field and click Search. The first result in the returns from whitepages.com describes the location and offers to show you a map (Figure 2-6).

Parcel tracking IDs, patents, and other specialized numbers can be entered into Google's search box for quick access to information about them. For example, typing a FedEx tracking number will return the latest information on your package. Other special search-by-number types are based on the number sequence and sometimes an operator. In this list, numeric characters are shown as "1", and text characters are shown as "X":

Number	String
FedEx tracking	111111111111
Telephone area codes	111
UPC codes	111111111111
UPS tracking	1X1111X11111111111
USPS tracking	1111 1111 1111 1111 1111 11
Vehicle ID (VIN)	XXXXX111X1XX11111

FIGURE 2-6   Google obligingly tells you the area code where the call originated and offers a map of the area.

TIP
There are more numeric searches you can do, such as FAA airplane registrations. Read more at http://tinyurl.com/yxsc.

Address and Phone Number Listings

Google lets you find US street addresses and phone numbers. For searches using specific keywords, public phone numbers and addresses are shown at the top of the results page.

To find listings for a US residence, type any of the following combinations into the Google search box and click Search:

- first name or initial, last name, city (state is optional)
- first name or initial, last name, state
- first name or initial, last name, area code
- first name or initial, last name, zip code
- phone number, including area code
- last name, city, state
- last name, zip code

The results page first shows local business results (read about local searches later in the chapter), followed by the first phonebook listings. Click the link to open a list of all returns that match your search terms (Figure 2-7).

Search for contacts using phone number, name, and address combinations.

NOTE   *You can have your number removed from the listings at this location:*
http://tinyurl.com/u8dc.

Special Searches for Travelers

Are you on the road to someplace exotic? Or perhaps you're going on a less-than-exotic business trip? Here are a few specialized searches that can help you prepare for your trip:

Are There Flight Delays Today?   What's more annoying than thinking you are going to make a flight with time to spare, only to run into freeway construction snags that make you run the 100-yard dash to the departure lounge? In the Google Search home page, type the airport's international three-letter code and the word "airport" and click Search to see any problems or issues.

TIP   *You can find a list of airport codes at http://www.world-airport-codes.com/.*

Is My Flight on Time?   Search using the airline name and flight number to display a result showing departure times and any problems.

TIP   *Use I'm Feeling Lucky instead of Google Search if you like. For the most part, you'll see the airline's page showing flight info.*

How's the Weather?   Weather Underground provides a link to weather you can access with a simple search. Type the terms **weather [city]** (including the brackets) and click Search or I'm Feeling Lucky. The results include advisories and a forecast.

NOTE   *You can also search for maps and other traffic information: read about Google Maps in Chapter 3.*

Just Ask the Question

If you aren't sure what sorts of keywords to use for a search, whether or not to use operators, or how to arrange the keywords, simply ask the question. Type the query as a phrase and click Search. The question has to be fact-based and quantifiable. For example, typing the phrase **people killed by bubonic plague** produces results including books about the plague and shows values in several search returns (Figure 2-8).

Use a slightly different strategy to define a term. If you want a quick definition type the word **define** and the words you want defined, separated by spaces. The first return is a definition. If you want to explore a word's definition use an operator. For example, typing **define: compound growth rate** produces the returns shown in Figure 2-9, which list definitions and their source web pages.

FIGURE 2-8 Ask a question to return results containing your answer.

Use Special Search Areas for Easy Information Access

If you are looking for information on a college extension course, or how to tweak some setting in an operating system file, don't bother slogging through general search results. Instead, go directly to the source. Google offers a method for searching in specific realms of interest, including universities, public service, and computer systems.

FIGURE 2-9 Use an operator for a list of definitions.

University and College Sites   You can begin a search for a college at http://tinyurl.com/j7rj on the Google University Search page. Scroll through the alphabetical listings and select a desired link; click to open a search window for querying the college site. If you know the URL and are looking for specific information, start from the Google home page. For example, to find extension courses at Harvard, type **extension site: www.harvard.edu** for returns like this example.

Public Service and Other Special Sites   Looking for information in a government website is often a time-consuming effort. Finding a setting for a system file is often time-consuming. Shave a bit of time from your searches by restricting the Google search to special areas starting from the choices at http://tinyurl.com/2lan9. On this page, click one of the images or links to open a specific page for the search (Figure 2-10).

Other entities, organizations, and individuals can create their own search engines using a beta service called Google Co-op. Click the Public Service Searches link on the special sites' page or open http://tinyurl.com/2dusnk to learn how to build custom search engines using Google Co-op.

Seek Wisdom Online

Check out the news, find information in a book, or dig up a periodical article using other specialized Google searches.

FIGURE 2-10   Use one of the links to open special search areas.

Book Searches

Google Book Search is a service that searches text of books stored in a digital database. In a regular search, if the Book Search finds results on the keywords used, up to three book listings are shown prior to the regular web page results, like the search results shown in Figure 2-8.

You can search using Google Book Search directly from the site at www.books.google.com. Type the name of the book, author, or keywords to return search results like the example shown here. The page results can also contain associated advertising for publishers and booksellers, depending on the author or title.

Different links are associated with the book listings based on the copyright status of the book. In all cases, you'll find links to booksellers and libraries.

The options include:

- Every listing contains the About this Book link. Click the search result's link or "About this Book" to view basic information such as the publication date, author, and so on.

- Full view shows you the entire content of the book for books that are out of copyright, in the public domain, or have permission from the rightsholder. Books in the public domain are available for download in PDF format.

- A Limited preview is shown for books whose publishers are part of the Google Partner Program. In partnered books, you can search repeatedly or browse through a number of pages (Figure 2-11).

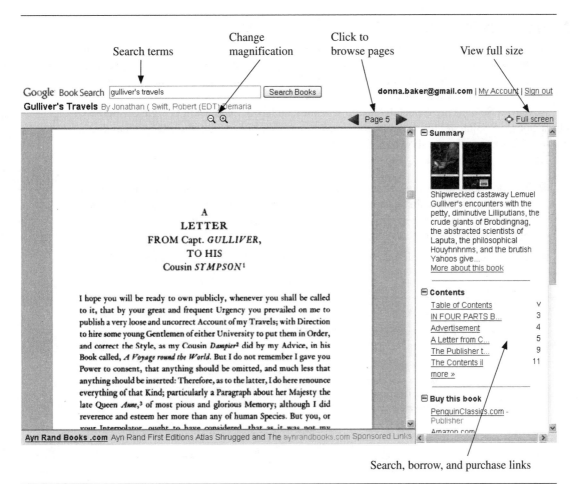

FIGURE 2-11   Access content in a Book Search.

■ The Snippet view doesn't let you see multiple pages of the book. Instead, if you search within the book you see up to three text snippets showing your search term in context.

■ The Table of Contents is listed for books having either full view or limited preview status.

NOTE   *Find out more about using Google Book Search at http://tinyurl.com/yqnlxd. If you are an author find out more at http://tinyurl.com/jqcgt. For publishers, read about the program at http://tinyurl.com/2egamk*

Search for Scientific and Scholarly Materials

For those involved in education, either as educators or students, or who want to dig into a topic in a serious way, Google offers a search type called Google Scholar. Use the search engine to find research results in the form of a bibliography. The results are ranked in terms of the article's text and how often an article has been cited in other works.

Advanced Settings are especially useful when a search is defined using Google Scholar. Open Google Scholar at http://scholar.google.com and click Advanced Scholar Search to display the search preferences page shown in Figure 2-12.

Here are some tips for using the Advanced Scholar Search:

■ Use operators to customize the results. To find an author, for example, type **author:"JK Heinz"** to return results for content written by JK Heinz. Similarly, restrict the author's name if it can also be a search term. In the example, **rosa** is a search term, and also an author's name for unrelated publications.

■ Restrict the date by typing a range of dates in the search field, such as **2006-2007**.

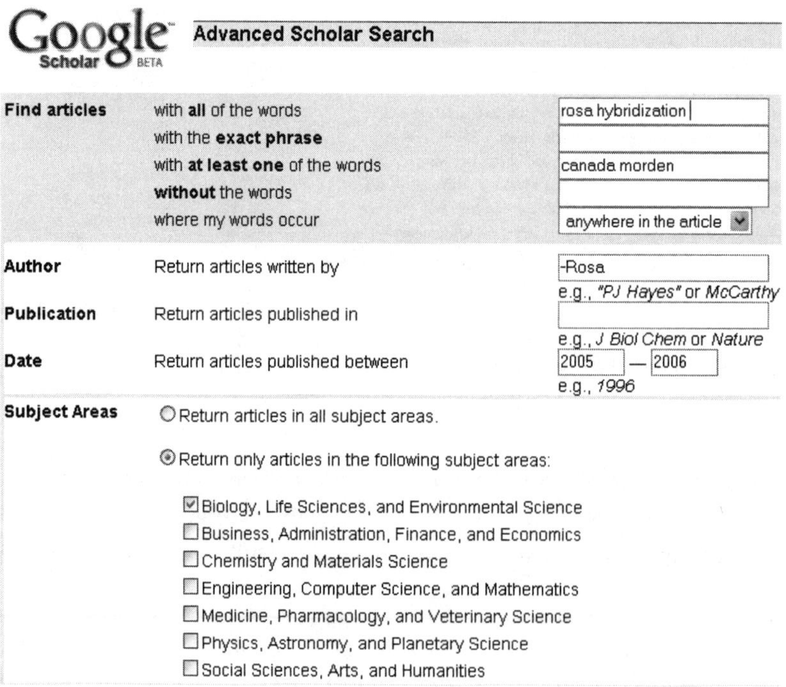

FIGURE 2-12   Customize a search for scholarly works.

■ Restrict the returns to a specific publication by typing the name of the journal, such as **New England Journal of Medicine**, but keep in mind that you have to search using the common abbreviation for a journal, such as **NEJM**.

■ Restrict the results based on the title by using an operator—typing **intitle: phosphorescence** returns only publications containing the word in the title.

■ Restrict a subject area by selecting one of the listed areas.

In the example shown here, the search string Google Scholar uses for the search is **rosa hybridization canada OR morden -author:Rosa**, restricted by dates, and searched in the Biology, Life Sciences, and Environmental Sciences fields.

NOTE *Find information for libraries at http://tinyurl.com/24wvmp, http://tinyurl.com/2yf85l*

Directory Browsing by Topic

The Google search tools are useful, but only if you know what you are looking for. If you find the vast wealth of information at your fingertips intimidating or overwhelming, try Google Directory to give you a starting point and sense of direction.

Open the service at directory.google.com. As you see in Figure 2-13, the Google Directory is broken into a number of broad topic areas from Arts to Sports, like the table of contents in a book. Click one of the topics to open a list of subtopics, like the sections in a book. Continue drilling down into the topics one layer at a time until you find the information you're looking for.

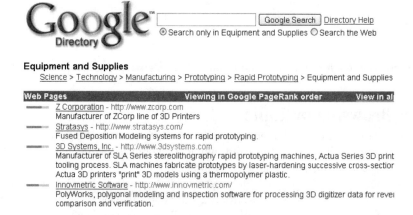

FIGURE 2-13 View information based on topics.

At its core, a directory search lists web pages ordered using Google PageRank. You also see the sequence used to pass through the directory structure.

The Google Directory is based on the DMOZ Open Directory project, which uses volunteer editors to review websites and classify them by topic. Find out more about Google Directory at http://tinyurl.com/2g5zbx. To read about serving as an editor for the Open Directory, visit http://tinyurl.com/6h91.

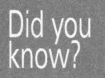

You Can Search Where You Live

Google Search helps you tap into the world's resources, but also helps you search closer to home. Craft your search terms to show local information, or search local directories to find businesses and services by including an address or zip code along with the terms you are searching.

In the search results, Google shows results from the specific area on a map (Figure 2-14). You can also find directions and other types of information in the results.

Read about working with maps in Chapter 3.

FIGURE 2-14   Add location information to the search terms to search locally.

Explore the Joys of Shopping—Online

Over time the internet has become a truly global marketplace. The advent of huge online shopping malls, countless products, and a proliferation of secure payment systems makes seeking the perfect item a realistic endeavor. Of course, millions of products make the quest for the perfect something elusive.

Google offers a number of services to help make shopping easier, including catalog directories, Google Product Search, and the Google Shopping Cart.

Catalog Shopping

Google Catalog lets you search within literally hundreds of catalogs. You can browse for the right catalog or product from the site at http://catalogs.google.com.

The interface offers two methods for tracking down a catalog: either type terms in the search field, such as **retail displays** and click Search, or choose a topic area from the directory listing, such as Business to Business.

Choosing a directory listing opens a window offering sections of the listing at the left of the page, and thumbnails and links to pertinent catalogs on the right side of the page, shown in Figure 2-15.

FIGURE 2-15   Choose catalogs from listings by category or type search terms.

If you are a merchant, check out http://tinyurl.com/2ahjoc for information on listing your catalog.

Track Down Products with Google Product Search

Your search for products isn't restricted to catalogs. Google offers Google Product Search (formally known as Froogle), a specialized search engine for purchases. You must have a Google Account to use Google Product Search, located at http://www.google.com/products.

Design the Product Search

The Google Product Search interface shows a search field and a selection of searches recently found using Google Product Search. Click the Advanced Product Search link to open the window shown here.

Consider these ideas for designing a custom product search in Google Product Search:

- Enter search terms and operators (see Chapter 1 for information on using operators).

- Type the price range high and low values to filter the search results.

- If you like, type a location for filtering the results, such as a city, state, or zip code.

- Specify where the search terms are to display in the search returns.

- If you are familiar with the Google Product Search categories, filter the results to a specific category.

- Select a view for displaying the results, either as a grid or a list.

Evaluate the Search Results to Find the Perfect Product

Click Search Search Products to conduct the search. The results for a sample search are shown in the grid layout you see here.

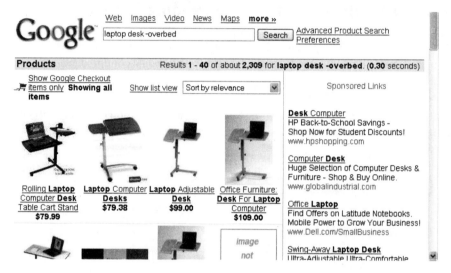

You see the choices made in the Advanced Preferences dialog box, such as the search terms and operators, reflected in the results page.

Click an interesting product to open a window describing the product in detail and details on the price and purchase locations.

Add Products to Your Shopping List

Use the Shopping List feature to store details about products you are interested in. The information is stored as a private list to which you can add notes and reminders.

Follow these steps to add a product to the list:

1. On the Google Product Search results page, click Show List View to display the search returns in a view offering information as well as the product's thumbnail as you see here.

2. Click Add to Shopping List below the description.

TIP *The Google Product Search Shopping List works like the Google Notebook extension. See how to use Google Notebook in Chapter 8.*

3. The details of the product are entered into the Shopping List.

4. Click Edit to open a text window to add details about the product for future reference.

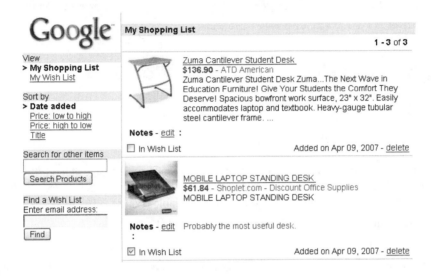

TIP *If your list is very lengthy, use the Sort by options at the left of the window to sort the results by date, price, or title.*

Add a Wish List

If someone is looking for gift ideas for you, add items from your Shopping List to a shareable Wish List. Click the In Wish List checkbox below the listing for the item in your Shopping List.

Anyone wishing to buy you a gift can type your e-mail address into the field on the Google Product Search Shopping List page, located at www.google.com/shoppinglist to display your public Wish List.

NOTE *If you want to sell your products on Google Product Search, check out the process at http://tinyurl.com/yxlqox*

Manage Accounts Using Google Checkout

Would you like to shop online, use a single user account and password, secure your purchases against fraud, easily track your orders and shipping, and prevent excessive commercial e-mail? Of course you would. Google Checkout offers all these features.

FIGURE 2-16 Start with search terms or browse the Google Checkup stores.

Follow these steps to use Google Checkout:

1. Log into your Google Account from the main Google Checkout page at http://tinyurl .com/3cy3w5. From this page, you can also type a search query to get started, or click browse Google Checkout stores to see what is available (Figure 2-16).

2. Fill the online form to provide shipping and credit card information.

3. Accept the terms of service and click Create my account. Time to shop!

4. In the shopping window, type search terms to see results for stores containing the type of products you are searching for. Search results are shown in Google Product Search.

Summary

This chapter explored Google's specialized products and services to search for many things in many ways. You saw how to find images, movies, and video using Google. There are a number of online communities that are supported using Google, such as blog and group searching. Google offers a number of ways to search for different types of numbers, such as addresses and phone numbers. Google includes specialized searches for books, scholarly papers, or a directory if you want to search in a systematic fashion. You saw the ways in which Google enhances shopping online through catalogs, Google Product Search, and Google Checkout.

In the next chapter, you'll learn more about finding and using information with Google Maps.

Part II

Communicate—Google Style

Google offers ways to communicate beyond the norm. You've become accustomed to using faxes, e-mails, and voicemails. Whether for business or pleasure, Google lets you communicate in various ways using maps, images, and a variety of voice processes.

In this part, you'll see how mapping has become integral to many parts of Google communications. From finding a business to plotting a vacation to searching for information about a specific location—there's a Google map application. You'll see how to use two-dimensional maps for defining routes, searching for businesses, and even plotting bus routes and fares in some cities. Take the world into three dimensions with Google Earth, and out of this world with Google Mars.

See how Google's communication products are making it simpler for us to keep in touch, or merely to keep up. Some content can be taken mobile, used online, or applied in a combination of ways. For example, pictures are a big part of our everyday lives, and Google offers Picasa, a well-featured program for managing and editing images. You can create a range of different outputs from web albums to blog pages and printed posters.

Take your message to the people with Google. See how to use Google AdSense to advertise your products, or host Google AdWords on your website as a source of revenue.

Chapter 3

Map with Google

How to...

- Navigate in Google Maps
- Modify the map views
- Create routes and itineraries
- Create and customize your own maps
- Check out upcoming travel planning programs
- Tour Mars online

Use Google Maps to first search for locations or businesses, and then develop an itinerary and driving directions—all from a single program interface. You can even send your maps to your phone for mobile use.

If the basic program offerings aren't enough, you can also make custom maps with a new Google Maps component. Two map-based Google Lab products are available for searching for public transportation and taxis, as you'll see.

NOTE   *Find out more about Google Maps at http://maps.google.com.*

Search for Locations

You always view a map layout when you work in Google Maps. When the most significant results in a general Google search include locations, you see a small map included in the returns page. Read more in the section "Decipher the Search Results" found in Chapter 1.

Get Around in Google Maps

Google Maps is popularly used to run an integrated search, where you look for content based on a combination of search terms, business names and directories, and map information. The results include relevant listings and a map.

Different Places Offer Different Features

The full-featured version of Google Maps is available in several countries, and includes satellite imagery, maps, local business searches, street level searches, and driving directions. Satellite imagery is available for the entire planet, although not to the same resolution.

Other countries can access map data or other combinations of content. A new service offers business users the opportunity to add a business listing to the Google Local Business Center site in some countries. Check for the list of features available for your country at http://tinyurl.com/yro4kw.

Follow these steps to get started in Google Maps:

1. Click Maps on the Google home page. You can also open the site directly at http://maps .google.com. The Google Maps search window displays.

TIP   *If you add search terms in the Google home page they are transferred to the Google Maps search field when you click the Maps link.*

2. The default display in Google Maps is the Search the map display, shown in Figure 3-1. The Search Results contain various types of information, including your past searches, and a number of sample searches for locations, directions, and businesses.

3. Click a link in the Search Results to display the content in the map area.

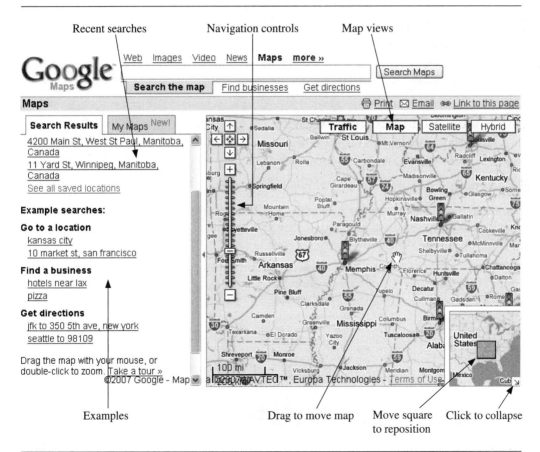

FIGURE 3-1   Google Maps provides information in a number of ways.

Navigate in Google Maps

The Google Maps interface shows a set of navigation controls, as seen in Figure 3-1. Click the slider to increase or decrease the map's magnification, or drag the indicator on the slider up to increase the zoom or down to decrease the zoom.

If you want to move the map directionally, click one of the arrows at the upper left of the Navigation controls. If you want to return to the previous view, click the central button within the directional arrows at the upper left of the Navigation controls.

You can move and modify the map view in a number of ways using these shortcuts:

- Drag within a map to drag the view to show other areas of the map; the cursor changes to a dragging hand as indicated in Figure 3-1.

- Zoom with the mouse—double-click the left mouse key to zoom in; double-click the right key to zoom out. On Mac, CONTROL+double-click the buttons.

- Use the scroll wheel on your mouse if you have one to increase or decrease the magnification.

- Use the keyboard arrow keys to pan up/down or left/right; pan larger sections using the PAGE UP/PAGE DOWN, HOME/END keys.

Check Out Different Map Views

The default map display shows a two-dimensional map with major highways and cities. There are several ways in which you can view map content.

Show a Traffic Overlay

Click the Traffic button at the upper right of the map to show an overlay of cities where Traffic features are included, as you can see next. Click a Traffic icon to show a pop-up window and click Zoom in to view local traffic.

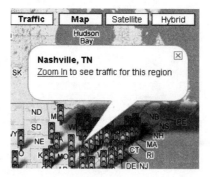

View Traffic Locally

Zoom in to the detailed level to view streets and intersections, shown in Figure 3-2. The map shows real-time traffic conditions in color. Each color represents traffic speed. Green means the

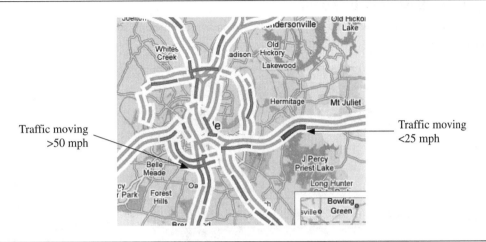

FIGURE 3-2   View traffic conditions in a city closeup map.

traffic is moving over 50 mph, yellow lines mean traffic is moving at 25-50 mph, and red lines indicate areas where traffic is inching along at less than 25 mph. Gray indicates areas without traffic data.

TIP   *Traffic conditions are especially valuable when you are in traffic, and Google Maps Mobile can show you potential problem areas. Read more about taking Google mobile in Chapter 5.*

Show Satellite and Aerial Images

Rather than a flat, two-dimensional map, click Satellite to show the satellite and aerial images view of your map. The map shown here is the same area as that seen in Figure 3-2.

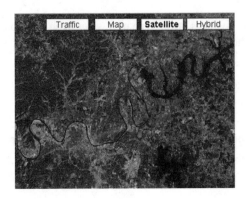

Display the Best of Both Worlds

The third view is a hybrid with the map data overlaid on the satellite and aerial images, as shown in this example:

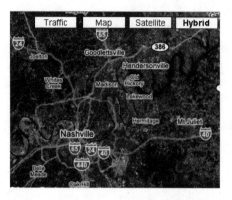

You can use Google Maps on your website, as long as it is free for consumer use. Find more information at http://tinyurl.com/hg2kj; check out the Google Groups Maps API discussion forum at http://tinyurl.com/q7m58.

Zoom In on Businesses and Locations

In the default Google Maps view, the Search the map option is active, showing a single search field. Enter terms and click Search Maps to generate a list of search results; click a result to display the area in the map view.

Follow these steps to make your search more specific and localized using the Find Businesses option:

1. Click the Find Businesses link below the search field on Google Maps to display the Find Businesses fields.

2. Type the name of the business or the type of business you are looking for in the left field, and the location in the right field. You can use a city, street address, or zip code.

3. Click Search Businesses to run the search and display the results.

4. The map is redrawn to show the most relevant listings in the Search Results, such as the example seen in Figure 3-3.

5. Click a result's link in the Search Results area at the left of the browser window. The balloon displaying information pops open above the company's placemark.

6. Choose a link from the balloon to get directions, save the information, send it to your phone, and so on, or select another return from the list of search results.

Search for a local business using a number of terms.

Generate a Route or Itinerary

The third type of search you can perform in Google Maps plots a route between two or more locations.

Create Driving Directions

Suppose you are leaving a Parisian parfumiér and want to stroll to the Eiffel Tower. Plot the route following these steps:

1. Click the Get Directions link below the Google Maps search field to display the Get Directions fields.

> **TIP** *If you have used the Find Businesses search, a selected business is shown in the left field.*

2. Enter an address in the fields and click Get Directions.

FIGURE 3-4   The route is plotted and numbered according to changes in the route.

3. The route is shown in the Search Results area of the window (Figure 3-4).

4. Scroll through the results to see your route. Notice in the example that the distances are shown in kilometers, as Paris uses a metric measuring system.

View the Results

Here are some suggestions for working with the results:

- Click a numbered location in the results to see a magnified view of the location in a pop-up balloon (shown in Figure 3-4).

- You can change the view of the pop-up by selecting one of the Map, Sat (Satellite), or Hyb (Hybrid) buttons. Zoom in and out using the (+) and (–) buttons, or drag within the balloon to pan the map.

- If you want to plot your course going back, click Get Reverse Directions.

Design an Itinerary

Why stop at two locations? Google Maps lets you plan an entire trip with multiple placemarks. Follow these steps to plan your summer motorcycle road trip using the Destinations feature:

Search Results | My Maps New!

Get reverse directions

From: Sturgis, SD 57785 ⊠ Edit

⊞ Drive: 54.4 mi (about 1 hour 10 mins

To: Mount Rushmore ⊠ Edit

Add destination ... New!

These directions are for planning purposes only. You may find that construction projects, traffic, or other events may cause road conditions to differ from the map results.

Map data ©2007 NAVTEQ™

1. Type the locations for your start and endpoints as in the previous section, such as **Sturgis, SD** to **Mount Rushmore** and click Get Directions.

2. The list of directions are shown in the Search Results area. Click the (–) to the left of the Drive link to collapse the directions list, replacing it with a (+) sign. As you see here, the Add Destination link is shown below the collapsed list.

3. Click Add Destination to display another search text field in the Search Results area.

4. Type the location, such as **Yellowstone National Park** and click Add Destination. The additional leg of the trip is routed.

5. To add another leg to the trip, click Add Destination to open another text field, type the next location, such as **Billings, MT** and click Add Destination to display the results both in the map and the Search Results.

TIP *Notice the different placemarks added to the map—there are different icons for the start location, trip segments, and the endpoint.*

6. Continue adding additional segments of the journey.

You can work with your itinerary as you like. Here are some tips:

■ Use a different map view to get an idea of the terrain you'll experience on your trip. In Figure 3-4, for example, the map is shown in the Hybrid view.

■ Click one of the placemarks on the map to show an information balloon with further links.

■ The destination field in the Get Directions search shows the string of search locations. In this example trip, the start point is Sturgis, SD. The right destination field shows a search string of intermediate locations, such as Mount Rushmore to:Yellowstone National Park to:Billings, MT.

■ To change one of the trip legs, click Edit in the Search Results to open a field for typing a new destination, such as **Bozeman, MT**; click Change to alter your itinerary.

If you are interested in more in-depth use and discussion you can participate in the Google Maps community and help groups at http://tinyurl.com/22v3ux.

Interesting Things to Do with Your Maps

Maps aren't static objects, and they certainly aren't static in Google Maps. You can define your default location, save your searches, and distribute maps in several ways.

Make Your Home the Default Map Location

Trips usually start from where you live. Rather than have Google Maps start with a country-wide view, set your home as the default location. That way, when you start a new search your address is automatically used as the starting destination when doing searches.

Follow these steps to reset the default location:

1. Click Search the Map on Google Maps home page to display the default search view.

2. Type your address in the text field and click Search Maps.

3. The map zooms into the specified location. Click the placemark to open the pop-up balloon.

4. Click Make This My Default Location. The information in the pop-up balloon then changes to indicate your preference.

If you want to reset your default location, click the Get Directions link to show the Get Directions view of Google Maps. In the Search Results area, notice that the Starting From Location area specifies the default location. Click Clear and the map resets itself to the default US view.

You can also reset your default location in the Saved Locations window, described next.

Save and Manage Your Searches

The Search Results on the Google Maps page lists links for your last ten search locations, but you can save additional searches and maintain your own list. Google Maps maintains a Saved Locations list that can hold up to 100 locations. Once you've saved 100 locations, newer search locations replace the oldest.

Follow these steps to manage your list of saved locations:

1. From the Google Maps browser window, click Saved Locations in the top right of the window.

2. Log into your Google Account, if you aren't logged in, and the Saved Locations window displays in the Google Maps browser window (shown in Figure 3-5).

Saved Locations

| New Location: | Location | Label | | Add | ☑ **Enable auto-saving of locations** |

Delete   Select: All, None

Default	Location		Label	
☐ ⇨	Gimli, MB		home, sweet home	[Edit]
☐ ⇨	Paris, France			[Edit]
☐	Don't use this location as the initial map view			[Edit]
☐ ⇨	39, Boulevard des Capucines, 75002 2ème Arrondissement, Paris, France			[Edit]
☐ ⇨	Eiffel Tower, France			[Edit]
☐ ⇨	Sturgis, South Dakota		Rally 2007	[Edit]
☐ ⇨	Mount Rushmore			[Edit]
☐ ⇨	Grand Canyon			[Edit]
☐ ⇨	Yellowstone National Park			[Edit]

FIGURE 3-5   Click the link to display locations saved in your Google Account.

3. Review and modify your Saved Locations as desired in the following ways:

    ■ Add a New Location by typing the location and an optional label in the fields at the top of the Saved Locations window. Click Add to include the location in your list.

    ■ Select the check box to the left of a location and click Delete to remove it from the list.

TIP   *Select multiple locations for removal at once. Click All to select your entire list, or None to deselect prior selections.*

    ■ Click Edit to open a new text field in which to type a label; Google Maps uses the labels to generate suggestions when searching.

    ■ Click the green arrow to the left of a location to define it as your default location.

    ■ Click a location to display it in the Google Maps view.

    ■ Select or deselect the Enable Auto-Saving of Locations feature, which is active by default.

Take Google Maps to the Next Level

You don't have to settle for ready-made maps. Instead, make your own maps using the My Maps feature. You can create and distribute personalized maps that can include content ranging from text to photos and video.

Create a New Map

Google Maps includes the My Maps feature tabbed with the Search Results frame in the Google Maps window. Follow these steps to add a map to your personal collection:

1. Display the location you want to use for creating your new map in the view.

2. Click the My Maps tab to display the frame and click Create New Map to display text entry fields.

3. Type a title for the map, and add text in the Description field if you like. At the very least, the new map needs a name.

4. Select Public or Unlisted. The default is a Public map, which is available to others online.

5. Click Save. The text fields collapse, and the new map is listed in My Maps as you see here.

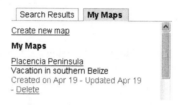

TIP   *If you add a map and decide you want to start over or you don't need it any longer, click the Delete link below the map's listing.*

Add Custom Content to Personalize Your Map

Once you have created the map it's time to add features to it using the toolbar that overlays your map (Figure 3-6). While you are working with a new map, use the Selection tool to select content or drag the map to reposition it in the view. At any time, you can click Save on the My Maps panel to save your work; Google Maps autosaves the content as well.

If you select a tool from the toolbox and change your mind, press ESC to deselect it, and reactivate the Selection tool.

NOTE   *The tools offered on the My Maps view are also included in Google Earth. Read about Google Earth in Chapter 4.*

Mark Locations with the Placemark Tool

Add custom placemarks to your map to indicate a point of interest, such as a business, residence, or a great mountain lookout.

Follow these steps to add a placemark to your custom map:

1. Select the Placemark tool on the view and position it where you want the placemark; click to add the placemark and open the pop-up balloon.

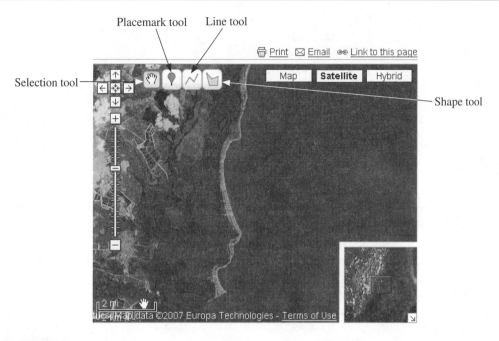

Placemark tool   Line tool

Selection tool

Shape tool

FIGURE 3-6   Use the tools to add content to your map.

2. Type a name for the placemark, such as **Cottage on the channel**, as shown here.

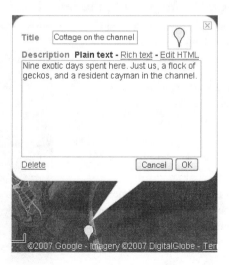

My Maps

FIGURE 3-7   The completed placemark is included in the map's listing.

3. Click the icon symbol at the upper right of the balloon to display a panel of icons. Select an alternate icon to use for the placemark; the panel closes automatically and the icon is changed.

4. Type text in the Description field. The default display uses plain text; you can use rich text or HTML instead, described in the upcoming section "Configure the Appearance of Your Descriptions for Interest."

5. Click OK to close the pop-up balloon. Your placemark is listed in the My Maps panel (Figure 3-7).

NOTE   *To reposition the placemark on the map, move the mouse over the placemark. When you see the cursor change to a pointing finger, click and drag to move it.*

Draw a Freeform Line on the Map Using the Line Tool

Perhaps you have found a great hiking trail and want to show a path on the map. Follow these steps to draw and customize your path:

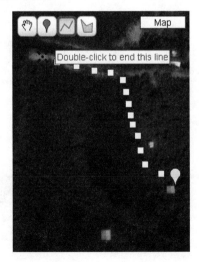

1. Select the Line tool and start drawing. Click the map with the Line tool for each segment of the route you are defining, shown here.

2. When you have completed the line, double-click at the last point to deselect the Line tool. In the My Maps panel, the object is named Line 1.

3. Click the Line 1 label in the My Maps panel to open a pop-up balloon. Type a name and description, for example, **Path to the lagoon**.

4. Click the line's icon at the upper right of the pop-up balloon to display customization settings. Change the appearance of the line in several ways. The line's appearance changes as you make changes, including:

    ■   Click the Line color's color swatch to open a color swatch panel and choose a color

    ■   Type the Line width in pixels

    ■   Type the Line Opacity as a percentage

5. Click OK to close the configuration pop-up balloon and return to the line's pop-up balloon; click OK again to close the line's balloon.

Identify an Area on a Map Using the Shape Tool

The Shape tool lets you identify a region of interest on the map. You might use it on the map to outline a park area, or, as in this example, a good location for spotting manatees. Follow these steps to draw a shape:

1. Position the map where you want to draw the shape.

2. Select the Shape tool and move it over the area; click to place the first point on the shape.

3. Continue adding additional points. The more points you add, the more detailed the final shape will be.

4. Double-click the tool over the first point to complete the shape and deselect the tool, shown here.

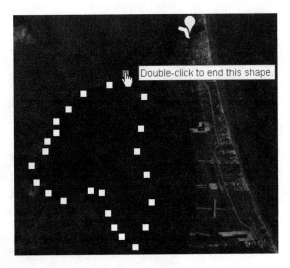

5. In the resulting pop-up balloon, add a title and description.

6. Click the color swatch icon on the pop-up balloon to open another pop-up balloon and select alternate colors for the line and fill, as well as the opacity and line width. Click OK to return to the shape's pop-up balloon.

7. Click OK to complete the shape.

8. The drawn shape is shown on the map, and its title and details are shown on the My Maps panel (Figure 3-8).

TIP   *If you want to adjust the shape, move the cursor over any point and drag to adjust its location.*

Configure the Appearance of Your Descriptions with Custom Text and Images

The descriptions for your objects added to the map are in plain text, but you can use rich text or HTML instead. Rich text, described in this section, offers a toolbar to customize the text appearance, add links, and insert images.

NOTE   *You can enter your own HTML code for more control of the appearance. Click Edit HTML to display a text field and type the coded content, including a tag for an image if you like.*

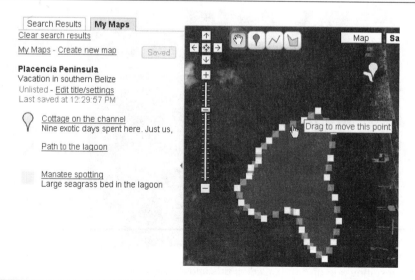

FIGURE 3-8   Add a shape to define an area of interest.

If you have images stored online, you can insert a photo into a map for extra interest. Use an online hosting program, such as PicasaWeb, to upload and store your images online. Refer to the section "Design and Upload a Web Album" in Chapter 6 to learn about using Picasa Web Albums.

Follow these steps to add zing to your map items:

1. Click one of your map locations in the My Map panel to open its pop-up balloon in the map view and click Edit.

2. The editing view reopens, showing the same pop-up balloon used to configure the object initially.

3. Click Rich Text to display a toolbar (Figure 3-9).

4. Select style options for the text appearance from the toolbar.

5. Click the Image icon at the far right of the toolbar to open a text field for inputting the location of your image.

NOTE *If you use PicasaWeb, click Link to this Photo on the PicasaWeb browser window to open the written link for the image you want to use. Then, copy the link text to paste it into the text field.*

6. Click OK to save your changes.

FIGURE 3-9   Configure the contents of the information using various tools.

7. To check the appearance, click on your map object. As you see here, the pop-up balloon looks much more interesting with some text changes and a photo.

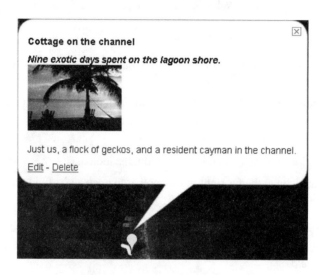

Add Businesses and Addresses to Your Custom Maps

You can add items to your map from search results. Select a listing in the Search Results tab to open the location's pop-up balloon. Click Save to My Maps in the balloon.

In the example map, searching for hotels in Belize included a result for the Turtle Inn. Clicking Save to My Maps in the hotel's pop-up balloon transferred the placemark to the custom map (Figure 3-10).

Here's another example—if you are building a custom map for a trade show exhibit, search for addresses or businesses using any of the methods described in earlier sections of this chapter and find points of interest to add to your map.

Distribute Your Map Collection

Your maps can be used online. If you choose to make the map public, others can locate your map as a search result. You can also share them with others directly, or export them for use in Google Earth.

Sharing Maps

Your My Maps collection can be shared with others. The example project, for instance, is available online at http://tinyurl.com/yrsfs9.

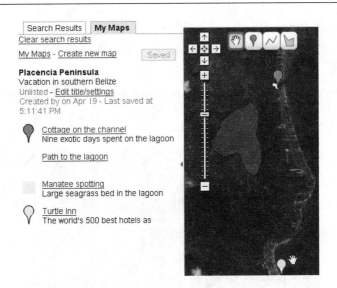

FIGURE 3-10   Import placemarks for other businesses or locations.

How to ... Add Video to Your Personal Maps

Your maps can include either Google Video or YouTube videos. You need some familiarity with editing HTML, but don't have to write the code yourself. You need video accessible from YouTube or Google Video.

NOTE   *Learn about working with Google Video in the section "Search for Moving Pictures" in Chapter 2.*

To add your own video to a map object, follow these steps:

1. Find the uploaded video you want on YouTube or Google Video. On YouTube, the code is an `<object>` tag; in Google Video, the code is an `<embed>` tag. The code snippets embed the video into a website or blog (Figure 3-11).

2. Click the object you want to attach the video to in My Maps, which will open the pop-up balloon. Next, click Edit to display the editing mode.

3. Choose Edit HTML.

4. Paste the snippet of code into the description field of your object.

5. Click OK to save your changes.

6. To test the content, click the object containing the video to watch it play.

FIGURE 3-11   Specify the content you want to include on your map's object.

> G http://maps.google.ca/maps?ie=UTF-8&oe=UTF-8&hl=en&tab=wl&q=
>
> @gmail.com | Saved Locations | Help | Web History | My Account | Sign out
>
>)s   News   **Maps**   Scholar   **more »**
>
> Search Maps
>
> Find businesses   Get directions
>
> ⬛ KML 🖶 Print ✉ Email 👓 Link to this page

FIGURE 3-12   Copy the page's URL to use in other programs or e-mail.

Follow these steps:

1. Select the map you want to share in My Maps.

2. Click Link to This Page in the upper right of the Maps title bar to place the URL for the map page in your browser's navigation field (Figure 3-12).

3. Copy the URL and paste it into an e-mail or post it to your blog or website.

Did you know?

You Can View a Map in Google Earth

If you have Google Earth installed on your computer, you can view your maps in Google Earth. Open your map and click the KML link or icon in the title bar (shown in Figure 3-12). Google Maps uploads a KML file to your computer that you can open in Google Earth.

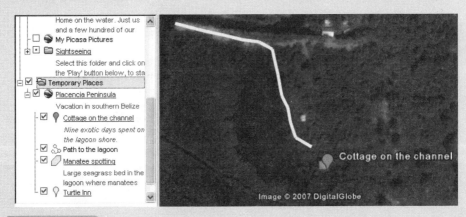

NOTE   *Read about working in Google Earth in Chapter 4.*

Click Print at the upper right of the Maps window to open a Print dialog. Click E-mail to open an e-mail message that includes the link for e-mailing your map to others.

Map Features Emerging from Google Labs

New features and products are always under development at Google Labs. Two map-based services that are currently in development let you find public transport options in some cities, as well as track down a cab or shuttle in other cities.

Plan a Local Trip with Google

Google Transit Trip Planner is a Google Labs product that offers local transit in several metropolitan centers. The Transit Trip Planner works like Google Maps, except the directions returned in the search results use public transportation instead of driving directions. Read about the service at www.google.com/transit.

NOTE
At the time of writing, the locations covered by the product are limited to cities in California, Florida, Hawaii, Minnesota, Nevada, Oregon, Pennsylvania, Texas, and Washington.

Suppose you are attending a conference in Austin and decide to take in some sightseeing and shopping on a free day. To find the most efficient route from your hotel to your shopping destination follow these steps:

1. Open Google Transit at www.google.com/transit.
2. Type the Start address and the End address. You can use a combination of the street address, city/town name, or intersection for the search. In this example, the start location is an Austin hotel and the end destination a street known for adventures in shopping.

TIP
If you want to plan the trip in reverse, click the double-headed arrow between the address fields to switch locations.

3. Select either Depart At or Arrive By, and type the date and time in the fields.
4. Click Get Directions to run the search.
5. The search returns display in a browser window, with directions for walking and public transport listed as you see here.

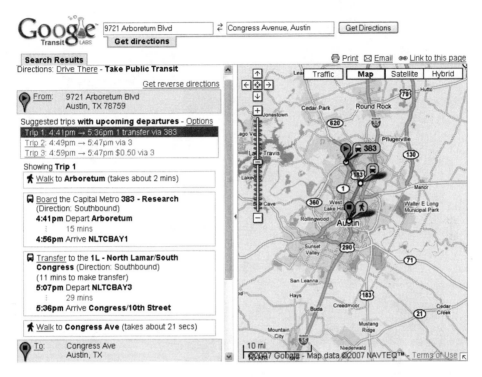

6. Click the links in the search results to make changes, such as addresses or times.

> **TIP** *Click Drive There at the upper left of the results window to generate a list of driving directions. Note on the returns that a comparison of driving versus using public transportation is shown. In the example, driving costs $5.30 while the most expensive public transport is $.50.*

Take a Taxi or Shuttle

Ride Finder is a Google Labs product that displays taxis and shuttles in a number of cities. If you are living in one of the cities included in the product, check out where to find the nearest taxi.

Open the Ride Finder at http://labs.google.com/ridefinder. You'll see a Search field to enter your location, a map showing tracked locations, and a list of cities linked to the map.

Select the city to search by clicking the map pin or the city's link in the list, or by typing the name in the Search field. Click Search. Use the navigation tool at the upper left of the map to zoom in and position the area you want to search as seen here.

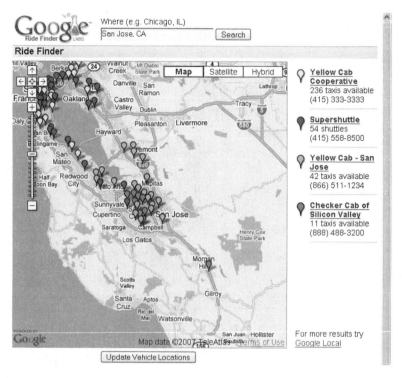

Click the Update Vehicle Locations link on the page below the map to see a trend in movement of vehicles.

Take a Tour of the Red Planet

Google Mars is a Google Labs product that lets you look at Mars in three-dimensional space, just as with Google Earth. Find the service at www.google.com/mars.

The Martian landscape shows three different types of image data. Click one of the options at the upper right of the program window (shown next).

Move around Mars

Use the navigation controls, as shown in the illustration, to move around the planet. Use the directional arrows to pan around the map. Drag the slider upward to zoom in, and downward to zoom out. Click the center icon to display the previous view.

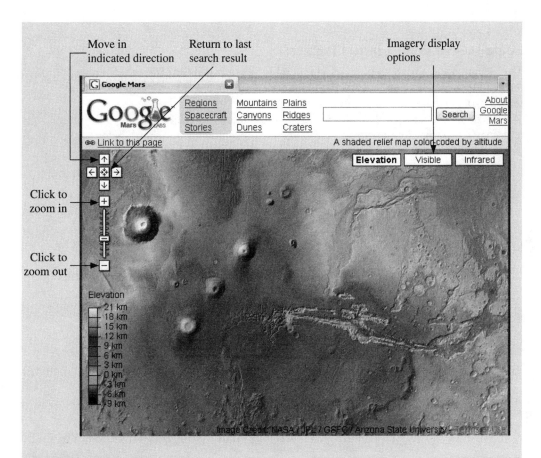

Choose a Planetary View

Your survey of the Martian landscape can be shown in three ways, including:

- The default display shows a brightly-colored relief map; use the Elevation key at the lower left to interpret altitudes corresponding to the color.

- Digital camera images make up the Visible display showing the surface, as well as dust and clouds.

- The Infrared images are the clearest as dust particles are transparent to infrared. The infrared map view shows brown patches indicating a high-resolution mosaic image has been constructed using the infrared data.

NOTE   *We all know that Mars is a dusty red color. Google Mars shows grayscale maps as contrast in surface detail is sharper in grayscale than color.*

Zoom into High Resolution Images

The Elevation and Visible displays let you zoom in as far as you can. The Infrared map, on the other hand, has a limited amount of data. Zooming in too close produces a tiled text image, explaining that imagery isn't available at that level of magnification.

The image includes a link to the closest high resolution area. Click the link in the image to display one of the close-up areas, such as the high-resolution image shown below.

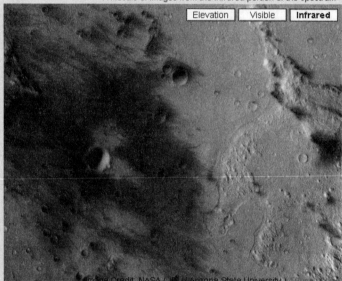

A mosaic of images from the infrared portion of the spectrum

Image Credit: NASA / JPL / Arizona State University

Search for Content

The Google Mars browser window offers different ways to search for content, including:

- Select a category from the directory links at the top of the page, then search in a particular category.
- Type a search term in the field and click Search.

For example, if you want to see how the Mars rovers are faring, type the rover's name in the Search field, type **rover**, or click the Spacecraft Directory link. The results of using the Spacecraft directory link are shown next.

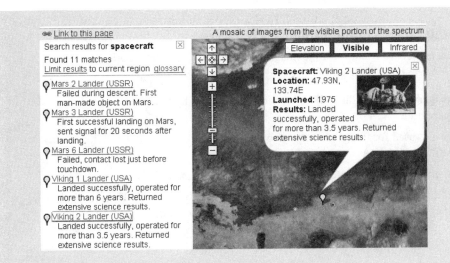

Los Angeles Basin

Fly through the Craters of Mars

Looking at areas of interest on Mars is entertaining, but fairly limited. You can't use the same features and tools as those provided in Google Earth, but you can experience a fascinating fly-through on Mars based on the imagery used to build Google Mars.

The University of Arizona is a part of the imaging consortium responsible for the Google Mars imagery. The fly-through is a collection of scenes built by the JPL (Jet Propulsion Laboratory) and make up a four-minute movie. Open the page at http://tinyurl.com/hoc3x and select a viewer. Follow any prompts that may display based on your chosen viewer, and watch the show.

Where the Images Come From

There are a number of sources for the images used in Google Mars that originate from different NASA systems, including:

- Imagery for Elevation and Visible view is collected by the Mars Global Surveyor spacecraft.
- Images used for Elevation maps also include data from the Mars Orbiter Laser Altimeter (MOLA).
- Visible images are captured by the Mars Orbiter Camera (MOC).
- Infrared images are captured by the Mars Odyssey spacecraft's Thermal Emission Imaging System (THEMIS) administered by Arizona State University.

Summary

In this chapter you've been all over the map, so to speak. You saw how Google Maps can be used to search for locations in different ways. You discovered the possibilities for searching for a business in a specific location, generating a route between two locations, and even planning an itinerary for your next trip or vacation. Google Maps includes the My Maps feature that allows you to create and configure your own maps. You learned how content can be added and personalized with custom text, images, and even video. For future reference, some of the map-related features coming from Google Labs were explained. Finally, the chapter ended with a trip to Mars.

In the next chapter, continue your travels in three dimensions with Google Earth.

Chapter 4

Travel the Earth

How to...

- Install and tour Google Earth
- Use different navigation methods
- Customize your Google Earth experience
- Search for locations and directions
- Add places in Google Earth

Google Earth is a new way of accessing information. The free program offers a view of our entire planet using satellite imagery. The Google Earth imagery database is enormous, and contains data for millions of square kilometers. Although not every square foot of the planet is visible at a high resolution, many locations are, offering a bird's-eye view of landscapes.

With Google Maps you can create your own map location information, plan vacation routes, or view information about places such as parks and historic locations.

Download and Install Google Earth

Unlike many Google services, Google Earth is downloaded and installed on your computer. Once you have installed the software, you access the satellite imagery from Google servers. There are four levels of Google Earth available that all use the same satellite imagery. This chapter describes using Google Earth Free, which is, as the name suggests, free software. Download the program from http://earth.google.com and follow the installation prompts.

There are other versions of the software as well:

- Google Earth Plus offers higher resolution printing. It also offers the user the ability to upload GPS information from their personal sources.

How to ... Choose Between Google Earth and Google Maps

Both Google Earth and Google Maps draw from the same satellite imagery. Google Earth is more interactive and includes more tools and content using its Layers feature, including the ability to use your own data. Google Maps shows two-dimensional maps; Google Earth is three-dimensional and offers flight features to simulate viewing buildings, landscape, and other features. In Google Earth, you can use tools for measuring distances and drawing.

- Google Earth Pro is a business tool. Users can export movie tours and import Geographic Information System (GIS) data.
- Google Earth Enterprise is business enterprise software used for mapping and satellite imaging work.

Take a Program Tour

When you open Google Earth, you initially see the planet from space, and the view zooms in to the United States (Figure 4-1).

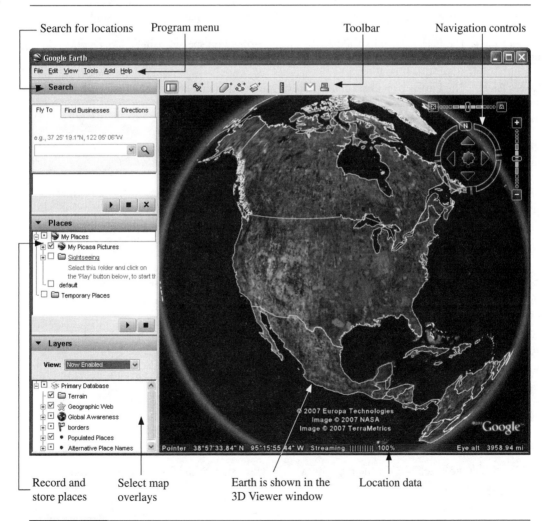

Search for locations   Program menu   Toolbar   Navigation controls

Record and store places   Select map overlays   Earth is shown in the 3D Viewer window   Location data

FIGURE 4-1 The default view shows the earth from space.

Check Out the Program Elements

The Google Earth program offers a great deal of information, and its interface is different from the usual sort of program you may be familiar with.

The different types of exploring you can do in Google Earth is covered in upcoming sections. For now, here's a brief rundown of the major components of the program:

Program Menus   Use the program's menus to set program options, toggle display items such as the Atmosphere, and choose options for playback and printing.

Search Panel   The Search panel offers three ways to find locations on the planet. You can choose the Fly To option using an address or coordinates; Find Businesses to locate a business in a particular location; and the Directions search to map a route from starting and end points.

Places Panel   The Places panel lists identified locations that you specify using a *placemark*. The Places panel offers a system of folders to store, locate, save, and organize placemarks.

Layers Panel   The Layers panel lists collections of information that have been created by Google and others you can use to overlay the data shown on the map. The choices range from Terrain maps to Parks and Recreation Areas to Shopping and Services.

Google Earth Toolbar   A toolbar of common features is included above the map window. Use the tools for adding placemarks, measuring, and printing, among other tasks.

3D Viewer   The largest part of the program window is taken up by the imagery. As you can see in Figure 4-1, the map is centered on the United States. Navigation controls are located at the upper right of the window. Since the world is round (!) the controls offer three-dimensional manipulation. That is, you can move horizontally, vertically, and also tilt the globe, which is especially interesting in terrain such as the Grand Canyon.

Location Data   Look for location specifications along the bottom of the map. You can see that the longitude and latitude of the mouse pointer's location at the lower left, and the altitude at which the map is viewed at the bottom right.

Be a Tourist on Planet Earth

To whet your appetite, and to give you a quick overview of the program, take a sightseeing tour. That way, you see how the imagery works and how Google Earth is used.

Follow these steps to take your first trip:

1. Click the (+) to the left of the Sightseeing folder in the Places panel to open a list of available tours.

2. Select the check box for the tour you want to view, such as the Forbidden City, China shown here.

TIP — *If you want to go on the Grand Tour, select the Sightseeing Places checkmark instead; all tour segments are automatically selected.*

3. Click Play at the bottom of the Places panel to start the tour.

NOTE — *The panels toggle open and closed as you see here. Click the arrow to the left of the panel's name to expand or collapse the panel. You can also drag the panel's edge up or down to resize the vertical space used by the panel.*

Click to view   Click to view   Click (+) to
added comments   image of location   zoom in closer

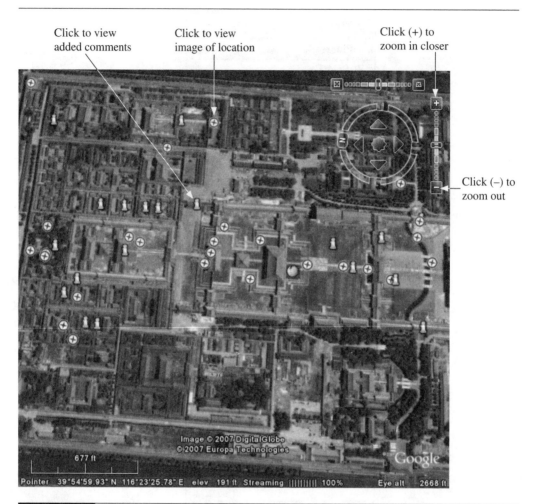

Click (−) to
zoom out

4. Sit back and relax. Google Earth rotates the globe and zooms in to the location in China (Figure 4-2).

5. Click the various locations identified on the map to see more information:

■ Click the compass icon to open a pop-up window, showing a photo that a Google Earth user has uploaded to the Google Earth Community for sharing.

■ Click the "i" icon to open a pop-up window containing comments about the location written by Google Earth Community members.

6. When you have finished viewing content, click Stop next to the Play button to stop the tour.

Did you know?

Google Earth Depends on Your System Files

Google Earth uses the software installed on your computer, as well as your system resources to display its map data and other information. Google Earth *renders*, or draws, its 3D content using the OpenGL driver platform, and requires drivers on your system to display smoothly.

If the program seems to be slow or isn't responding to your keyboard or mouse commands, you may need different video drivers. If you connect to the Internet using a dial-up connection, the slow response is related to the rate of data transfer, and new drivers won't improve the situation!

Read more about drivers, graphics cards, and other similar issues at http://tinyurl.com/235alb.

> **NOTE**   *There are thousands of animations, tools, tours, and other points of interest that organizations, businesses, and individuals have added to Google Earth. Check out the contributions at http://earth.google.com/showcase.*

Travel the Globe

The 3D Viewer shows the planet and terrain. There are a number of ways in which to locate specific locations, as you'll see in the next sections. To help you check out different points of interest, or if you want to explore the globe, Google Earth offers a Navigation console in addition to mouse navigation.

Navigate in Google Earth

The Navigation console is shown at the upper right of the 3D Viewer when the mouse cursor is in the upper right area of the window. In its inactive state, the console is hidden and a compass identifies North. To toggle the compass visibility, choose View | Compass.

Orient Yourself with a Mini-map

Choose View | Overview Map (or use the CTRL+M shortcut keystroke combination) to toggle a small overview map's visibility. As you see here, the overview map identifies your global location with crosshairs.

FIGURE 4-3   The Navigation console offers several ways to manipulate the 3D Viewer.

TIP

If you want to move to another location on the 3D Viewer, you can double-click the general area on the overview map to move the view.

Take Control of the Navigation Console

Navigation controls in Google Earth are fairly intuitive if you are familiar with moving in 3D space on a computer screen. Move the mouse cursor toward the upper right of the screen to display the Navigation controls (Figure 4-3).

The numbers in Figure 4-3 correspond to the following descriptions of the navigation functions:

1. Click the direction arrows to move the view in the corresponding direction.

2. Click the North button to reset the view, placing North at the top of the window.

3. Drag the navigation ring to rotate the view.

4. Click the center of the joystick and move it in any direction with the mouse button depressed. Notice here how the center of the joystick moves away from the center point in the direction you are moving.

5. Click or drag on the Zoom slider to increase or decrease the magnification. Click (+) the center point to zoom in; click (–) the center point to zoom out.

6. Click or drag on the Tilt slider to modify the horizon. Drag the slider left to view top-down; drag the slider right to view the horizon.

> **TIP** *Double-click the icons at the ends of the sliders to make the maximum zoom or tilt change to the view.*

Hands-on Navigation with Your Mouse

The simplest way to learn to use your mouse for navigation is to experiment. Different mouse configurations and operating systems work in different ways, as does using clicks in combination with mouse button presses.

> **NOTE** *You can set the navigation in the preferences on the Navigation Mode pane of the dialog box, described in the section "Customize Your Global Travel."*

Tips for Basic Mouse Navigation

Pan and Zoom is the Google Earth default. To return to the default from the other navigation types, press CTRL-T (COMMAND-T on Mac).

Here are some general mouse navigation tips using default Pan and Zoom settings:

- To drag the view in any direction, press the left or main mouse button and drag

- To *drift*, which simulates a globe spinning, press the left/main mouse button and drag in any direction; release the mouse and repeat to keep drifting.

- Double-click the mouse to zoom in. Single-click to stop the zoom or double-click to zoom more.

- If your mouse has a scroll wheel, scroll towards you to zoom in or away from you to zoom out. Press ALT (ALT/OPTION on Mac) as you scroll to decrease the zoom speed.

- Move the mouse to the center point of your desired zoom location and press the Right mouse button (CONTROL-CLICK on Mac) to display the double arrow cursor seen here. Now you can move the mouse toward you to zoom in, or away from you to zoom out.

Some Macintosh laptops let you drag two fingers across the trackpad to zoom in or out.

Buzz Around Using GForce Navigation

If you have used a joystick, you're going to enjoy GForce navigation. Like a joystick, moving the mouse in GForce mode specifies the direction in which the view moves. Click the 3D Viewer with the mouse to make it the active area on the program, and press CTRL-G (COMMAND-G on Mac) to invoke the mode.

When you enter GForce mode, you'll see that the cursor changes to an airplane. The motion effects are more obvious the closer you are to the surface. The actions you need to fly include the following:

- To pan across the view, left-click the mouse and move it right of center to pan right, or left of center to move left.

- To tilt to the top-down view, left-click and drag the mouse away from you; to tilt to the horizon view, left click the mouse and drag toward you (Figure 4-4).

- To speed up, right-click the mouse (CONTROL-CLICK on Mac) and move the mouse forward, or away from you.

- To slow down, right-click the mouse (CONTROL-CLICK on Mac) and move the mouse backward, or toward you.

- Press SPACEBAR to stop the motion in the window.

FIGURE 4-4   Change your perspective from top-down (shown left) to the horizon view (shown right).

How to ...   Find Your Way Back Home

Sometimes you can get lost—even in a program. To find your way back, click the default placemark in the My Places folder and click Play, as shown here. The 3D Viewer moves the view back to the middle of the country, or another country that uses your language.

Specify a location and name for the Default placemark if you like. Read how that's done in the section "Save Places for Future Reference."

Click-and-Zoom to Move In and Out

Suppose you are interested in opening a coffee shop in a particular area of the city. Google Earth offers Click-and-Zoom navigation to let you zoom in and out at will. Use a controlled rate of magnification to zoom in to see a business location; zoom out to see what else is available in the neighborhood.

To start the Click-and-Zoom mode, choose Tools | Options | Navigation | Navigation Mode | Click-and-Zoom; on Mac, choose Google Earth | Preferences | Navigation | Navigation Mode | Click-and-Zoom.

The cursor now changes to crosshairs as you see here, along with several coffee shops marked with labels. Left-click the mouse to zoom in, right-click the mouse to zoom out, and press SPACEBAR to stop the action. Your mouse is restricted in this view—use the Navigation Controls for other actions.

NOTE   *The labels on the map show search results. See how to search in Google Earth in the later section "Search for a Business or Directory Listing."*

Customize Your Global Travel

As with most computer programs, the more you work with Google Earth, the more you become interested in showing and using specific features that fit your workflow and habits. There are a number of different view options you can try, as well as a collection of preferences for setting features ranging from the mouse speed to the detail area.

Work with Different Views for Different Purposes

Zooming around the world is an entertaining way to spend time, but Google Earth certainly isn't just a toy. There are a number of ways to change your view for different purposes. Some configure the display in the 3D Viewer, while others show playback options or print output views.

Modify the 3D Viewer Experience

Several of the viewing features are shown on the 3D Viewer by default, including the Status Bar at the bottom of the window, the Scale Legend above the Status Bar, and the Compass at the upper right of the window.

Choose the commands from the View menu to toggle the features on and off. The Overview Map, described in the previous section, displays a small map in the upper left of the 3D Viewer to orient you to your location. You can also toggle the Atmosphere on and off. By default, you see the Earth's atmosphere as a glow around the curve of the planet when you are zoomed out sufficiently.

For those accustomed to showing projection lines for longitude and latitude, choose View | Grid to overlay the grid as you see here.

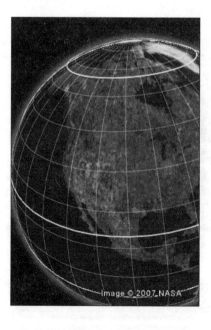

Image © 2007 NASA

You'll also find settings to toggle the Toolbar and Sidebar on and off, as well as view the map at Full Screen size.

Choose View Sizes for Different Purposes

Google Earth offers choices to view your data according to computer playback, TV playback, and print output size options.

Specify a Computer Monitor View Sometimes a program you view on your monitor looks entirely different under other circumstances. For instance, if you want to include a satellite imagery view of your business locations on a small monitor or projector, take the time to check out the view displayed on your tradeshow equipment. Choose View | View Size | Computer Playback and choose one of three aspect ratios (also called proportional displays) to use for showing the view (Figure 4-5). The program window is resized automatically, although you can resize it manually as you like.

Choose a TV Playback Option Choose View | View Size | TV Playback and select an option for video display. Use NTSC (720 × 486) for TV playback in North America; use PAL (720 × 576) for European TV playback.

Choose Print Settings To specify one of four page sizes for printing, choose View | View Size | Print Output and make your selection. The default uses a regular 8.5 × 11 Landscape view. Choose the larger 11 × 17 page size, or smaller 4 × 6 and 5 × 7 page sizes.

Customize Program Preferences

Google Earth offers a panel of preferences you can adjust to make your experiences more life-like and smoother flowing. To start, choose Tools | Options on Windows/Linux, or Google Earth | Preferences on Mac from the Google Earth menu to open the five-tab Google Earth Options dialog box.

Set 3D View Options

The Google Earth Options dialog box displays the 3D View tab when it opens. On this tab, configure visual settings such as label or icon sizes, the format for elevations, and the size of the detail areas and Overview Map.

FIGURE 4-5 Specify an aspect ratio for sizing the screen appropriately for playback to a device.

Here are some tips for adjusting 3D View options:

- If your monitor uses a high resolution and you have a quick graphics card, use the Large Detail Area to increase the size of the image shown in high quality detail.

- The default font used in Google Earth is Arial at 20px. Click the Primary 3D font or Secondary 3D font buttons to select an alternate font from the Select Font dialog box if you prefer another text appearance. Regardless of the font chosen, the text displays in white with a black stroke as seen here.

- Boost the Elevation Exaggeration if you are traveling in the mountains. The range is from 0.5 to 3; 1.0 is the elevation at its true height. In Figure 4-6, the mountain at the left is shown at an Elevation Exaggeration value of 0.5, whereas the right image shows the same mountain with a value of 2.

FIGURE 4-6   Adjust the appearance of a mountain's elevation from the default (left) to twice as high (right).

If you are looking at 3D View buildings and they don't look quite right, be sure the Elevation Exaggeration is set to 1 as the building may have default terrain settings.

■ If you like working with the Overview Map, adjust its size smaller or larger to fit your screen.

Adjust Storage Using Cache Settings

Google Earth automatically optimizes the cache size, which is the amount of memory allocated to Google Earth to perform its tasks. You can improve performance by increasing the cache size, but as a result, you may find other programs process data slower. If you like to work with Google Earth offline, consider increasing the Disk cache anywhere up to 2000 MB, which is the maximum setting.

Pick Touring Preferences

Use the Touring preferences to adjust how you want to watch the Fly To and Tour features. The default uses slow speeds for both features, and a pause time of 1.7 seconds at each change of roadway. Drag the sliders to increase the flight speeds and the pause time.

Change the way you watch a route flyover using the Driving Directions Tour Options. By default, the camera is tilted at 45 degrees, as shown here. You can change the camera view, speed, range, and angle while doing a flying tour of your driving directions by dragging sliders.

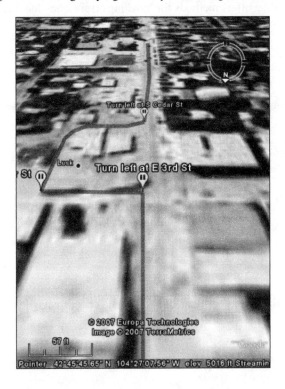

Fine-Tune Navigation Controls

For the power mouse users, increase the speed of the mouse wheel setting in the Navigation tab. The default speed is rather slow; be sure to experiment with the speeds as Fast moves the map at supersonic speeds. Also on the Navigation tab, look for settings to select different Navigation modes, described earlier in the chapter (Figure 4-7).

TIP   *Depending on your personal preference, choose the Invert Mouse Wheel Zoom Direction check box to swap the mouse wheel directions. For some people, the inverse feels more natural when maneuvering in three-dimensional space.*

Select General Settings

The final group of preferences are on the General tab. On this tab, choose:

- Display options, including Show Tooltips and Show Web Results in External Browser, both chosen by default. When you click a web link on a placemark, a new browser window opens by default.

- Select a language and specify whether to send usage statistics to Google.

- E-mail program options for sending e-mail through Google Earth; the choices include Thunderbird, Gmail, or Select Each Time.

- KML Error Handling offers methods for handling errors when loading layer data, such as 3D Viewer drawings.

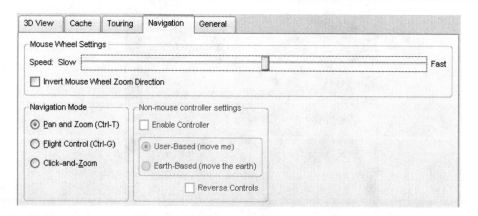

FIGURE 4-7   Adjust the speed for the mouse wheel and choose navigation modes.

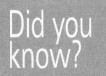

Google Earth Can Display Google SketchUp Models

Google SketchUp is a program that you can use to draw and save three-dimensional objects and models. There are thousands of models available to place on your Google Earth locations. Find help for integrating SketchUp models in Google Earth at http://tinyurl.com/2z4gxc.

Download Google SketchUp at http://tinyurl.com/e8a4e.

Search for Locations All Over the World

The Search panel is one of the default Google Earth panels and one you may use most often. There are three ways to find a location—using an address, a business name, or by defining a route.

Use combinations of search terms with or without commas. For greater accuracy, use two terms such as a city and state, street location and city, city and country, longitude and latitude, and so on. In each type of search Google Earth offers an example, as shown here.

TIP   *Street-level searching isn't supported throughout the entire planet yet.*

Fly To a Location

You can use the Google Earth Search panel to find places on the globe. To conduct a search and view the results, follow these steps:

1. Type the location in the Search field. For example, type **MoMA, New York** and click Search.

2. The search returns are shown in the lower part of the Search panel. Several locations are identified by letters (Figure 4-8). Google Earth shows icons for ten results on the 3D Viewer at a time.

3. Scroll through the results to find the location you are looking for. Your search results are stored in the Search entry history on the Search panel, and shown in pages of 10 results at a time. As you see in Figure 4-8, the returns are shown in page by page views; click a number below the list of displayed results to view another page of results in the Search panel.

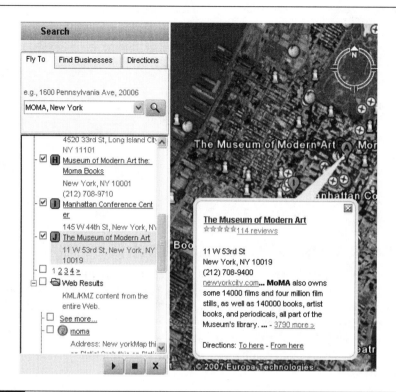

FIGURE 4-8   Search for an address and select the return to view the map location.

4. Click a result to zoom in on the 3D Viewer. Basic information about the location is shown in a balloon.

5. To find out more about the location, click a link on the balloon.

6. To clear the search results from the map and the Search panel, click Clear Searches on the Search panel's controls.

Search for a Business or Directory Listing

You can search for directory listings and business locations using the Find Businesses tab in Google Earth. Specify the type of business and where it is located to yield a list of search results and numbered markers on the view.

Use the features described in Chapters 1 and 2 for designing search terms. For example, use the exact name of a business in quotations "Bob's Furniture Emporium" to narrow the results to those exact terms in that order. A search conducted in the same area for *furniture* will produce a much larger number of returns.

The Find Businesses feature uses Google Maps search to search a combination of Yellow Page listings and web page information for the location. The search starts from the location specified in the Search fields, and can be a city, street, or the current view shown on the 3D Viewer. For example, if you are meeting with clients at their office and want to entertain them for dinner, type **restaurants** as the What term, and the office location as the Where term to view a list of results.

NOTE *Read about using Google Maps in Chapter 3.*

Conduct the Search

Follow these steps to look for a business or type of business:

1. Type your search term in the What Text field, for example, **antiques**.

2. Type your location terms in the Where field, such as **New Orleans**. Alternatively, if you have already displayed a region in which to search in the Fly To search, use the default Current View as the Where search term.

TIP *My preference is often to Fly To the location where I want to start looking and then use the Current View option. Google Earth will look for a number of results, and expand the search beyond the current view to collect returns.*

3. Click Search. The returns are shown in the Search panel, and identified locations are identified with lettered markers on the map (Figure 4-9).

Explore the Search Returns

Once the search is complete, select a result link in the Search panel or click a marker on the current view in the 3D Viewer to show a balloon, as shown here.

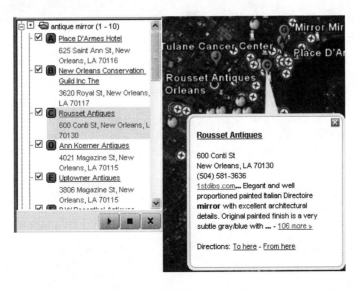

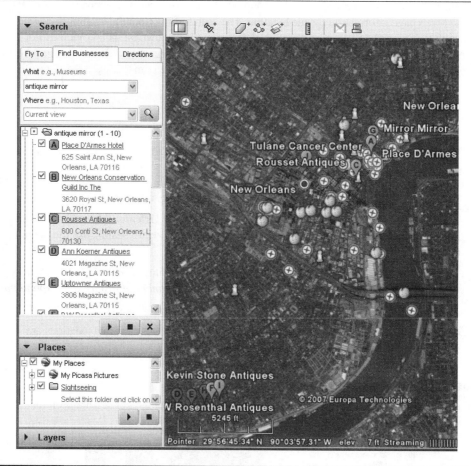

FIGURE 4-9 The 3D Viewer shows lettered markers and resets the view if necessary.

TIP

Some of the results may not directly relate to your quest, although the web pages searched by Google Earth include your search terms. The example search for an antique mirror in New Orleans returned results for antique shops, as well as hotels that describe antiques used in their décor. Deselect the check boxes for those unnecessary results to clear the view if it seems too cluttered.

A search for an antique mirror shows information about the results in the balloon. To continue the search, choose one of these options:

■ Click the link to the business' website, which opens in Google Maps (Figure 4-10).

■ Click the link to the web page describing the item—when one is shown, as in this example—to open a web page showing the quote and additional information about the search match.

■ Click the link listing additional results to display the Google Maps information shown in Figure 4-10.

Store Your Search Results

Your search terms for both What and Where are saved in the Search history, shown in the results area of the Search panel. The search results from the current search that are displayed in the 3D Viewer are indicated with a dot in the check box next to the search terms, shown here.

Link from the business listing to a Google Maps page offering more information.

The next time you open Google Earth, the last ten searches are displayed. The Find Businesses search storage is independent of the Fly To search results.

Get Directions to a Destination

Use Google Earth to map a route to and from a placemark in the 3D Viewer, including turn-by-turn directions.

Take a Shortcut

Right-click/CONTROL-click a listing result on the Find Businesses tab and then choose either Directions To Here or Directions From Here from the shortcut menu. The Search panel transfers the information to the Directions tab, and the route and directions are shown in the Search results window, seen here.

To Here/From Here

On the 3D Viewer, click a search result listing or placemark to open an information balloon. Click To Here or From Here to add the location details in the To or From field in the Directions tab (Figure 4-11). Repeat with the other address and click Search. You find the route and directions in the results area of the Search panel.

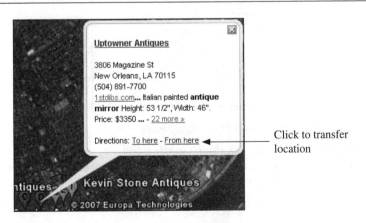

Click to transfer location

FIGURE 4-11   Use a placemark as an endpoint for a route.

Ask for Directions

Type start and end locations in the Directions tab and click Search. The route and turn-by-turn directions display in the search window. On the 3D Viewer, the route is indicated with a line.

If your route includes intercontinental travel, Google's search returns take you to one shore, suggest you "swim across the Atlantic Ocean" and then resume when you reach dry land again!

Print the Driving Directions

Take your route directions along with you on your tour. Print your route following these steps:

1. Select the directions you want to print in the Directions tab.

2. Choose File | Print to open the Print dialog box.

3. Select Most Recent Driving Directions as shown here.

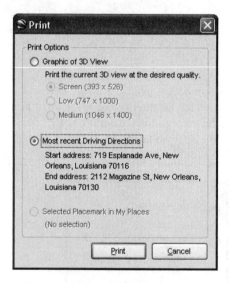

4. Click Print to open your system's Print dialog box.

5. Specify the print settings and click Print. Google Earth maps your route point and transfers the data to a print version. Your directions are printed, along with images of intersections where you have to turn (Figure 4-12).

6. When you are finished, deselect the check box next to the directions summary or delete the Search results.

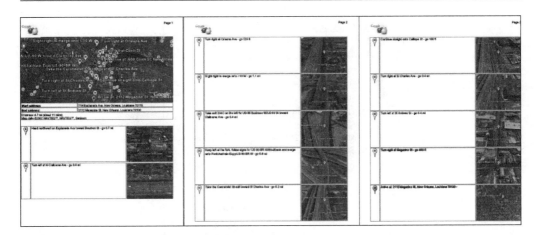

FIGURE 4-12   Take a well-featured map with you to show your route.

Play a Tour

Instead of simply viewing directions on a map, let Google Earth take you on a tour of your journey. Click Route at the end of the list of directions as you see here, and then click the Play Tour button.

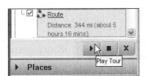

Your tour starts in the 3D Viewer from your departure point. The globe is rotated to orient the route toward your destination. Once the tour is finished, the map zooms out to show you the entire route.

Save Route Directions for Future Reference

If you are plotting a number of routes, or want to share your directions with others, save them in the My Places folder in the Places panel for future reference. To save your route, select the folder labeled with the To and From search terms. Right-click (CONTROL-CLICK on Mac) to display the shortcut menu and choose Save to My Places (Figure 4-13).

The directions, now stored in the My Places folder, can be edited as with any other place data.

Take Your Place in the World

Use the Places panel to hold placemarks for locations you want to save. There are several different ways to save the information from searches done in the Searches panel, manual searches, and from items imported from Picasa.

Use the Places panel to keep track of places you have experienced in Google Earth. You can save Places data to your hard drive, work with saved placemarks, and organize the data in a number of ways.

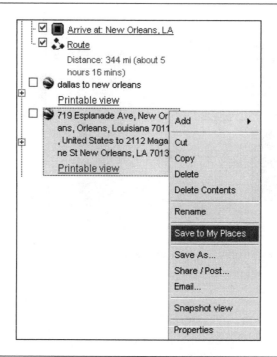

FIGURE 4-13 Store content from your searches for future reference in the Places panel.

NOTE *For an additional discussion of adding content such as placemarks, or drawing shapes and lines, see the section "Add Custom Content to Personalize Your Map" in Chapter 3.*

Save Places for Future Reference

Add content to your Places panel storage as new placemarks or as points of interest.

Add a New Placemark

If you are doing a manual search, or have found a location via a Search panel process, apply a placemark to keep track of the location. To add and customize a placemark, follow these steps:

1. Zoom into the location in the 3D Viewer.

2. Click the Pushpin icon on the toolbar, and move it over the viewer. The Google Earth-New dialog box opens and the New Placemark icon is shown on the viewer inside a yellow square, as you see here.

3. Drag the view in the 3D Viewer until the icon overlays the location you want to mark.

4. In the Google Earth-New dialog box, type a name for the placemark. The Latitude and Longitude are automatically specified for the placemark's location.

5. You can choose a custom icon as well. Click the icon shown next to the name field to open a dialog box containing several dozen icons. Make a selection and click OK to display the new icon on the view.

> **TIP** *You can also import your own icons into the program to use for your placemarks.*

6. Type notes or identifying information in the Description if you like. Content added here is shown in the placemark's balloon.

7. Add additional customizations to the placemark as desired by using settings on the remaining tabs in the dialog box:

■ On the Style, Color tab, choose a color for the Label and Icon by clicking the color swatch and then choosing a color in the respective color pickers; specify the opacity and scale as you see here.

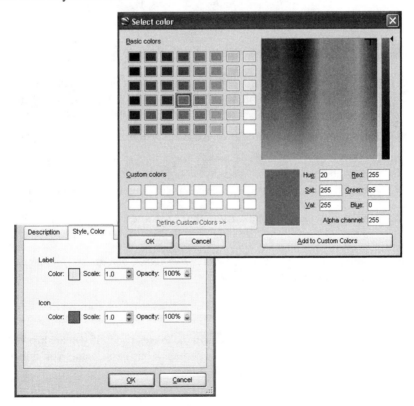

FIGURE 4-14   Your completed placemark is shown on the view.

- On the View tab, the location values such as Longitude, Latitude, and Tilt are shown by default. Choose the Center in View check mark to set your placemark center in the view when the placemark is selected from the Places panel.

- Change the Altitude if you like on the Altitude tab. By default, your placemark is clamped to the ground.

8.   Click OK to close the dialog box and save your placemark. To test the placemark, click it on the view; information added to the description is shown in the pop-up balloon (Figure 4-14).

If you want to modify the placemark, right-click/CONTROL-click the listing in the Places panel or on the icon on the 3D Viewer and then choose Properties to open the dialog box.

NOTE   *Read more about customizations for the placemarks, places, and folders at*
http://tinyurl.com/3bf7og.

Saving a Point of Interest

Placemarks aren't the only way to store listings in the Places panel. If you are browsing search results and come across something on the view, perhaps a business contact you'd like to make on an upcoming trip, save the Point of Interest (POI) as a placemark.

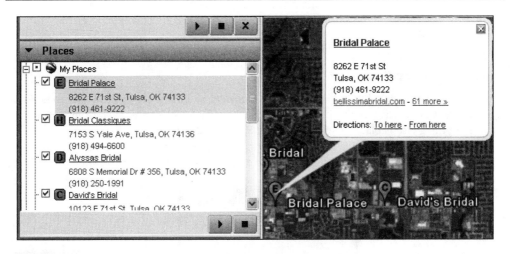

FIGURE 4-15 Store placemarks for storage in the Places panel.

NOTE *Read about Points of Interest in the next section "Layer Information on the 3D Viewer."*

Right-click/CONTROL-click the placemark on the 3D Viewer to open the shortcut menu and select Save to My Places. In your Places folder, the new listing displays the placemark information from the 3D Viewer (Figure 4-15).

NOTE *If you want to publish a placemark for public use, you can share it on the Google Earth Community BBS website. Right-click/CONTROL-click the placemark and choose Share/Post. Follow the prompts in the Google Earth Community posting wizard to post the placemark.*

Save Search Return Results

Your searches can be saved, as described in the previous section. If you want to make a list of locations to visit on your next business trip, move the results from the Search returns list in the Search panel to the Places panel.

You can use any of a number of options to select a result, copy it, and paste it to your My Places folder, or simply drag it. Select the result from the Search panel and drag it to the Places panel. Release the mouse and the location is stored.

Images geotagged in Picasa can be used as placemarks in Google Earth. Read how that's done in the sidebar "How to Tag an Image to Its Location on Earth" in Chapter 6.

Saving Temporary Places

When you first start Google Earth, the Places panel includes an empty My Places folder to hold places that you want to save. Items that are within the My Places folder are saved from session to session; everything else is placed in the Temporary Places folder.

Temporary items are discarded if you close Google Earth without saving them. Fortunately, you'll see a prompt to save the content if you try to close the program as you see here.

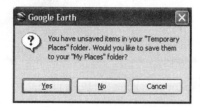

Layer Information on the 3D Viewer

The Layers panel is a treasure house of information generated by individuals and organizations. By far, the best way to appreciate the layers that overlay the 3D Viewer is to experiment with them.

Don't turn on dozens of layers at one time. It takes longer for the information to display on the view, and also clutters up what you see.

Turn a few layers on at a time at most, and make sure to turn them off when you are done. When you see placemark icons for some information, make sure you try clicking on some of them. Some of these layers provide a lot of information in the descriptions of the placemarks.

Here are some suggestions for basic geographic information:

- **Terrain** You may want to keep the Terrain layer on at all times as it shows the 3D terrain you see when you "tilt" your view and lets you see things like mountain, valleys, and canyons.

- **Roads** Google has detailed roads and streets for many countries including the US, Canada, much of Europe, Japan, and Brazil. More countries are becoming available every few months. As you zoom in you get more detail. From higher altitudes you'll see fewer (or no) roads with this layer turned on.

■ **Borders**   This lets you see the outlines of countries, island names, coastlines, and administrative orders (states, counties, provinces, and so on). It even includes details on some disputed border regions. Again, as you zoom you may see more or less border information.

■ **Populated places**   This is what shows the labels and locations for towns and cities world-wide

■ **Geographic features**   This category contains sublayers for things like locations of volcanoes, names of mountains, and water bodies.

Another selection of the layers serve the purpose of highlighting points of interest if you are traveling. This is the same kind of information you get with a modern car navigation device (or GPS) for finding hotels, restaurants, etc. Examples of these kinds of layers in Google Earth are: Dining, Lodging, Shopping and Services, Transportation, Travel and Tourism, Parks and

How to ...   Find In-depth Information and Assistance

This chapter offers a brief introduction to what Google Earth has to offer. To use the program terms, this is merely a "high altitude fly-over." Here are some links to online sources:

■ The Google Earth Help Center is a good place to start, located at http://tinyurl.com/38j6pn.

■ Download a PDF version of the User Guide from http://earth.google.com/userguide/v4/google_earth_user_guide.pdf.

■ Google Earth User Guide at http://tinyurl.com/29ep3v.

■ Hands-on tutorials for using Google Earth at http://tinyurl.com/2aokbh.

■ Lists of frequently asked questions (FAQ) about Google Earth at http://tinyurl.com/dd3vp.

■ Troubleshooting information for error messages, graphics cards, configuration, and other issues is at http://tinyurl.com/2d26tw.

■ The Google Earth Community is a collection of dozens of forums for connecting with other Google Earth users at http://tinyurl.com/beq5z.

In addition to the official Google sites, there are many personal blogs and sites about working with Google Earth.

Recreation, and Community Services. As with the roads, Google has been steadily deploying this kind of information for more countries during the past several months.

All of the layers mentioned previously are useful and important, but the really interesting layers are coming from a variety of sources not originally maintained or created by Google. Google recently released the Geographic Web layers, which consist of a careful selection of useful information and pictures and references to web-based information on places all over the Earth.

And, when that isn't enough, you can turn to the Google Earth Community layers, which show placemarks from posts made by hundreds of thousands of contributors about virtually everywhere on the Earth.

And finally, Google Earth has Featured Content layers, which highlight content from a variety of organizations. Here you will find information from Rumsey Historical Maps, National Geographic Magazine, Discovery Channel, European Space Agency, and even the United Nations. These layers highlight information of human interest, science, history, the environment, and even restaurant reviews.

Summary

This chapter showed you how to travel the globe from the comfort of your office or home. You saw how to take a tour of different locations in the program, and learned how to navigate using different types of navigation tools and features. You discovered how to work with the 3D Viewer and how to customize the program's preferences to maximize your experience with Google Earth. Like other Google products, Google Earth offers searching, helping you readily locate businesses, locations, and find directions. You saw how the Google Earth program saves and stores your searches, and how to add your own places.

In the next chapter, see how you can keep up to date and communicate with others using tools like Google Group, News, and Google Talk.

Chapter 5

Talk It Up

How to...

- Contribute to, and start your own Google Group
- Manage news using Google News
- Get up to date financial information with Google Finance
- Use mobile services, such as Google SMS, maps, and product information
- Communicate instantly with Google Talk

Look to Google for tools, services, and features to strengthen the backbone of your personal, business, and social communication systems. Google offers specialized information exchange features in Google Groups that let you communicate with others online or via e-mail. Search and locate targeted information with Google News. Take your information with you using Google e-mail and search features on your phone.

Participate in Discussion Groups

Google Groups is a convenient way for connecting and communicating with like-minded users and accessing information, either by e-mail or by browser.

If you are interested in something—from aardvarks to zoology and all points in between—there is sure to be a Google Group for you. Tap into the resources of Google Groups using searches, join a group, or start your own.

 For detailed information, check out the Google Groups Help site at http://tinyurl .com/yvlarz.

Search Google Groups

Google offers specialized searches for tracking down groups and content in postings. Google Groups offer a range of features that include:

- The ability to create custom pages and web pages within the group
- Customization of the appearance and graphics used in the group's page
- Uploading files to Google's servers for sharing with the group
- Storing profiles that other group members can access or search

To get started, click Groups from the links above the text search fields on the Google home page to display the Google Groups home page (Figure 5-1).

Search the contents
of group posts

Click for an
overview

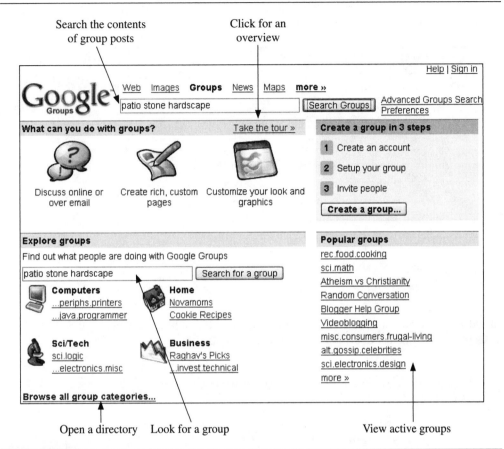

Open a directory   Look for a group

View active groups

FIGURE 5-1   The Google Groups home page offers several ways to get started.

Search Posts in Existing Groups

If you want to read opinions, advice, and information given by users and consumers rather than sifting through general searches, give the posted content from Google Groups a try.

Type your search terms in the text field and click Search Groups to conduct the search. Your returns are displayed in the Google Groups Search window as with other types of Google searches. As you see here, the results identify the locations of keywords, and include a link to the group where the post originated. Below the listing, the time of the posting, its author, and the number of associated messages are displayed.

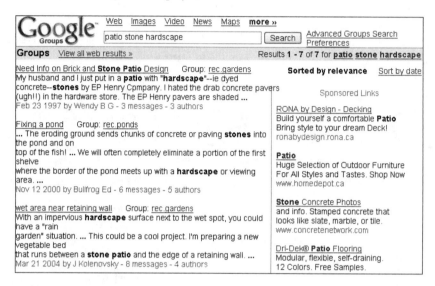

Targeted ads are shown at the right of the returns window. If you like, click View All Web Results in the blue title bar to explore general search results.

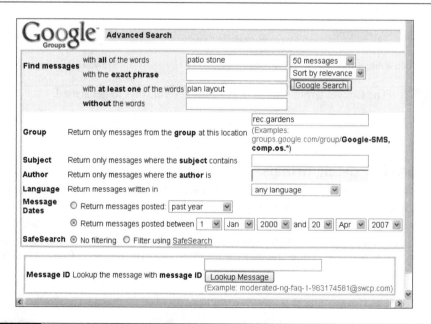

FIGURE 5-2   Customize the search results using advanced features.

How to ...   Take Advantage of Google Groups Searching

Why bother with searches in Google Groups? Many experts in different fields are involved in Google Groups and help point out important issues. Here are some examples to help answer that question:

- You are involved in product marketing and want to see what the consumer thinks of your product, and that of the competition.

- You are looking for new product ideas and want to find out what your consumer base is looking for or asking about.

- You are facing a business management situation, such as retooling a workflow, and want to find out if other businesses have faced and dealt with the same issues.

- You are looking for advice on a home improvement project and would like to read unbiased information and user experiences.

- You need information to help you make an important life decision, whether that be taking a medication or how successfully others have home-schooled their children.

- Your dog (or cat, or fish, or kid) has a skin condition and you'd like to explore dietary options.

- You're planning a vacation with your family who live in a number of cities, and you'd like to communicate in a convenient way that lets you keep track of the details.

- Anything else you can think of—the list is virtually endless.

Use Advanced Search Terms to Narrow the Returns

Google offers an advanced searching form for all of its search types. When you scan the search results, you may find some returns that deal with the subject you are looking for, while others may use your search terms in passing. You might also find a particular group that has several postings about your search topic.

Instead of sifting through the returns, click Advanced Groups Search to the right of the search text field to open the form (Figure 5-2).

Customize the elements of your search in the Advanced Search window. Combine combinations of different keywords that should or shouldn't be present; specify a search in a particular group; define a date range for searching, and so on.

For highly-targeted searches, you can search by the subject, author, or by typing the message ID, a number assigned to each post to a Google Group. In the example shown in Figure 5-2, the keywords used in the initial search are used again in a different configuration, and the group that seemed to have the most useful posts in the general search, **rec.gardens**, is typed to constrain results to that group.

Click Google Search to conduct the search using the string of terms you specify. In the example, the search is typed as **patio stone (plan OR layout) group:rec.gardens** and includes the specified date range, as you see here.

NOTE   *Read about using operators and conducting searches in Chapters 1 and 2.*

Search for an Interesting Group to Join

From the Google Groups home page you can search for a group to explore and join. Type the search terms in the Explore Groups section of the home page (shown in Figure 5-1) and click Search for a group.

The search returns offer several methods to sort through the returns. In Figure 5-3, a search for **car repair** hunts through Google Groups' directory and returns 49 groups that feature the terms.

Choose one of these methods to narrow the list further:

- Select a topic to view groups according to a category; if you are looking for information on the cost of car repairs, you aren't likely to find what you need in the Computers topic.

- Specify a region to narrow the group list to your part of the world.

- Choose a language from the list if there are multiple languages.

- Select a group on the basis of its level of activity or its number of members.

The Ins and Outs of Participating in Google Groups

To participate in a group you need to have a Google Account. Click the Sign In link at the upper right of the Google Groups home page to open the Sign In page. You can create an account from this page if you don't have one.

NOTE   *Read about Google Accounts in Chapter 8.*

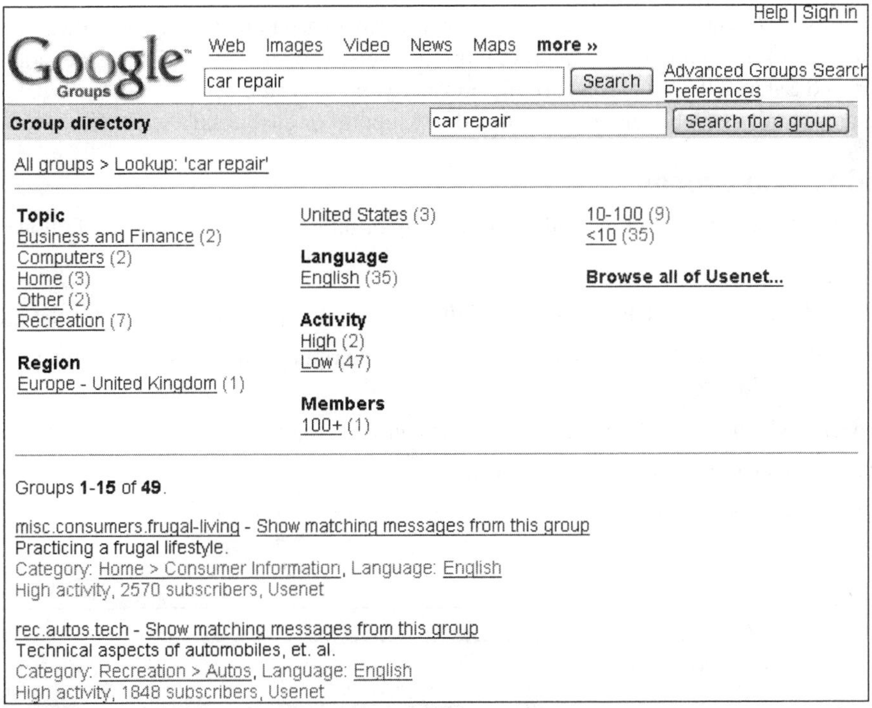

Google Groups directory screenshot showing:

Help | Sign in
Web   Images   Video   News   Maps   **more »**
car repair   [Search]   Advanced Groups Search / Preferences

Group directory   car repair   [Search for a group]

All groups > Lookup: 'car repair'

Topic   United States (3)   10-100 (9)
Business and Finance (2)   <10 (35)
Computers (2)   **Language**
Home (3)   English (35)   **Browse all of Usenet...**
Other (2)
Recreation (7)   **Activity**
                              High (2)
Region   Low (47)
Europe - United Kingdom (1)
                              Members
                              100+ (1)

Groups **1-15** of **49**.

misc.consumers.frugal-living - Show matching messages from this group
Practicing a frugal lifestyle.
Category: Home > Consumer Information, Language: English
High activity, 2570 subscribers, Usenet

rec.autos.tech - Show matching messages from this group
Technical aspects of automobiles, et. al.
Category: Recreation > Autos, Language: English
High activity, 1848 subscribers, Usenet

FIGURE 5-3   Track down groups of interest listed in the Google Groups directory.

Did you know?

Usenet Newsgroups Pioneered the Online Newsgroup

The Usenet system began as an online bulleting board system in 1979 at Duke University. Users post messages to the bulletin boards for reading via newsreaders. There are thousands of Usenet groups that can be distinguished by their names. Group names are written in a hierarchical format, such as rec.garden.cactus, meaning the *cactus* Usenet group which is part of the larger *garden* group, which is in turn part of the larger *recreation* group.

Usenet postings from 1981 and on are archived by Google Groups. The archives can be searched as with other Google searches and read in a browser rather than a newsreader. Posts to the groups are handled within Google Groups. Google Groups have a group owner who can control the content of the posts, while Usenet groups may or may not be moderated.

What You Need to Get Started

In addition to your Google Account, you need a browser that can support group activities. Google Groups is fully supported by Internet Explorer, version 6 and newer; Firefox version 1.5 and newer, and Safari 2.0.3. Regardless of the browser you use, you must have cookies enabled. Some features aren't available on browsers that don't support or enable JavaScript 1.3.

Join and Post to Groups

Once you have done some searching and found a group of interest, joining is simple. Follow these steps:

1. Click the group's name in the search results or listing to open the host page for the group.
2. Click Subscribe to This Group from the panel at the right of the browser window to display the Join form (Figure 5-4).
3. Specify whether to receive e-mail, and how you want to receive it.
4. Type a nickname to use for the postings.
5. Click Subscribe to This Group.

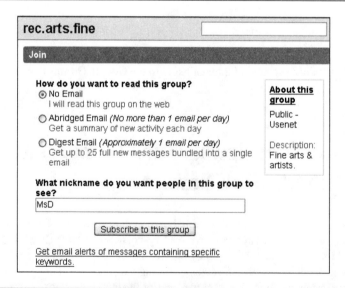

FIGURE 5-4   Subscribe to a group using the form.

TIP *You can receive alerts from different Google services via e-mail. Refer to the section "Keep Up to Date With E-mail Alerts" for more information.*

Manage Your Groups

Some of us enjoy participating in groups a great deal. Whether you are a member of three or thirty groups, Google Groups offers tools to manage your subscriptions. Once you have joined one or more groups, links are listed at the top right of the Google Groups home page, shown here.

TIP *If you belong to a large number of groups, click the My Groups drop-down arrow from the links at the top of the Google Groups page and select a group.*

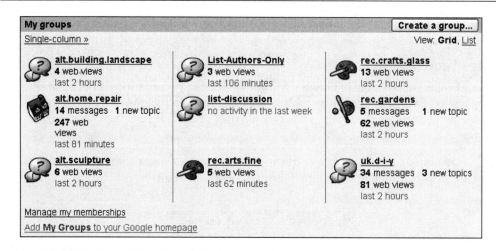

My groups   Create a group...
Single-column »   View: **Grid**, List

alt.building.landscape   **List-Authors-Only**   **rec.crafts.glass**
4 web views   3 web views   13 web views
last 2 hours   last 106 minutes   last 2 hours

alt.home.repair   **list-discussion**   **rec.gardens**
14 messages 1 new topic   no activity in the last week   5 messages 1 new topic
247 web   62 web views
views   last 2 hours
last 81 minutes

alt.sculpture   **rec.arts.fine**   **uk.d-i-y**
6 web views   5 web views   34 messages 3 new topics
last 2 hours   last 62 minutes   81 web views
                                                                   last 2 hours

Manage my memberships
Add **My Groups** to your Google homepage

FIGURE 5-5   Expand the view of your group memberships on the Google Groups home page.

To manage your groups, click Expand to display the My Groups section on the Google
Groups home page seen in Figure 5-5.

> **TIP**
> *If you are viewing any page but the Google Groups home page, you can click the My
> Groups drop-down arrow at the top of the page to open a list of all your groups, or click
> the My Groups link to display the Google Groups home page.*

From the My Groups area on the page, you can

- Specify the group display as either a grid, as in Figure 5-5, or in a list
- Click the link to a group to display the group's page
- Click Manage My Memberships to open a window where you can specify the nickname
  used for each group as well as how you want to receive mail
- Add My Groups as a component to your Google home page
- Create your own group, described in the upcoming section "Start Your Own Group."

Read Messages and Post Replies

Although you can search and read postings from any public group, you must belong to a group to
post messages. Open the group's page to view a list of the topics and sort options (Figure 5-6).

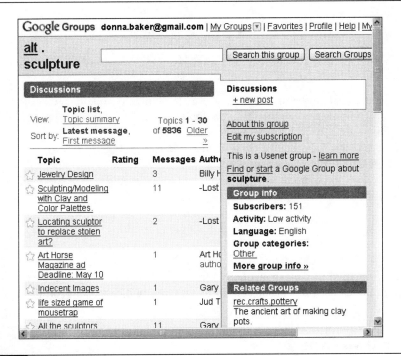

FIGURE 5-6   Work with the group's postings in a number of ways.

Specify how you want to view the messages by choosing either a Topic Summary or Topic List view. Click the listing for the message you want to read, and click Reply as you see here. Type your response and then click Send.

You Can Create and Share a Personal Profile

Constructing a personal profile increases the sense of community and offers other group members information about you, although you don't need a personal profile to participate in Google Groups.

Click Profile in the listings at the top of the Google Groups home page to open a list of information, including your recent postings. Click Edit My Profile to open the window. Here you can add a photo, information about yourself, and a link to your website or blog. Click Save to store the profile.

For more information on the group, click More Group Info to display an archive list for the group. From the list you can select links to archives by date, posters' profiles, and related groups.

Start Your Own Group

While many groups are associated with a particular interest or field, others are more personal or restricted to a specific group of people, such as your family or your office workgroup. Choose from three membership structures according to how you intend to use the group.

Specify Group Structure and Membership

Create a group to communicate and collaborate with others following these steps:

1. Click Create on the Google Groups homepage.

2. Type a name for your group. Google Groups suggests an e-mail address for the group automatically, but you can change the name if you like.

3. Type a description for the group as desired.

4. Select a type of group membership. You can choose from three types, as you see here:

Google Groups   **Create a group**

1 Set up group   **2** Add members

Name your group
Vacation plan November 2007

Create a group email address
vacation-plan-november-2007   @googlegroups.com

Group web address: http://groups.google.ca/group/vacation-plan-november-2007

Write a group description
Information and planning ideas for our family cruise, November 2007

Letters remaining: 233

☐ This group may contain content which is only suitable for adults.

Choose an Access level

○ Public - Anyone can read the archives. Anyone can join, but only members can post messages, view the members list, create pages and upload files.

○ Announcement-only - Anyone can read the archives. Anyone can join, but only managers can post messages, view the members list, create pages and upload files.

◉ Restricted - People must be invited to join the group. Only members can post messages, read the archives, view the members list, create pages and upload files. Your group and its archives do not appear in public Google search results or the directory.

Public Group   A public group has open archives and membership; membership is required to post messages, create pages, upload files, and view the member list. Use this type of group for public communication on a topic of interest, such as a profession.

Announcement Group   Use an Announcement group to distribute information; membership is open but only group managers can read the member list, create pages, upload files, and post messages. If you have a system of groups, the group leader might use the Announcement group for distributing meeting notices, company policies, and the like.

Restricted Group   Restricted groups are by invitation only, and aren't included in Google searches or the Google Groups directory. Members can post messages, read the archives and members list, create pages, and upload files. A restricted group is useful for a work group to discuss topics of interest among themselves.

Invite Members to a Restricted Group

To invite others to an invitation-only group, you can either send invitations or directly list members:

- Type the e-mail addresses for those you want to invite to join the group and click Invite Members.
- Click Add Members Directly, type (or copy and paste) the members' e-mail addresses, and click Add members.
- Type a message and choose an e-mail subscription option for members added directly.

Google will send the messages to your group members. Your group information is shown in the Google Groups window.

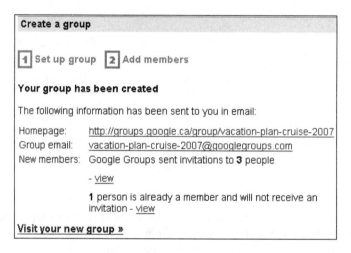

Create a group

1 Set up group   **2** Add members

Your group has been created

The following information has been sent to you in email:

Homepage: http://groups.google.ca/group/vacation-plan-cruise-2007
Group email: vacation-plan-cruise-2007@googlegroups.com
New members: Google Groups sent invitations to **3** people

 - view

1 person is already a member and will not receive an invitation - view

Visit your new group »

Customize Your Group's Features

The Google Groups service offers a number of options for configuring the appearance and function of your group, ranging from the colors used on the pages to the navigation used in the group. Tools for managing the group and the group's content are accessible from the home page (Figure 5-7).

TIP   *You can access the same tools from different locations on the window. For example, clicking the Tune Your Group's Settings link at the bottom of the window opens the same options as clicking the Group Settings link at the right of the window.*

NOTE   *Find detailed information about configuring your group's settings at http://tinyurl .com/225lth.*

Posts to the group   Content management   Group management

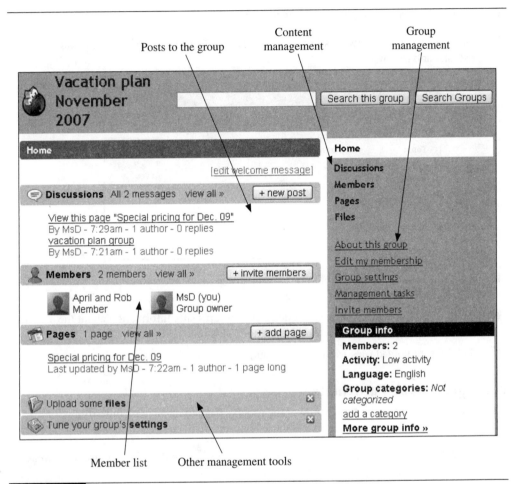

FIGURE 5-7   Control and manage your group from the home page.

Member list   Other management tools

Manage Your Group

The features included in the group's page breaks down into two categories: views and tasks related to the content and tools and tasks related to the group membership. From the group's page, click one of the links on the right frame to open different dialog boxes and pages.

Take Care of the Group's Content

Choose one of the links at the upper right of the group page, shown in Figure 5-7, to display further settings and views of the group's contents. The default view is the Homepage, shown in Figure 5-7.

Choose one of the remaining links, described next.

■ Click Discussions to view existing posts listed to the page as shown here, respond to a post, and add new posts

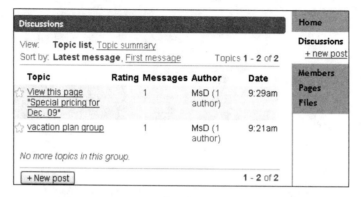

■ Click Members to open a list of your existing group members; you can also invite additional members to join on this page.

■ Click Pages to open a list of pages added to the group's site. Information about the added material is listed, as well as the Add New Page link to add additional pages

■ Click Files to upload files from your computer or storage area to share with the group.

Manage the Group's Particulars

Use the lower set of links in the right frame of the group's page to manage memberships, settings, and the page's appearance. Look for these features:

■ About This Group displays the selections you made when configuring the group, such as the description, e-mail, and access types.

■ Edit My Membership shows selections you made as a group member for receiving e-mail and your nickname.

> **TIP** *The Edit My Membership page offers the option to unsubscribe from the group; if you are the group owner you can't unsubscribe.*

■ Group settings lets you select various features for the structure of the group's page (Figure 5-8). The categories of settings are listed in Table 5-1.

■ Management tasks lists pending messages and pending members for a monitored group.

■ Invite members opens a form to fill in and e-mail to prospective group members.

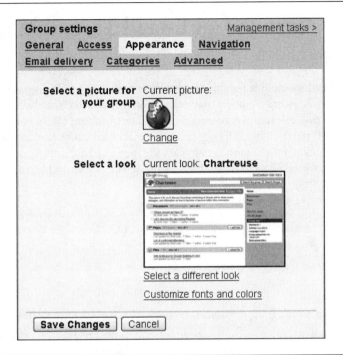

Choose configuration options to customize the group's page and function, such as the appearance.

Group Setting	Tasks and Options
General	Lists basic data, such as group name, e-mail address, and description
Access	Defines who can view listings, members, invitations, upload rights, post message rights, rights to edit and upload pages, and message moderation
Appearance	Select a picture for the group as well as a font and color scheme
Navigation	Reorder or delete the links at the upper right of the group window, including Home, Discussions, Members, Pages, and Files
E-mail delivery	Displays a message footer and subject prefix for the e-mail which can be edited
Categories	Lists the Google Group categories for classifying the group if desired
Advanced	Offers features to specify a language for the group, manage a remote archive, or delete the group

Group management tasks and settings

How to ...   **Turn Off an E-mail Thread in Gmail**

Your group memberships include options for receiving e-mail, either as digests or as they are posted. Sometimes, group members may embark on a thread that simply doesn't interest you. For those less than relevant e-mail threads, Gmail lets you turn off, or *mute* the thread.

When the e-mail arrives in your Inbox, select the message's check box and press M to mute the conversation. Future messages bypass the inbox and are directly archived, although they are not marked as read. That way, you can still search and locate the thread of messages.

Here are some more mute features:

- If an e-mail arrives with your address in the To or CC fields, the conversation is moved into your Inbox

- You can search for muted conversations by using the search phrase:

  `is:muted`

  in the Gmail search field; any muted conversations are listed in the returns.

- If you want to restore the conversation, select it in the archives, and choose Move to Inbox from the More Actions menu. All subsequent conversations are delivered to the Inbox.

Use Google News to Manage Newsworthy Information

Google News is another specialized search that offers you news according to your interests. You can search current news and archived news from 4500 news sources.

> **TIP**   *The Google News service uses the analogy of a paper newspaper, in that it divides the content into sections, similar to those found in a traditional newspaper. It also uses the idea of editions to identify news from different countries and in different languages.*

Click News from the links above the search field on the Google home page, or open news. google.com in your browser. In the default Google News layout shown in Figure 5-9, categories of news are listed at the left of the Google News window, snippets of news headlines and links are listed in the center column, and headlines and top keywords are listed in the right column.

The In The News list on the page shows you top keywords in the news at the time. Click a keyword to open a number of articles about the topic.

FIGURE 5-9   View news in different ways in Google News.

Conduct a News Search

Like all Google Search tools, you can use a combination of terms and operators to zero in on a topic of interest. There are also several ways in which to search, from simple browsing, to personalized and archival searches.

Perform a General Search for a Topic

For a basic search, type the terms in the search field and click Search News to display returns in a News Results window. As you see here, the returns are sorted by relevance; one return can have additional links associated with the same terms from different news sources.

The left column of the returns window includes several options for browsing top news stories in different time frames. As shown here, you can quickly get up to date with all that's been happening in the last hour, day, or week.

> **TIP** *You can also search blogs from the Google News home page to read what the movers and shakers are saying about the news of the day. Click Blog Search from the links above the Top Stories to open the Google Blog Search home page. Read about searching blogs in Chapter 2.*

Create a Search Using Advanced Terms

From the Google News home page, click Advanced news search from the links above the separator bar to open the Advanced Search form (Figure 5-10).

To customize a search, you can:

■ Specify the order and content of the search terms used, such as using the phrase *Earth Day*

■ Narrow the results by specifying a date, such as the last week

■ Choose a specific news service or source

■ Restrict results to a named location, such as Florida

■ Define where your search terms should appear in the results by choosing an option from the Occurrences drop-down list. The default is to return results when the terms are included anywhere in the article; choose headline, body, or URL options to narrow the results.

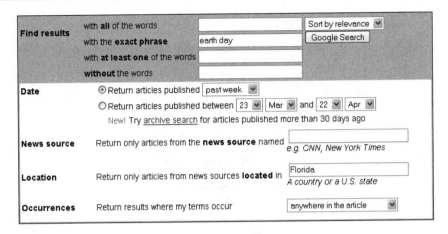

| FIGURE 5-10 | Customize the search terms for more relevant results. |

Once you have set your search parameters, click Google Search. In the returns page, you'll see only those returns that meet your search criteria.

Personalize Your News Search

One person's idea of important news and top stories doesn't always jive with another's. Google News lets you customize what you read by defining a personalized page that is displayed along with the default Top Stories section.

Select Basic Personalization Options

Click the Edit This Personalized Page link at the top of the right column on the Google News home page.

The personalization form displays in the link's location, and can be customized in a number of ways (Figure 5-11).

The changes you can make to your news page include:

Reposition the Labels   Click one of the eight label areas on the page and drag it up/down, or left/right to reformat the page layout—the cursor shows a four-ended arrow when you can move the label.

NOTE   *You can reposition the section objects, but you can't reposition or remove the Top Stories section on the page.*

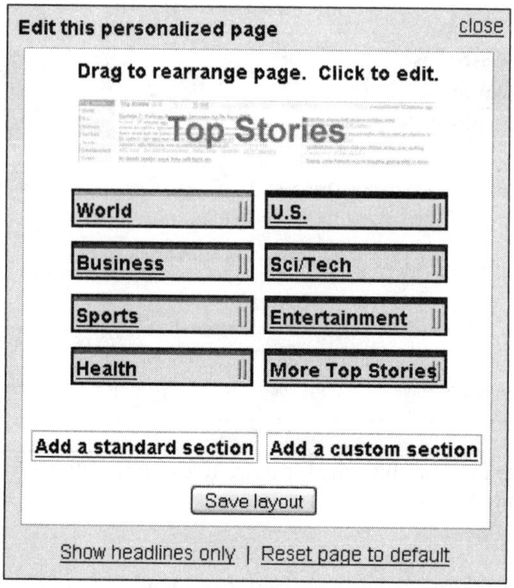

FIGURE 5-11 Use the links and objects to organize and define your custom news page.

Customize a Section   Click a Label link to open a further personalization form (shown next) on which you can specify a location (called an Edition), the Section, the number of stories, or delete the section by selecting the check box. Click Save changes to return to the customization form shown in Figure 5-11.

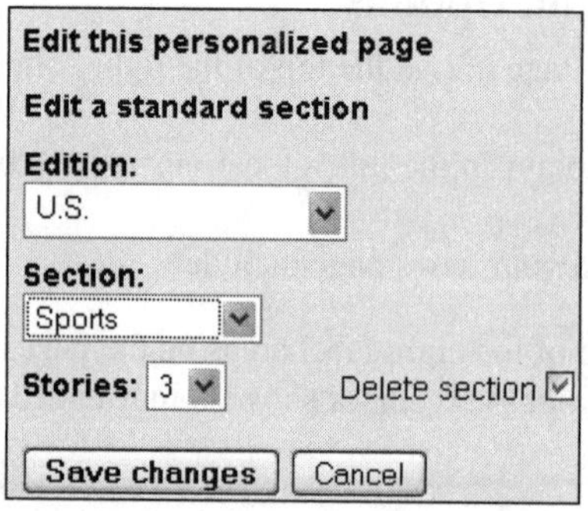

Add Another Section   If you have deleted a section, and decide you would like to restore it, click Add a Standard Section to open a list where you can choose the edition, section, and the number of stories. Click Add Section to close the list and return to the main configuration form.

Toggle the Page Display   The default view shows small images as well as text and links. If you prefer, click Show Headlines only at the lower left of the form to restrict the page display.

Insert Custom News Categories for Targeted News

Whether you are looking for information on a competitor's product launch or following the career of your favorite band, customize the search using keywords.

The next example shows how to customize the news to find out about travel bargains. Follow these steps to keep up with news that's important to you:

1. From the Edit This Personalized Page form shown in Figure 5-11, click Add a Custom Section to open a form where you can insert keywords (Figure 5-12).

2. Type your keywords in the Keywords field. All returns will include your keywords.

3. Click Advanced to display several additional fields.

4. Choose other features, such as a Language and a Section to restrict the results further.

5. Type a label for the section rather than using the default, such as **travel plans**.

TIP   *By default, the keyword string is used as the label.*

6. Click the Stories drop-down arrow and choose a number of items to show on the news page.

7. Click Add Section to close the form and return to the main personalization form, which now includes your custom section.

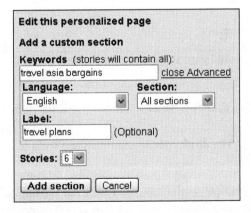

FIGURE 5-12   Create customized news sections to keep up-to-date on topics of special interest.

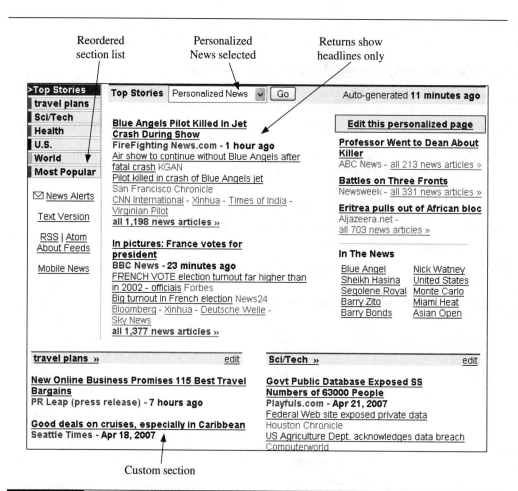

FIGURE 5-13   The reconfigured page shows the custom news display.

8. When you have finished, click Save Layout; click Close to return to the Google News homepage.

9. Check out your news. The display shows the topics and areas of interest in the layout you planned (Figure 5-13).

> **NOTE**
> *You can edit any of the sections by clicking Edit in the heading bar for each section. If you want to return to a default view, click Edit This Personalized Page to reopen the editing form, and click Reset Page to default.*

Explore History with Archive Searches

Suppose you are tracking information about a product launch, or want to find out how a competitor's product has fared in the news over time. Google News includes an archive search feature that lets you view content over time. The results contain both freely accessible content as well as content that is fee-based.

NOTE   *To condense the content and provide a better perspective on the event, articles about a single story are collapsed into one listing.*

Conduct an Archival Search

To conduct a News Archive search, follow these steps from the Google News home page:

1. Click News Archive Search from the links above the returns section of the page to open the News Archive Search window shown here.

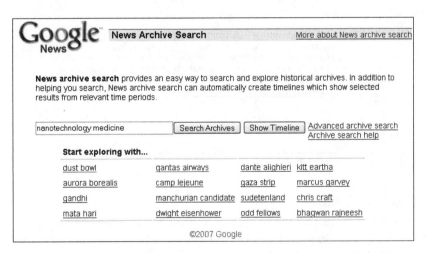

2. Type your search terms in the field, such as **nanotechnology medicine** and click Search Archives.

TIP   *If you like, experiment with archive news displays by selecting one of the example searches listed on the page.*

3. Results are listed as with other search results showing the title linked to the full piece, as well as a snippet of the article, links to news sources, and other related web pages and articles (Figure 5-14).

4. Select an article to read, or click a date range or publication link in the left frame of the results page to sort the returns further.

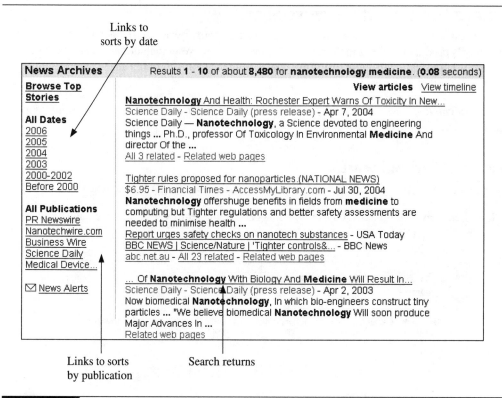

Links to
sorts by date

Links to sorts
by publication

Search returns

FIGURE 5-14   Search for news trends over time.

View Results Over Time

An archival search can also display the results on a timeline, handy if you are looking for a particular reference and can only remember the year it was produced. From the results page, click View Timeline to open the results page ordered by date. The left frame shows the year or year range with the results for that time period shown in the right frame.

Convenient Ways to Manage Your News

Like many Google products, Google News offers ways to stay current with information that is important to you. You can receive regular updates using news feeds, get breaking news of importance to you using News Alerts. As described in the later section "Take Google with You," you can send the information to your phone when you are on the road.

Subscribe to News Feeds

Feeds are summaries of web content along with links to the full version of the content. Google News supports RSS and Atom feed formats. At the time of writing, the feeds were in Atom 0.3 and RSS 2.0 formats.

There are three types of Google News feeds that vary according to the page displayed in Google News:

- Feeds by Section sends summaries of a type of news, such as Business or Sports, if you select the feed link while viewing the Business or Sports section.

- Feeds by Search Results creates a feed if you select a feed link while viewing a page of Google News search results.

- Feeds by Customized Search Results creates a feed if you click a feed link while viewing a custom news page you created.

Follow these steps to subscribe to a feed:

1. Click either the RSS or Atom link in the left frame of the page in Google News.

2. In the resulting window, select an option for reading the news from the drop-down list at the top of the page. You can choose from Live Bookmarks, Bloglines, My Yahoo, or Google Reader (Figure 5-15).

TIP *An option to select a check box to always use the chosen feed is included on the page. If the Live Bookmarks option is chosen, the option is to Always use Live Bookmarks to subscribe to feeds. If Google Reader is chosen, the option is to Always Use Google Reader to subscribe to feeds, and so on.*

3. Click Subscribe Now.

4. Depending on the options chosen, follow the resulting prompts and dialog boxes. For example:

   - Live Bookmarks opens your Bookmarks folder to select a storage location.

   - Google Reader opens a page for choosing whether to add your feed to your Google homepage or to Google Reader.

NOTE *You can set up a Google News feed for your blog or website for noncommercial use. Read about the service and terms of use at http://tinyurl.com/dqgm5.*

Reading Your Feeds in Google Reader

You need to use a news reader, such as Google Reader, to display the feed content. (See the results shown next for an example feed subscription.) Google Reader doesn't require any installation—if you specify using the service, your feeds are shown automatically.

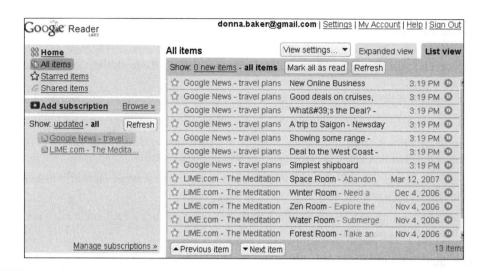

NOTE   *Read about features and configurations for Google Reader at http://tinyurl.com/s7jff.*

FIGURE 5-15   Subscribe to a feed to receive custom news summaries.

Google Brings Information to You with Alerts

One of the coolest Google tools, currently in beta, is Google Alerts. Use a Google Alert to deliver information from a selected range of sources right to your e-mail inbox.

Click the News Alerts link in the left column of the Google News homepage (shown below the sections in Figure 5-13).

To set up an alert, follow these steps in the Google Alerts Beta window:

1. Type the Search terms in the field. The alerts returned will use the search string you specify, so if there are variations in your terms, be sure to use operators.

TIP   *Read about operators in Chapters 1 and 2.*

2. Click the Type drop-down arrow and choose a service from the list. You can select News, Blogs, Web, Groups, or Comprehensive, which searches all listed services.

3. Specify how often you want to receive alerts. You can choose once a day, once a week, or as-it-happens from the How Often drop-down list.

4. Type the e-mail address where you want the alerts sent. Your Google Accounts default address is used automatically.

5. Click Create Alert (Figure 5-16). Your settings are stored, and new updates are sent to your e-mail according to the schedule you selected.

NOTE   *Your alerts from all sources (News, Groups, Blogs, and Web) are listed on a Google Alerts page for convenience.*

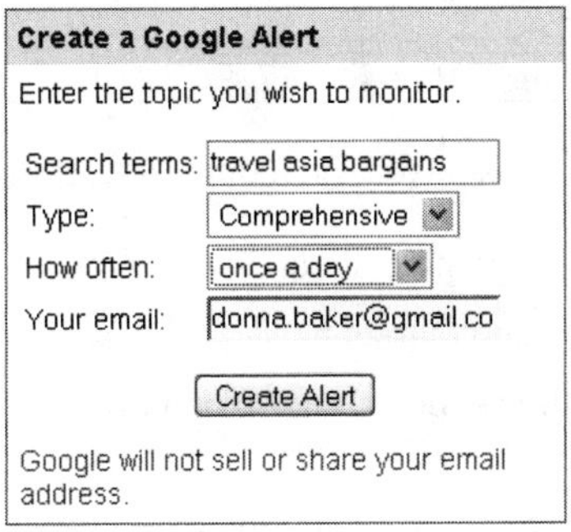

Create a Google Alert

Enter the topic you wish to monitor.

Search terms: travel asia bargains
Type: Comprehensive
How often: once a day
Your email: donna.baker@gmail.co

[Create Alert]

Google will not sell or share your email address.

FIGURE 5-16   Use an alert to receive information by e-mail.

Read Google Finance to Stay Up to Date

Whether you are into finance, involved in an industry sector, or following your stocks, you'll find something interesting in Google Finance. You can find the service at finance.google.com.

NOTE *Google Finance is a beta product. As the service's disclaimer specifies, the content is for informational purposes and not for advice or trading. Quotes are posted with a 15 minute NASDAQ delay and 20 minute delays for AMEX and NYSE. Read more about the disclaimer at http://tinyurl.com/qtqm7.*

What's on the Overview Page

A portion of the Google Finance home page is shown here.

You see a variety of information displayed, including (not all items are seen in the example):

- A market summary displayed graphically and numerically

- Headlines to the top finance and market news

- A sector summary, which shows industrial sector activity—green bars indicate sectors showing increased performance; red indicating decreased performance

- Recent quotes for a number of stocks including their share price, change, and market caps

- Top moves listing those companies that were the largest gainers and losers

- Windows to play video from some top business and finance broadcast outlets

Search Google Finance for Targeted Information

You may have special interest in certain companies or stocks. Instead of sifting through general information, zero in with a search.

Type the search terms in the field on the Google Finance homepage and click Search Finance. The results are shown in a segmented returns page (Figure 5-17).

The results page contains several sources of information, including:

■ A summary of the company's trades numerically and graphically

TIP *Move your cursor over the graph to see prices and volumes for a particular point in time.*

■ News about the company

■ Links to related companies; for example, search results for Adobe include Microsoft, Apple, Avid, and Autodesk in the list of related companies

■ Discussions on the company created by Google Finance users

■ Financials, including a link to the company's Income Statement and cash flow data, key stats and ratios

■ A collection of blog posts

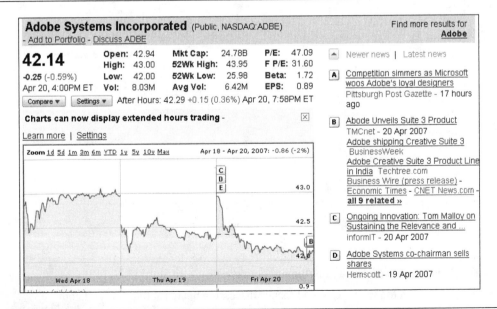

FIGURE 5-17   Read financial information about a particular company or industry.

- A summary of the company's history and development, as well as links to the company's website
- A list of the company's key management people
- Links to even more resources

 **There's Much More to Google Finance**

Google Finance provides a large number of options and services beyond the simple search outlined, such as My Portfolio, which is shown here. In My Portfolio you can track your stock and investments portfolio and read news associated with your stock.

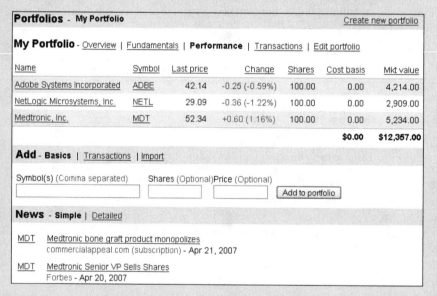

Here are some links to areas of interest for Google Finance:

- My Portfolios at http://tinyurl.com/jnofz
- Google Finance FAQ at http://tinyurl.com/opc7a
- Application to join the Google Finance discussion boards at http://tinyurl.com/33xb4n

Take Google with You

Google isn't confined to your home or office computer and Internet connection. You can take Google mobile using Google Mobile (pun intended). With Google Mobile you can send information to your phone, search from your phone's browser, and even check your e-mail.

NOTE *Google collects information on your transmissions, including the IP address, cookies from your computer, the telephone number, and the carrier.*

Find out about the ways you can take Google with you at www.google.com/mobile.

Track Down Information Using Google SMS

Many of the features you use in Google's services are available via Google Short Message Service (SMS). You can experiment with Google SMS from the test page at www.google.com/sms. To try it, type a search term—choose your own, such as **bed and breakfast san francisco** or select one of the example searches and click Send. The mobile phone mock-up on the page shows the results as you'd see on a phone interface (Figure 5-18).

TIP *Need help using Google SMS? Text the word "help" to the SMS number.*

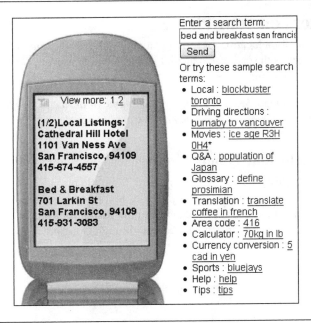

FIGURE 5-18 Test Google SMS or try it on your phone.

For real-life Google SMS, follow these steps:

1. Start a new text message and type in your search terms.
2. Send the message to the number **466453** (just remember GOOGLE).
3. Read the results on your phone.

Google Product Search on the Move

Sometimes you come across a product in a store that you think might be a bargain, but you aren't sure. Take the guesswork out of your decision-making using Google Product Search Mobile.

To check out competing prices for your product online from your phone, follow these steps:

1. On your phone's browser, load Google Product Search at http://google.com/products/wml.
2. Type the search term in the field, and click Search Products.
3. Check the results using the phone's keypad arrows; sort by price or best match using the links at the bottom of the search results.

NOTE   *If you don't want to receive text messages from Google Maps, ask your service provider to block Maps-results@google.com.*

Use Map Content on Your Phone

Whether you are looking for a location, or trying to avoid traffic snarls, nothing beats a good map. Fortunately, you can both send map content to your phone or use Google Mobile Maps to help you get where you are going.

NOTE   *You can access Google Mobile on any mobile phone or device that supports XHTML (WAP 2.0). Find out more at the homepage located at google.com/gmm.*

Send Web Content to Your Phone

Use the Google Send to Phone service with all major US mobile providers to send web content such as directions or addresses to your mobile phone as text messages. Google Send to Phone started life as an extension to Firefox in 2005, and is now part of the Google Maps business listings service. There is no charge to send a message through Google but you may have carrier fees.

When you've located content you want to send to your phone, click Send to Phone, as shown here, or click Call.

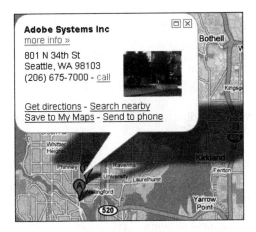

Not all placemark balloons offer a Call link, but all will include the Send to Phone link.

Type the phone number in the field, select the carrier, and click Send Message (Figure 5-19).

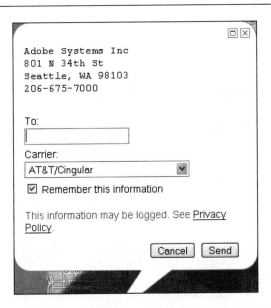

FIGURE 5-19   Specify the phone number and carrier for the call.

Find Out What's Happening in Traffic

Find out what's happening locally by phone using Google. Follow these steps on your phone:

1. Type **http://mobile.google.com/local**.
2. Type your search terms in the What box.
3. Type your location in the Where box.
4. Click the Google Search button.

   In the results, you can get driving directions, or place a call to the business by highlighting and selecting the phone number.

Even More Mobile Services

There are a growing number of mobile services offered by Google beyond the ones described in this chapter. Here are some links to other services and sources of information:

- Starting with Google Mobile at http://tinyurl.com/epfz3
- Help for Google Mobile Maps at http://tinyurl.com/2xxszs
- Google Mobile web searching at http://tinyurl.com/2eph4z
- Google Mobile personalized home for your phone at http://tinyurl.com/2m2gcm
- Google News mobile (beta) at http://tinyurl.com/2k2rts
- Gmail for your mobile browser at http://tinyurl.com/yute3v

You Can Test a New Voice Local Search

Google Labs is experimenting with a system used to search for local businesses by voice. The Google Voice Local Search service is currently available in the US for American business listings in English. To try it, dial 1-800-GOOG-411 (1-800-466-4411) from any phone.

Search for a business by name or category. The service connects you to the business free of charge. If you are using a mobile phone, you can have your results by SMS—say "text message." There is no charge for the call or connecting you to the search result, although your regular phone charges may apply.

Read more about Google Voice Local Search at http://tinyurl.com/ywo3sk.

Integrate Google Talk into Your Communications Repertoire

Google Talk is an online chat client that comes in two versions—either you can use the Google Talk Gadget online through your Google Personalized Homepage, or download the Google Talk Client to make high quality PC-to-PC voice calls and transfer files.

> **TIP** *Google Talk is a terrific business tool if you use it in conjunction with Gmail. Your talk scripts are stored in Gmail along with other e-mail, giving you a permanent record of your communications with clients.*

Open the Google Talk homepage at www.google.com/talk. On this page, you can launch Google Talk, download the Google Talk Client for more features, or copy code to use Google Talk on your website or blog (Figure 5-20).

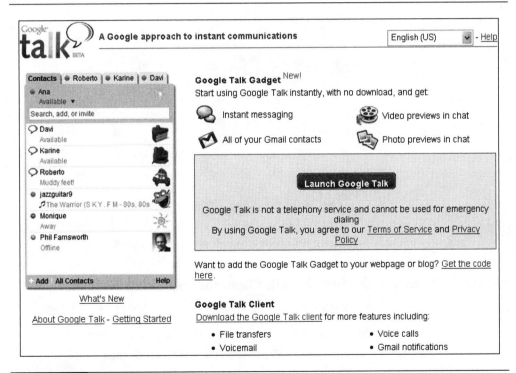

FIGURE 5-20   Choose a Google Talk option from the homepage.

Talk It Up with Google Talk

To get started with Google Talk, click the Launch Google Talk button on the Google Talk homepage to display Google Talk in a pop-up window. You have to sign into your Google Account if you aren't already signed in.

NOTE *Find details about using Google Talk in the Help files at http://tinyurl.com/2zhn5b*

Add Google Talk to Your Homepage

You can use the Google Talk Gadget from your iGoogle home page following these steps:

1. Open your iGoogle home page and click Add Stuff to open the gadgets directory page.

2. Type **Google Talk** in the search field and click Search Homepage Content.

3. Click the Google Talk Add It Now button to place the gadget on your homepage.

4. Click Back to Homepage to see the new gadget, shown here.

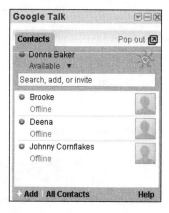

NOTE *Read more about personalizing your iGoogle home page in Chapter 8.*

Download and Install the Google Talk Client for Expanded Features

For more expansive instant messaging, download the Google Talk client following these steps:

1. Click the Download the Google Talk client link from the Google Talk homepage.

2. In the resulting dialog box, click Save File to store the 1.5MB application file on your hard drive.

3. Locate the file and double-click to install the program.

4. When the installation finished, sign in with your Gmail or Google Account username and password.

If you use a Gmail account, your Gmail contacts are displayed in the Google Talk window.

Using Google Talk

Here are some tips for using the Google Talk client:

■ Select a contact from the list to communicate with.

■ If your contact isn't online, you can send a voicemail or call from the pop-up window, shown in Figure 5-21.

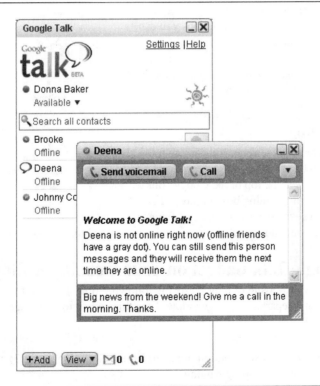

FIGURE 5-21   Send messages or voicemail to contacts on your list, whether or not they are online.

■ Click the Gmail icon to send e-mail from Google Talk; click the voicemail icon to open Gmail, displaying the results of applying a *label:voicemail* filter.

Read about using labels and filters in Chapter 10.

■ Click the drop-down arrow at the upper right of the message pop-up window to open a list of options, ranging from sending files to blocking the contact, shown here:

■ Click the Search all contacts link to open a field for you to type a contact name to add to the list.

■ Click Add at the bottom left of the window to add others to your contact list.

■ Click View to view contact pictures, show contacts on a single page, show offline contacts and address book contacts, and sort by name.

■ Click the drop-down arrow next to your status to display a list, shown here, of options you can specify for your status.

NOTE *You can view several demos of Google Talk in action at http://tinyurl.com/cwfsj.*

Choose Your Settings

Google Talk offers a panel of settings you can use to configure the program to suit how you prefer to work. To get started, click Settings at the top of the Google Talk window to open the Settings dialog box (Figure 5-22).

Choose settings in seven panels, as listed in Table 5-2. When you have made your choices, click OK to close the dialog box.

Place the Google Talk Gadget on Your Website or Blog

Place Google Talk in your website or blog. Paste the following line of code into your page's code to show Google Talk in a separate pop-up window. Type this code into your page's XHTML:

```
<script src='http://talkgadget.google.com/talkgadget/button'></script>
```

When you publish the page you see a button linked to Google Talk (Figure 5-23). Click the button to open the Google Talk pop-up window.

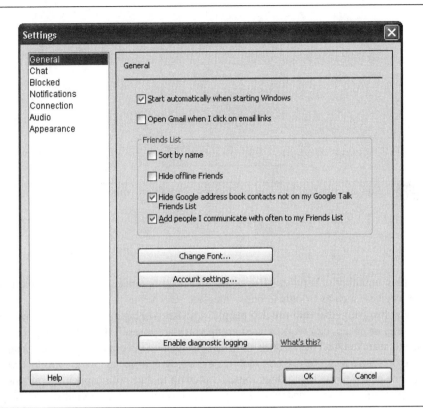

Configure Google Talk according to your needs.

Panel	Settings to Configure
General	Specify when Google Talk starts, how the Friends List is displayed, and link to dialog boxes to change fonts and choose account settings.
Chat	Choose whether or not to save chats in your Gmail account.
Blocked	Any contacts blocked from Google Talk are listed on this panel; you can unblock contacts from this list.
Notifications	Choose how you want to be notified—by sound or a pop-up notification for incoming calls, chats, when a friend comes online, or for new e-mail.
Connections	Specify automatic proxy detection or input proxy settings if you are behind a firewall.
Audio	Choose input and output devices for microphones and headsets.
Appearance	Select a chat theme from a drop-down list to use instead of the default display.

TABLE 5-2   Settings available to configure Google Talk

FIGURE 5-23   Add a script that lets you use Google Talk from your blog or web page.

Summary

Google provides a number of services offering ways to communicate, as this chapter explains.
Many of the services, such as Google Groups, integrate searches as part of their features. Google
Groups lets you bring together like-minded people, whether sharing a common concern or issue,
a personal family or group, or a work-related group you start yourself. Google Groups can be
customized and searched, and the information exchange can be via browser or e-mail. You also
saw how Google services can be used on mobile devices, such as using Google Product Search
from your phone and viewing travel directions. To keep up to date with happenings around your
world, Google offers news in a variety of ways you can customize to meet your needs. Why
settle for talking by phone? Google Talk lets you communicate instantly by IM or voice.

In the next chapter, learn how to communicate visually in Picasa, Google's image editing and
management program.

Chapter 6

Say It in Pictures

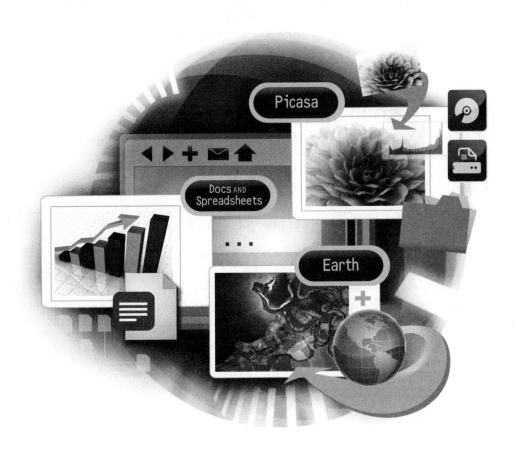

How to...

■ Scan your computer for images and videos

■ Organize your collections

■ Label and search images

■ Correct image, color, and lighting flaws

■ Add special effects for interest

■ Export images in a number of ways

■ Create products such as posters, collages, and Web Albums

Picasa is Google's answer to your general image collection, editing, distribution, and archiving needs. Use the program to collect and organize all the images on your hard drive into folders. Make touch ups and edits to your images, and add effects to enhance their appearance.

Once the images are ready, you can use several different types of output—from posters and collages to Web Albums and e-mail—to distribute your images. Save collections of images to CD or DVD for archival storage using Picasa.

Install the Program

Picasa is a free download, just like other Google programs. Download the program at http://picasa.google.com/ and follow the installation prompts.

Perform the Initial Scan to Find Images

The first time you open the program it scans your computer or designated folders for images and video to add to the library. Choose one of two options for finding images:

■ Use the Completely Scan for Pictures option if you save images all over your hard drive or on multiple drives.

■ Choose the Only Scan My Documents, My Pictures, and the Desktop option if you use default settings for your computer and cameras, because in this case the images are usually added into My Documents or My Pictures folders.

Once you have made your selection, click Continue. The contents of your folders are checked and images and other content collected. Folders are created according to the dates of the images or video. When the scan is complete, click OK to close the message describing how many folders and files have been included.

Get Around the Program

The Picasa program window is composed of several sections. The main components of the program are shown in Figure 6-1.

FIGURE 6-1   The Picasa program is made up of several functional areas.

Picasa Supports Numerous File Formats

You can manage image, movie, and RAW image data files in Picasa. The supported file types you can work with are

- Image formats including BMP, GIF, JPG, PNG, PSD, and TIF files
- Movie formats including ASF, AVI, MOV, MPG, and WMV files in Picasa
- RAW data files produced by several manufacturers, including Canon, Kodak, Minolta, Nikon, and Pentax cameras. The program recognizes several camera formats as RAW file formats, including Nikon NEF, Canon CRW and CR2, Kodak DCR, and Sony SRF.

Check out the entire list of supported cameras and file formats at http://tinyurl.com/yttlma.

Organize Images and Videos

You can add photos or video to the Picasa Library via existing folders or as new folders from other locations on your hard drive, from media such as a CD or card, or directly from your camera or scanner. Once the images are added to the program, you can use a range of features to organize, maintain, and catalog your files.

Import Images from a Camera

Importing images from another folder is the same as moving content between folders in general, so I'll only describe how to import images from a card or camera. To import photos into Picasa from your camera drive, follow these steps:

1. Click the Import button to display the Import screen, which replaces the Picasa program interface.

2. Click Select Device to open a menu. What you see in the menu will vary according to the devices installed on your system.

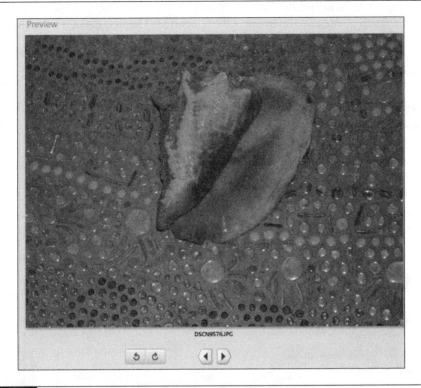

Preview

DSCN9576.JPG

Look through the images before importing them in the Preview area.

3. Select the device from the list to open its drive. The content is shown as thumbnails in the Import Tray. A thumbnail with an overlaying "X" indicates an image that is already in the Picasa library.

4. To check through the images, click the Previous and Next arrows below the Preview image, as shown in Figure 6-2.

> TIP *You can click Rotate Clockwise or Rotate Counterclockwise buttons to rotate an image in the Preview.*

5. SHIFT-CLICK/CTRL-CLICK the thumbnails to select specific files. Each thumbnail selected is framed by a bounding box, shown here.

Import Tray

6. Click Import All to import the contents of the drive, or Import Selected to import a selected group of images. The Import All or Import [##] Item(s) dialog box opens depending on your selection.

> **TIP** *Click Exclude Duplicates to save time deleting extra images later.*

7. Choose import settings, shown in Figure 6-3. The settings let you type a name for the folder, specify a storage location or select an existing folder, and add more information such as the place or a description.

8. Choose a camera or card action after copying the files. You can leave the source files as they are on the camera, delete copied pictures, or delete all pictures on the card or camera.

9. Click Finish to close the dialog box and import the images into Picasa. The Import screen returns to the regular Picasa window.

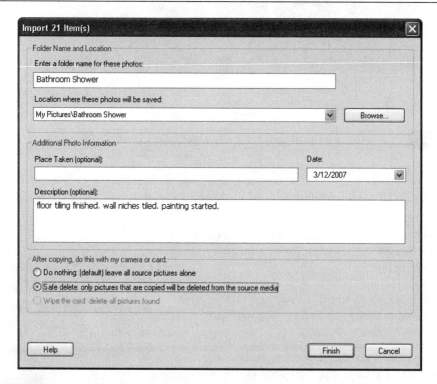

FIGURE 6-3 Select storage settings to use for imported images.

Manage Images and Folders

Get your files and folders in order using the organizing tools and features in Picasa. All the folders in the Library, except for Albums, are folders on your hard drive. Move, rename, combine, or delete folders in the Library panel as you would on your hard drive: The only difference is that Picasa asks for confirmation before completing a task.

Choose a Different View

The default Library view shows flat folder arrangements named according to year—an example was shown in Figure 6-1. Instead of listing folders, click the Folder Tree Structure button at the top of the Library panel to display the images in large groupings, like you see here.

If you want to look for files that have been changed, or need to locate a specific group of files by name, click the drop-down arrow at the right of the Library panel to display the View options. Choose an option to sort the Library in other ways than the default Sort by Creation Date.

Rename Files to Keep Track

Cameras name images using a string of alphanumeric characters, which are difficult to differentiate. To make it simpler to find specific images, you can rename files either individually, or as a batch.

Rename a Single Image   To rename a single image, select the folder in the Library to display the thumbnails. Select the thumbnail in the Lightbox, and press F2 to open the Rename Files dialog box, shown in Figure 6-4. Type a name for the file. You can include the date or resolution if you like, which is handy if you have several versions of an image for online or print purposes. Click Rename to make the change.

Rename Multiple Images   If you want to change the names of several files simultaneously, select the folder in the Library; if you want to change some of the images, select their thumbnails in the Lightbox. Press F2 to open the Rename Files dialog box and type a common name, such as **mural**.

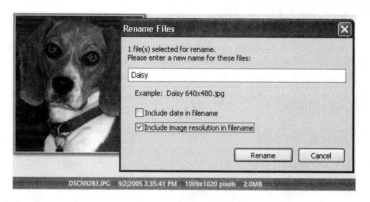

FIGURE 6-4   Rename images using descriptive names for easy searching.

Next, select the date and image resolution if desired. Click Rename to close the dialog box and rename the files. The names of your files are changed to the common name with a numbered suffix, such as mural-2, mural-3, and so on.

Name the Thumbnails   Your filenames can be used as thumbnail captions to help you find images faster. Choose View | Thumbnail Caption and choose an option from None, Filename, Caption, or Resolution. The example here uses the filename as the thumbnail's caption.

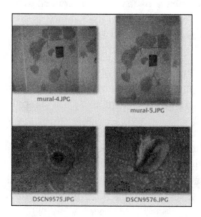

Organize Your Image Folders

Folders use a name and date by default. To change the name of a folder, double-click it in the Library to open the Folder Properties dialog box. Change the name, date, and add place and description information if you like. Click OK to close the dialog box.

If all you want to do is add information, click the Add a Description label below the folder's label in the Lightbox.

The label is replaced by an I-beam cursor. Type the description and press ENTER or click off the area to finish.

Find Your Folders

If you want to open a folder of images on your hard drive, select the folder in the Library and press CTRL+ENTER to open the folder on your computer. If you just want to see where the folder is located, hold your cursor over the folder's name in the Lightbox to see the folder path in a tooltip.

Organize with Albums

An Album is a Picasa tool you use for organizing content within the program. You can't find an Album file on your hard drive, nor do you save an Album as a hard drive folder. The program includes two permanent albums named Screensaver and Starred Photos. Add a new album to use for assembling images for a project, or to upload to a Web Album, for example.

How to ... **Hide Folders**

If you have more images than you can manage at one time, or want to store older images for safekeeping, take advantage of the hidden folders feature in Picasa. Hiding a folder has no effect on the images, they are simply hidden in the Library. If you share your computer with others, you can even attach a password to the hidden folders that prevents them from being seen.

Follow these steps to hide a folder using a password:

1. Right-click the folder's name in the Library panel and choose Hide Folder to open the Add Password dialog.

    Click No to close the Add Password dialog box and then add the folder to the Hidden Folders collection if you don't need a password.

2. To add a password, click Yes in the Add Password dialog box and type the password. Click OK.

3. Retype the password in the next dialog box to verify. Click OK again.

Your folder of images is safe, but it's now listed in the Library under Hidden Folders. To unhide a folder, right-click it in the Hidden Folders listing and select Unhide Folder.

Click Create a New Album on the Library panel to open the Album Properties dialog box. Type a name for the album, and add other information including the date, location, and a description. Click OK.

Drag a thumbnail from the Lightbox to the album to add a copy, or *instance* of the image to the album. Images can be used in multiple albums.

 Picasa offers different ways to use the contents of the folders or Albums. The menu locations are different, although the commands are the same. Select an album and choose Album from the main menu; select a folder and choose Folder from the main menu.

Maintain the Image Library

Bringing images into the Picasa library isn't a one-time event. As you add more images from your camera and other sources, set the program to look for those images automatically using the Folder Manager.

Follow these steps:

1. Choose Tools | Folder Manager to open the dialog box shown in Figure 6-5 and select the folder in the Folder List.

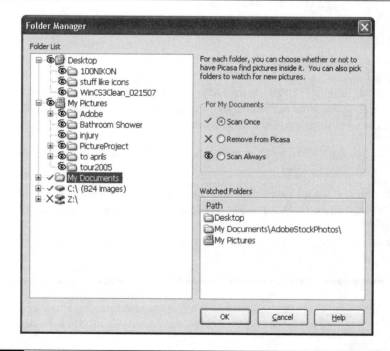

FIGURE 6-5 Specify folder locations to check automatically for new images and videos.

2. Specify when and how to check the selected folder:

■ Choose Scan Once to check for files one time.

■ Choose Remove from Picasa to delete a folder from the watched list.

■ Select Scan Always to add the folder to the Watched Folders.

3. Click OK to close the Folder Manager dialog box. Any folders marked as Scan Once are checked; any new files found are imported into the Library.

A Watched Folder is checked each time the program is opened, and is a handy way to check for new content automatically. If you have different storage folders for cameras and scanners, add those folders to the Watched Folders list. If Picasa is open when you add new content to your watched folders, it is added to the program instantly.

Keep Track of Your Files

Like many image management programs, Picasa offers a cataloging system you can use to filter, sort, and search for images quickly.

Add Different Types of Labels

Customize how you label files using one of three types of data. Your choices depend on how you want to work with your images and videos, and include stars, keywords, and metadata. One image or video file can have a star, metadata, and multiple keywords.

Tag Files with Stars

To add a star, select the image or images in the Lightbox, and then click Add/Remove Star in the Photo Tray, as shown in Figure 6-6.

FIGURE 6-6   Add a star to tag an image or video file.

When you want to collect the starred images together, click the Starred Photos album in the Library to see the starred images listed in the Lightbox, as you see here.

Label Files with Keywords

Use keywords as terms for searching your image collections. You can add multiple keywords to your images.

Don't worry about capitalization, as Picasa converts all keywords to lowercase automatically.

Select the file or files in the Lightbox and then choose View | Keywords or press CTRL+K to open the Picasa : Keywords dialog box. Type the keyword text and click Add or press ENTER as shown here; continue with additional keywords.

Use Metadata for Precise Descriptions

Picasa lets you view an image's Exchangeable Image File Format (EXIF) metadata, which is information about the content and structure of a file. EXIF is a standard for storing interchange information in image files. Most digital cameras now use the EXIF format and store information such as the camera and flash settings.

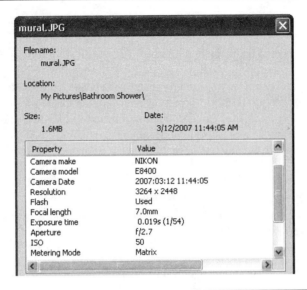

FIGURE 6-7   Metadata varies according to the type of image and the camera data attached to the file.

To view an image's metadata, select the image in the Lightbox and then choose Properties from the Shortcut menu or the Picture menu to open the dialog box shown in Figure 6-7.

Track Down Images

Adding information, keywords, sorting folders, using Albums—all these features are designed to help you manage your image resources. Instead of scrolling through the Lightbox looking for images, search for them by name or visually.

Search for Files

Use the Picasa Search feature to find a file quickly. Choose View | Search Options or use the Search field at the upper right of the program window, shown here.

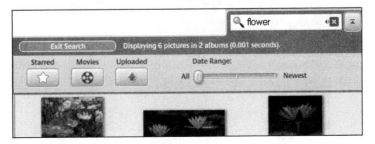

How to ... Tag an Image to its Location on Earth

Picasa offers an incredibly cool way to identify images. You can *Geotag* an image to include its Global Positioning Satellite (GPS) information, shown as the locale's longitude and latitude, along with other EXIF metadata. To do this, you work with both Picasa and Google Earth—read how to download and use Google Earth in Chapter 4.

Use the same method to Geotag one or multiple selected images, following these steps:

1. Choose Tools | Geotag | Geotag with Google Earth. Google Earth opens, and your image displays in a small Picasa window, as shown in Figure 6-8.

2. Display the locale corresponding to your image by dragging the map so the crosshairs overlay the locale, shown in Figure 6-8.

> **TIP** *If a value is entered in the Place Taken field in the Picasa folder, the map zooms to the geographic coordinates automatically.*

3. Click Geotag on the Picasa window.

4. Click Done to add the information to the image's metadata.

In Picasa, images that have been Geotagged show a crosshairs icon in the Lightbox, as you see here. To delete the information, choose Tools | Geotag | Clear Geotag info.

FIGURE 6-8 The selected image is shown within Google Earth.

Use these search options to zero in on your images:

- If you want to filter your images, click one of the buttons on the Search Options to display a subset of your files. For example, click Starred, Movies to search only movie files, or Uploaded to list only those images uploaded to a Web Album.

- Narrow the results further by filtering on a date range. Drag the Date Range slider left to include older content, and right to include newer content.

- Type a keyword or keywords as search terms. As you type, Picasa completes the words using text that has been typed previously, and displays the results as you add letters. Add or remove keywords to zero in on your images.

When you are finished searching, click the Show/Hide Search Options button to toggle the dialog box closed.

Look for Images in a Full-Screen Slideshow

You generally run through your images using the thumbnails in the Lightbox. If you are on the hunt for particular images for a project or doing some spring cleaning, try the automatic slideshow feature.

NOTE   *The viewing slideshow is different from the slideshow exported as a product from Picasa—read about exporting slideshows later in the chapter.*

To start, click the Slideshow task button or press CTRL+4 to display the Slideshow screen, shown in Figure 6-9.

The Slideshow screen shows the first image in a folder or a selected image with a toolbar overlay. Move the cursor over and away from the toolbar to toggle its view. The tools are similar to working with any sort of media controller; read about the tools in Table 6-1.

FIGURE 6-9   View and flag images in your collections in the Slideshow screen.

Tools	Description
Exit Slideshow	Return to the program window.
Navigate controls	Use the arrows to reverse or advance the playback; click the center arrow to play the slides automatically.
Star	Add stars to flag images from the slideshow for convenience.
Rotate image	Click the left button to rotate the image counterclockwise; click the right button to rotate the image clockwise.
Show captions	Click the Captions button to toggle captions on or off.
Set time	Decrease or increase the display time using the (–) and (+) buttons.

TABLE 6-1 The Slideshow tools and their functions.

Find Images on a Timeline

If you can remember roughly when an image was taken, or its subject or location, try the Timeline window. Click the Timeline task button to look through your Library in the Timeline screen, shown in Figure 6-10.

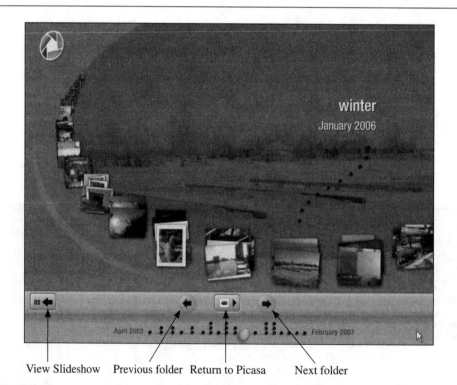

View Slideshow   Previous folder   Return to Picasa   Next folder

FIGURE 6-10 Use the Timeline to locate images and folders visually.

Here are some tips for using the Timeline:

- Drag thumbnails or click the Timeline to locate a folder; the thumbnails representing the folders in the Library slide to the left to show a newer folder or to the right to show an older folder.

- Click one of the columns on the Timeline shown at the bottom of the window to jump to the time location.

- After you make a selection on the Timeline, the folder's name and date are shown in the background, as is a grayscale version of the first image in the folder.

Improve Your Image Quality in the Edit Picture Screen

Most images can use some touch up, such as correcting the lighting or straightening the photo. For some quick edits, use the Edit Picture screen to improve the appearance of your images.

Double-click the image in the Lightbox to open it in the Edit Picture screen. This is where you can start editing (Figure 6-11).

FIGURE 6-11   Open the image in the Edit Picture screen to modify its appearance.

When the Edit Picture screen displays you will see:

- The image is shown at full size below a thumbnail strip. Look for different images in the active folder or album by clicking the arrows at the ends of the thumbnail strip.

- Click Back To Library at the upper left of the screen to return to the Picasa interface; click Slideshow to view the folder of images in a Slideshow view.

- The Basic Fixes tab is visible by default at the left of the Edit Picture screen; use its settings to apply corrections automatically.

- There are two additional tabs for editing: for adjusting the light in the image, use the Tuning tab's settings; to apply special effects like color tints and shadows use the settings on the Effects tab. Read about using each of the different sets of edit tools next.

- Click Make a Caption! below the image to activate an I-beam cursor and type a caption. Toggle the caption between Visible or Hidden using the icon at the left of the preview area. Click the Trash can at the right of the preview area to delete the caption.

Adjust the Image Preview to See Detail Clearly

You can adjust the preview to display the images in custom views. The default shows the image sized to fit the screen, as shown in Figure 6-12. Use the view tools shown here to zoom in and out of the preview for making repairs.

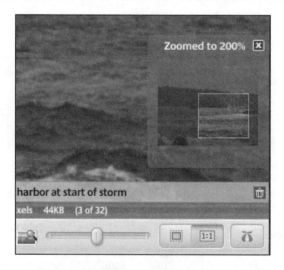

FIGURE 6-12   Adjust the magnification to see details clearly.

From left to right, here's how to use the tools:

- Drag the Zoom slider right to increase the magnification of the image. As you drag the slider, an overlay shows you the portion of the image that is showing in the preview area.

- Click the Fit Photo to Viewing Area button to view the image at the default size, fitting within the window.

- Click Display Photo at Actual Size to resize the image at its full size. The displayed area is shown in an overlay.

- Click Show/Hide Histogram and Camera Information to view a graph showing the color distribution in the image. Read about the histogram in the sidebar, "Did You Know: You can View Color Information on a Graph?"

TIP   *Depending on the image source, you may see camera data, as well as other EXIF or metadata information.*

Correct Basic Image Flaws

The tools you are likely to use most often are the Basic Fixes, shown in Figure 6-11. To return to a previous image state, click the Undo button; click Redo to restore a change. You can apply, reverse, and redo several fixes in sequence.

Make Changes with Simple Correction Tools

Some Basic Fixes are applied with a single mouse click and others are nearly as easy to apply, including:

I'm Feeling Lucky   Click I'm Feeling Lucky to adjust the image's color and contrast to the best balance based on the picture's color information.

Auto Contrast   Click Auto Contrast to adjust the contrast in your picture, making a greater distinction between light and dark areas.

Auto Color   Click the Auto Color button to adjust the color levels in your picture automatically. Auto Color is handy for images that have a color cast, such as green or red.

Balance the Light in the Image   Drag the Fill Light slider to balance the light in the foreground and background of your image, showing more detail in the dark and light areas. In the example shown here, the image at the left is the original picture; the one at the right shows the balanced light when the Fill Light slider is moved to the halfway point.

Remove Red Eye   One common image flaw is red eye, resulting from the reflection of the camera flash on the retina of the eye. To correct the problem, click Red Eye on the Basic Fixes menu, and then drag a rectangle around the red areas in the subject's eye, shown in Figure 6-13.

Release the mouse to correct the flaw. Repeat with the other eye, or other subjects in your image. Click Apply to change the color and return to the Basic Fixes tab.

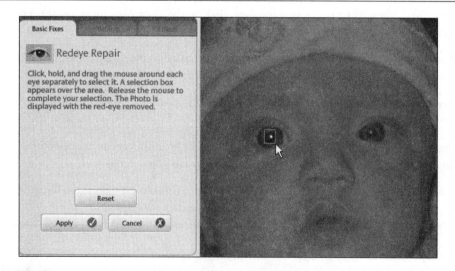

FIGURE 6-13   Specify the area for correction with the Red Eye tool.

 *Red Eye correction only works with red eye reflections, not with nonred reflections. Cats, for example, often have a green retinal reflection.*

Crop the Image

You can decrease the contents displayed in an image using the Crop tool. Follow these steps to crop off uninteresting backgrounds, or balance the subject in an image:

1. Click Crop in the Basic Fixes tab to display the Crop Photo tab.
2. Choose the crop dimensions in the Crop Photo tab:
   - Click a preconfigured size for the crop dimensions.
   - Drag the mouse over the image to draw a crop box, as shown next. Release the mouse and make adjustments to the crop box as necessary. You can drag a corner or side of the box to resize it, or drag the entire box to reposition it.

3. Click Preview to see how the crop appears after it is applied. You see the cropped image briefly, and then the full image displays again.
4. Click Apply to crop the image and return to the Basic Fixes tab.

Straighten a Crooked Image

Sometimes you shoot an image on an angle purposely, while other times the tilted angle isn't at all what you want.

Follow these steps to straighten your image:

1. Click Straighten on the Basic Fixes tab to display the Straighten Picture view.

FIGURE 6-14   Use the grid overlay to straighten a tilted image.

2. Drag the slider to rotate the image and align the picture's content with the grid, shown in Figure 6-14.

3. Click Apply to make the correction and return to the Basic Fixes tab.

NOTE   *You can apply some effects as a batch. Choose your images, choose Picture | Batch Edit, and select the effect.*

Use Tuning Tools to Refine Light and Color

The Tuning tab offers a number of tools for correcting light and color, shown in Figure 6-15. Drag the sliders to adjust the settings individually. Alternatively, you can click the upper button to instantly correct light, or click the lower button to correct color.

The image shown in Figure 6-15 shows the "before" image, and several "after" versions. Apply the Tuning tools to produce changes like these:

■ Use the Fill Light slider to balance the light in the foreground and background of a picture. The example shows the effect of using 60 percent Fill Light.

■ Drag the Highlights slider to the right to add areas of brightness in the image. The example shown here uses Highlights applied at 90 percent.

■ Drag the Shadows slider to the left to darken and expand dark areas of the image. The example shows Shadows applied at 80 percent.

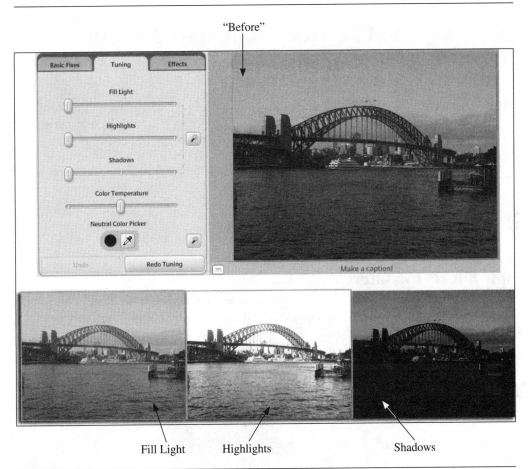

FIGURE 6-15   Use the sliders in the Tuning tab to make color and light adjustments, or click the buttons for automatic adjustments.

■ Drag the Color Temperature slider left to make the image cooler, or more blue; drag the slider right to make the image warmer, or more red.

■ Click the Neutral Color Picker eyedropper on the Tuning tab and then click a point on the image to sample an area that is considered neutral. Picasa uses the color you sample to balance the color in the image.

TIP   *Instead of using the picker, click the Color Auto Fix button to balance the color automatically.*

You Can View Color Information on a Graph

Color information called the RGB (Red/Green/Blue) histogram is derived from the image's data. The RGB histogram is a real-time graph that shows the distribution of colors in your picture.

Click the Show/Hide Histogram & Camera Information button on the Photo Tray to display the histogram in an overlay window, as shown in Figure 6-16.

As you experiment with adjusting color and light, watch the graph to see how adjusting the sliders modifies the amounts of color shown in the graph. For example, the histogram will show the color and light shift to the right of the graph as the amount of Fill Light and Highlights is increased.

Apply Effects for Interest

Click the Effects tab to display the list of effects to apply to your image—either alone or in combination. Notice how the image displayed in the Picture Edit screen shows thumbnail views of the effect applied to the image (Figure 6-17).

After choosing an effect, before you can return to the Library or another tab on the Edit Picture screen, Picasa asks whether to apply the changes; click Yes or No.

FIGURE 6-16   Use the histogram to show color distribution in the image.

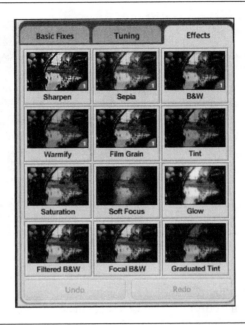

FIGURE 6-17   View the outcome of applying the effects in the thumbnails.

> **TIP**   *If you always want the changes applied, select Don't Ask Me Again, Always Apply Changes to Save a mouse click.*

Use the One-click Effects for Quick Changes

The effects showing "1" at the bottom of the thumbnail indicate that the filter is applied when selected without configuring. There are five absolute effects you can use for quick changes:

- Apply the Sharpen effect to make the edges of objects in your pictures more distinct.
- Use the Sepia effect to remove the color in the image and apply a brownish-red tone.
- To remove all color, use the Black and White (B&W) effect.
- If you find the skin tones in your image a bit on the blue side, click Warmify to replace some of the blue tones with red tones.
- Apply the Film Grain effect to make the image look like a frame from an old film.

Configure Image Effects for Impact

The remaining effects each display a dialog box overlaying the Effects tab when you click the effect's thumbnail. Experiment with these options to create a specific look, add emphasis to areas of your image, or place focus on the subject.

FIGURE 6-18   Choose a color tint and define how much is applied to the image.

Tint an Image with a Specific Color   Use the Tint effect to produce an image with an overlying color. You might want to use the effect if you have a set of images on your website, for example, that are used as buttons and tinted the same color for consistency. To add the tint, drag the Color Preservation slider to define how much of the original image color to maintain—anywhere from none of the color to all of it. Click Pick Color to open a set of swatches and a color display and then choose a color to use for the tint by clicking on it. In the example shown in Figure 6-18, the duck has maintained about half the original color and uses a dark lavender tint.

Saturation   Change the intensity of color for a dramatic effect. Drag the Saturation Amount slider left to remove color from the image (like the left side of the example shown here), or right to increase the depth of color in the image, as in the right side of the example.

Soft Focus   You can use the Soft Focus effect to highlight objects in the image. Drag the Size slider to define the size of the focus area; drag the Amount slider to define the amount of blur. Set the center point of the effect by dragging the crosshairs, as you see here.

Glow   Make your new puppy's face glow using the Glow effect. Adjust the Intensity slider to set the brightness and the Radius slider to define the size of the brightened area on the image. The Glow effect is subtle, especially on warm-colored images.

Filtered B&W   The Filtered B&W effect strips the color from your image. Choose a color from the color filter that is applied like an overlay to the grayscale image.

Focal B&W   The Focal B&W effect strips the color from the image except for an area you specify, a terrific way to emphasize a subject in an image. Define the size of the colored area by dragging the Size slider and the sharpness of the edge of the colored area by dragging the Sharpness slider. Move the crosshairs to identify the center of the effect.

Graduated Tint   Choose a color to apply as a gradient to the image. Drag the Feather slider to adjust the sharpness of the color changes; drag the Shade slider to define the intensity of color used in the gradient.

Save and Export Edited Images

Picasa doesn't save images in the same way as other common photo processing software. When you save an edited image, the original is moved into a hidden subfolder named Originals. The saved image in the folder is actually your edited copy. Here are some more features of edited images:

- The original and saved copies are the same size.
- An edited file is saved as a JPG file at 85 percent quality, regardless of your original file format.
- When you make a change to an image, the Save Changes button is active on the Lightbox.

The subfolder containing the original files is hidden. If you want to see it in Windows Explorer, specify that hidden files and folders are shown.

Distribute and Print Your Photos

Picasa offers different ways to send images that can save you time and effort. For example, you can save your files to a portable hard drive, export them directly to e-mail, or send them to your blog. You can also use one of several features to create items like a collage or poster.

Regardless of how you plan to use or distribute your photos, you have to assemble and hold the images in the Photo Tray. All the images in a folder can be used, or you can choose images from different folder locations.

CTRL-CLICK or SHIFT-CLICK to select groups of images which are shown in the Photo Tray. The thumbnails display a small target icon at its lower left edge, meaning they are attached to the Photo Tray. If you select any single images, the thumbnail is added to the group, and you'll have to click Hold again to store the single thumbnail. Your set of images will look like this example.

If you don't click Hold, each time you make a selection you replace the image currently in the holding area.

If you want to change the images, click Clear to remove a selected thumbnail from the Photo Tray; to remove all the thumbnails you are holding click Clear without selecting any thumbnails. Click Yes in the confirmation dialog box, and the images are removed.

Choose Tools | Configure Buttons to add, remove, and reorder buttons on the Photo Tray to suit the way you want to work. Click OK to change the layout; choose Restore to Defaults to reset the tools.

Create a Poster from an Image

Some images or cropped segments of images are perfect as posters. Picasa lets you configure a tiled layout to build a poster up to 1000 percent larger than the original image.

To create a poster, follow these steps:

1. Select the image you want to use for the poster and choose Create | Make a Poster to open the Poster Settings dialog box.

2. To configure the Poster settings, specify the percentage from 200 to 1000 percent; click the Paper Size drop-down arrow and choose either 4 × 6 or 8.5 × 11 as the paper size. To easily assemble the tiles, click Overlap Tiles.

3. Click OK to close the dialog box and produce the poster tiles. These are stored in the same folder as the original image, like the example shown in Figure 6-19.

Assemble a Collage

Picasa lets you combine a group of images into a collage that can be used as a single image or as a screensaver.

Select the images you want to include in the project and follow these steps to produce a collage:

1. Click the Collage button on the Photo Tray or choose Create | Picture Collage to open the Make Collage dialog box.

2. Click the Type drop-down arrow and choose a collage template. You can choose from Picture Pile, Picture Grid, Contact Sheet, or Multi-Exposure, as shown in Figure 6-20.

> **NOTE**   *If you select the Picture Pile template, you can specify a background from the Options drop-down list.*

3. Choose a storage folder from the Location drop-down list.

4. Click Create to build the collage.

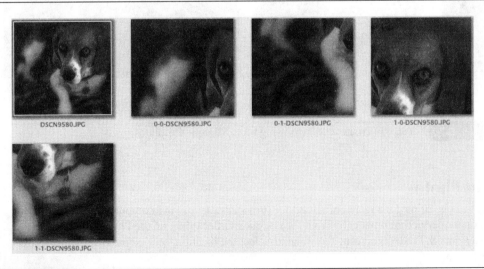

FIGURE 6-19   Produce a set of tiles to blow up an image to poster size.

Picture Pile   Picture Grid

Contact Sheet   Multi-Exposure

FIGURE 6-20   You can create a collage using four different templates.

Print Photos

Photos can be printed using an online service provider or from your computer. To send photos to an online service automatically from Picasa, click Order Prints on the Photo Tray to open the Picasa Prints & Products screen, shown next. Select the location, service provider, and account information.

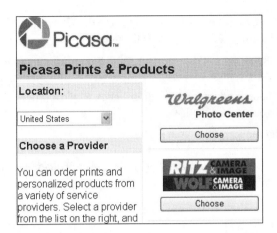

If you prefer to print your images yourself, select one or more images for printing and follow these steps:

1. Click Print on the Photo Tray to open the Print Screen, shown in Figure 6-21.

2. Choose the print size in the Print Layout area, and choose either Shrink to Fit or Crop to Fit to size the images proportionally. You can only use one size of image for each printing process.

FIGURE 6-21   Specify settings to print one or more images from Picasa.

3. Select the number of copies of each photo by using the Copies per Photo (–) and (+) buttons. The print settings use one copy as the default.

4. Click the arrows below the Preview to view other pages if there are more images than those that fit on a single page.

5. To view a list of names and image resolutions, click Review. Then click OK to close the dialog box when you've read the list.

6. Click Print to send the images to your printer.

> **TIP** *Choose Tools |Options and click Printing to find print choices, such as more image sizes, printer settings, and resampling quality.*

Send Photos by E-mail

Picasa's process for resizing and attaching pictures to e-mail is a real timesaver. Picasa uses Gmail as its default program though you can use others too (read about Gmail in Chapters 9 and 10).

Select the images to send and then click E-mail on the Photo Tray. The first time you use the E-mail process a dialog box opens, asking you to choose an e-mail program. Picasa selects Gmail automatically, but also allows you to choose Picasa Mail or your default e-mail client, such as Thunderbird or Outlook. Then, respond to any dialog boxes or login screens required by your e-mail program.

> **TIP** *If you use the same e-mail all the time, select the Remember This Setting, Don't Show This Dialog Again checkbox.*

Most of the information for the e-mail is added automatically in the e-mail, including the Subject and body of the message. You can leave the default content, or change it if you prefer.

Design and Upload a Web Album

A Web Album is an online account stored at Google used to store and display image albums. You register for the service the first time you try to upload a set of images.

> **NOTE** *Picasa offers two Mac Uploaders. Use the Picasa Web Albums Exporter for iPhoto to upload images from iPhoto. The Picasa Web Albums Uploader is another uploading program. Find the Mac Uploaders at http://picasa.google.com/web/mac_tools.html and click Free Download. If you prefer, upload images one at a time using your web browser.*

Select the images you want to use and click Web Album on the Photo Tray. The Send [xx] Photos to a Picasa Web Album dialog box opens, shown in Figure 6-22.

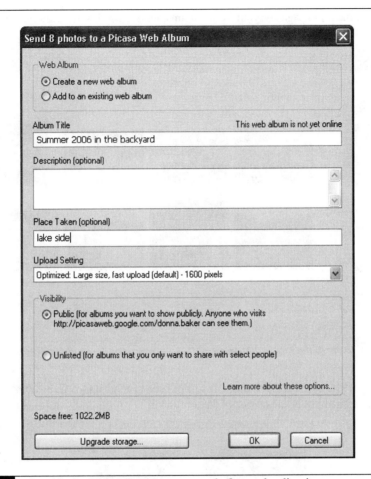

FIGURE 6-22 Specify the Web Album appearance before uploading it.

Select Create a new Web Album or Add to an existing Web Album and specify settings, including:

- Type a custom name for the Album Title; the default uses the folder name.
- Select an Upload Setting, including the size and upload speed.
- The album is public by default. If you prefer, click Unlisted and restrict the access to the album.

Click OK to close the Web Album dialog box. The Upload Manager dialog box opens, and shows the upload progress. Once the images are uploaded, click View Online to close the Upload

Manager and open the main page for your Web Albums, named My Public Gallery. Click the name of the Web Album to open it, shown here.

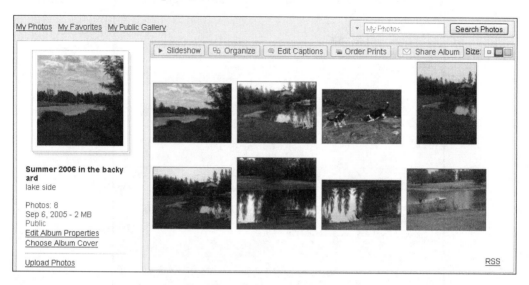

You have to close the Upload Manager dialog box manually when you return to Picasa.

In the Lightbox, you can see that images that have been uploaded to a Web Album are identified with a green arrow at the corner of the thumbnail.

Create a Web Page Automatically

If you have ever had to manually create a web page displaying a collection of images, you know how time-consuming it can be. Instead, use the Picasa feature to produce a web page from a folder or Album in a few steps.

Follow these steps to generate the web page and its code:

1. Either select a folder and choose Folder | Export as HTML Page, or select an Album and choose Album | Export as HTML Page to open the Export as HTML Page dialog box.

2. Specify the image size to use in the Export Pictures at this Size option, ranging from the Original Size to 1024 pixels wide.

3. Customize the web page's title and storage location rather than using the folder or Album name. By default, the web page and its pictures are stored at My Documents\Picasa HTML Exports\[Album or folder name].

4. Click Next at the bottom of the Export as HTML Page dialog box to open the Select a Web Page Template dialog box.

5. Select one of the seven templates from the Template Name list, shown in Figure 6-23. Read about the templates in the sidebar "Did You Know: Picasa Provides Album Templates?"

6. Click Finish to create the web page. The finished web page opens in your browser automatically.

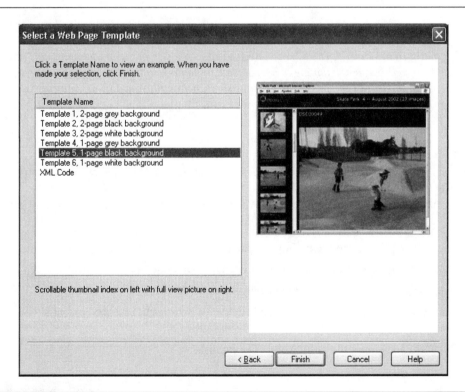

FIGURE 6-23   Picasa produces a Web page complete with a thumbnail index and slide show controls.

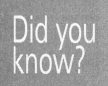

Picasa Provides Album Templates

Picasa provides seven templates for creating a web page to display images:

- Templates 1, 2, and 3 include two separate pages. The first page shows thumbnails linked to a full-size image on a separate page. The background choices are gray, black, or white.

- Templates 4, 5, and 6 offer grey, black, or white backgrounds as well. These templates use a single page with a list of thumbnails at the left and display a full-sized image at the right.

- Use the XML Code template to generate XML code for another page or application.

NOTE　*An experimental feature in Picasa lets you upload files to an FTP server. Choose | Experimental | Publish via FTP. You need to know the size of the image, web page title and storage location, template to use, and where to display the web page, along with your username and the password for your site. Check with your ISP as many are opting for secure FTP, which isn't supported in Picasa.*

Transfer Images to Blogger

Picasa offers the Blog This! command to automatically transfer selected pictures and text to a Blogger site (learn how to use Blogger in Chapter 14).

Select the images to upload, and then follow these steps to transfer images to your Blogger blog:

1. Click Blog This! on the Photo Tray to open the Picasa: Blog This! dialog box.
2. Follow the instructions for creating a new blog, or sign it to your account.
3. Select the blog where you want to display the images.
4. Choose a layout and an image size, and click Save Settings to pass the content to your blog's input page.
5. Type text content for the posting and click Publish.

The images are processed and uploaded to your blog, as you see in the example.

Make a Movie from Your Images

Make a movie instead of a slideshow to impress your friends and family. Select the images to use, and follow these steps:

1. Choose Create | Movie to open the Create Movie dialog box. Choose a time from the Delay Between Pictures drop-down list, ranging from 1 to 5 seconds, or choose Just Raw Frames. Select Small, Large, or Widescreen movie size; Small is the default size.

2. Click OK to close the Create Movie dialog box and open the Video Compression dialog box.

3. The default Compression option is Full Frames (Uncompressed). Choose a codec from the Compression drop-down list.

4. Choose codec options for movie quality, key frame, and Data Rate (Figure 6-24). Click Configure to open further configuration settings to specify how the codec deals with transparency, color, and so on.

5. Click OK to close the Video Compression dialog box when you have finished choosing settings. The movie is rendered and saved in your default location.

Make a Slideshow or Archive CD

Assemble your images into a slideshow for ease of viewing and distribution. Use the slideshow Gift CD command, following these steps:

1. Click the Gift CD task button below the main menu to open the Create a Gift CD dialog box.

2. In Step 1, choose folders to include in the Gift CD and then choose an image size from the Photo Size drop-down list rather than the original sizes of the images.

3. In Step 2, type a name for the Gift CD that is 16 characters or less.

4. If you don't want to include Picasa on the Gift CD, deselect the Include Picasa check box at the bottom of the dialog box.

5. Click Burn Disc to process your files and transfer them to the CD or DVD program.

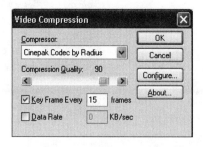

FIGURE 6-24   Select the type of compression to use for the movie.

If your project depends on your images or video, use Picasa's backup feature to archive files. Choose Tools | Backup Pictures to open the Backup Your Photos screen. Use the default record named My Backup Set, or select your existing backup. Then, select the files to back up. Click Burn. The archive is transferred to CD or DVD.

Send images to your portable hard drive for easy transport. Select the images and click Export on the Photo Tray to open the Export to Folder dialog box. Specify a folder location and name, image size, and quality; click OK to process the files and save them.

Summary

Picasa is an easy-to-use image management program you use to assemble images and collections, sort them using a variety of tools, and search for content using different methods. The tools used to correct images problems or enhance an image with effects were described. You discovered different methods for distributing and sharing images, from movies to slideshows, Web Albums to posters.

In the next chapter, learn about two services offered by Google—AdSense for web publishers to generate income displaying targeted ads on their pages, and AdWords for web advertisers to create advertising campaigns using keyword-based ads.

Chapter 7

Host Ads and Advertise
with Google Ads

How to...

- Use the AdSense program to increase site revenues
- Design and customize ads for your site
- Define channels to target site traffic
- Generate site reports to evaluate your efforts
- Advertise your business using AdWords

If you browse through a few random websites you are sure to come across Google ads on the pages. You've seen them placed in every location on a page, in a host of color combinations, some using images or video, and others simply a collection of links.

In this chapter, learn about the two sides of the Google Ads coin—hosting AdSense advertising on your site as a source of revenue, and advertising via Google AdWords. To track the effectiveness of your ad placements, you can use Google Analytics for all sorts of analysis.

> **NOTE** *You can add content directly from your blog hosted at Blogger. See how that's done in Chapter 14.*

Increase Your Site's Revenues with AdSense

Many website owners and publishers have turned to Google AdSense as a convenient way to earn money by displaying targeted ads on their web pages. The ads may be text, images, and video.

The ads are related to the content on the page, and each time a visitors clicks an advertising link, the site owners share in the advertising revenue. Google's search technology matches the page content with ads based on the website's content, the geographical location of the site, and other factors.

> **NOTE** *Where new advertising is included on a web page, or the page hasn't been crawled by a searchbot for classification, temporary ads for public service announcements are displayed.*

How AdSense Works

Each time a visitor visits a page with an AdSense tag, a piece of JavaScript provided from Google accesses the ad servers at Google. Using either a cache of the page or keywords in the URL itself to determine the high-value keywords, ads are served based on the AdWords bidding system. Read about AdWords later in the chapter.

Join the AdSense Program

You can't decide to simply insert ad code into your site—Google requires an approval process. The Google AdSense homepage is located at www.google.com/adsense.

Before you decide whether or not to join AdSense, take the tour to provide yourself with a high-level view of the program.

Read an Overview to Get Your Bearings

To get an overview of the program, follow these steps:

1. Open the What's AdSense? window shown here, which is located at http://tinyurl.com/hosns.

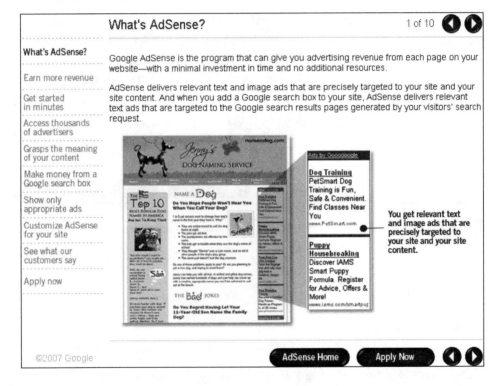

2. The overview comprises ten frames of information, outlining the different aspects of the program, the requirements for joining, customization, and so on. Click one of the headings in the left frame, or the directional arrow buttons above and below the text to move through the tour (Figure 7-1).

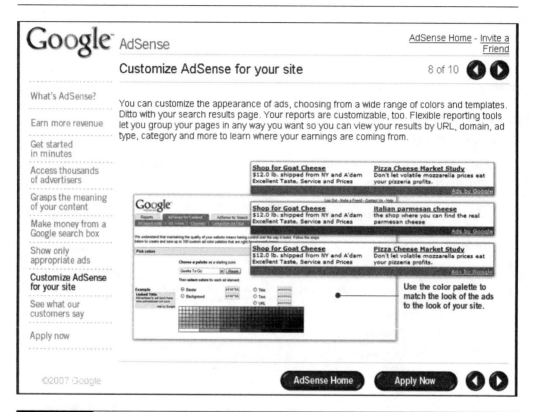

FIGURE 7-1   Take a quick AdSense tour to get an overview of how the program works.

3. Click AdSense Home to return to the start page. You can also click Apply Now to start the application process.

Make Your Application

To make an application to display Google AdSense ads on your website, follow these steps:

1. Click Apply Now from the Google AdSense homepage or the tour pages.
2. Enter the required information on the application form, part of which is shown next. You need to provide the website address, contact information, and product choices—either AdSense for Content, AdSense for Search or both.

Jody Starts a Business: The Online Entrepreneur's Tale

How To...

- Decide which Google tools to use
- Create an online presence using Blogger
- Use other Google tools to work online
- List a business in Google Maps
- Design a placemark for Google Earth

Jody Hart owns Hart of Glass, a shop selling her art glass pieces and those of other designers on consignment. Jody decides she's going to expand her horizons (and income) by taking her business online.

Although Jody is an experienced artist and business person, she isn't a programmer or web designer. She wants to display her work online, and decides a blog is the way to go, because she can easily update it to feature new works. She's interested in other ways to support her online presence, such as a calendar showing class and demonstration days. She works with other designers, and would like to communicate with them online, too.

How Google Tools Can Help

Jody uses Google Tools to help launch her online enterprise. Many elements of her business can be designed, managed, and published using Google Tools. Jody decides that:

- Using Picasa to collect and manage her image catalog allows her to easily locate, edit, and upload her images from Picasa to her blog.

- Publishing her blog using Blogger offers a convenient way to create new content online and keep it up to date.

- Uploading an inventory form to Google Spreadsheets lets both Jody and her subcontractors keep up to date with current inventory.

- Applying a custom signature in Gmail is a simple way to promote her business, and adds a professional look to e-mail messages.

- Providing customers and blog readers a custom Google Calendar advertises upcoming shows, demonstrations, and classes.

- Increasing her company's visibility by listing her business in Google's directory offers details about her products to potential customers looking for local businesses.

- Offering public information about her studio that customers can access through Google Maps or Google Earth searches increases her studio's visibility.

Create an Online Presence

The key element of Jody's online presence is a web address. She's decided to use a blog for its ease of updating, and for the ability to communicate with her prospective clients and buyers. Before building the blog, she has some images to edit in Picasa, and she's planned a Picasa Web Album to showcase her work.

Prepare Images in Picasa

Jody imports her images into Picasa, edits them as required, and prepares them for use on her blog. She also assembles some images into a Web Album, as an interesting way to present her work.

Import the Images into Picasa

Files are checked and imported into Picasa following these steps:

> **NOTE**
>
> Read about using Picasa for collecting and managing images, editing, and preparing output products such as an album in Chapter 6. Read about importing in the section Organize Images and Video; read about editing in the section Improve Your Image Quality in the Edit Picture Screen; read about Web Albums and uploading images in the section Distribute and Print Your Photos.

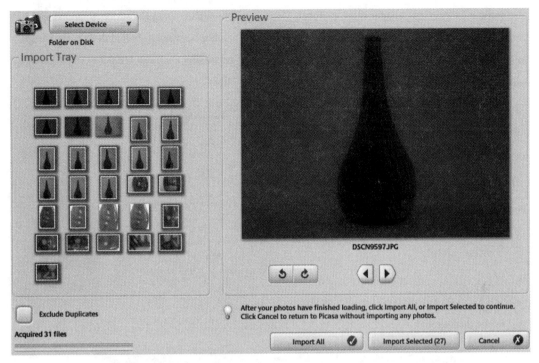

Figure 1. Review and select the images before importing them into Picasa.

1. Choose File | Import From from the main Picasa menu to open the Import Tray and Preview dialog box (Figure 1).

2. Use the controls below the preview area to view the images; rotate the images with the rotation tools.

3. Select the images for importing from the Import Tray.

4. Click Import Selected (xx). The Import [xx] Item(s) dialog box will now open.

5. Add identifying information about the group of images. Name the folder and storage location; add additional photo information if desired.

6. Click Finish to close the dialog boxes and import the images into Picasa. The images are shown as thumbnails in the Library (Figure 2).

Crop and Edit Images

Jody imported 27 images, although she needs fewer than ten images for her project. Once the images are

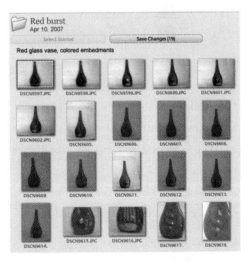

Figure 2. The imported images are shown in a thumbnail view in Picasa.

in Picasa she can examine the images more closely and compile her set of finished images.

Follow these steps to apply some basic color and contrast corrections to the batch of images:

1. Double-click the first image in the Library thumbnails view to open the Edit window.

2. Make basic corrections to the image in the Basic Fixes tab, shown below.

   ■ If the images are shot in poor light; click the I'm Feeling Lucky button to correct the contrast and color.

   ■ If the background light is poor; drag the Fill Light slider to increase the brightness of the background.

shown here. Drag the sliders to adjust the balance between light and dark in the image, and modify the color temperature, or green-red balance.

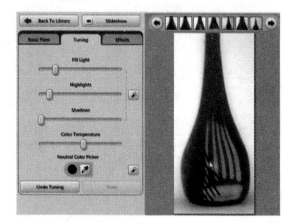

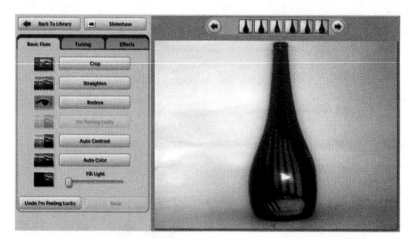

3. Click Crop Photo to open the Crop Photo settings in the tabs. Click Manual to allow cropping to any size, and drag a marquee over the image to define the cropping area. Click Apply to remove the extra content from the image and return to the default Edit window.

4. Click the Tuning tab to open a list of customizations for the image's color, as

5. Click the Make a Caption notation below the preview to activate the cursor and type a caption. Jody types **side 1**.

> **TIP**
>
> Captions aren't necessary, but Jody uses them as a way to identify the finished images she wants to use from the "spares" she imported.

6. Click the arrows in the thumbnail slider view at the top of the window to display the next or previous image and continue correcting images as required.

7. Click Slideshow to display the images at full size against a black background (Figure 3).

8. Click Exit Slideshow on the slideshow controls to return to the Edit window.

9. Click Back to Library to return to the main program window. Select images for deletion from the thumbnails, and press Delete. Jody has a finished set of eleven album images and one album cover image.

Save Copies for Online Use

Jody decides to collect the images she wants to use in her blog in one location to make it simpler to find the files later.

Follow these steps to create a new album and move the files:

1. Choose File | New Album to open the Album Properties dialog box. Add the date and description if desired, and click OK to create the new Album, listed in the Albums category of the Library.

2. Locate the images for the project in the thumbnails view.

3. Select and drag the images into the new album.

Create the Web Album

Jody wants her potential customers to have a sense of the beauty of her pieces. She's going to make a Picasa Web Album that she can use from her blog.

Follow these steps to create the Web Album:

1. Select the Picasa Album file containing the images; Jody assembled the files together in a new Picasa album folder.

2. The Photo Tray at the bottom of the Picasa window shows the selected content as you see here; click Web Album.

3. Picasa connects to the online Picasa Web Album storage site, and the Send x Photos to a Picasa Web Album dialog box opens.

4. Choose the settings for the Web Album in the dialog box, including the Album Title,

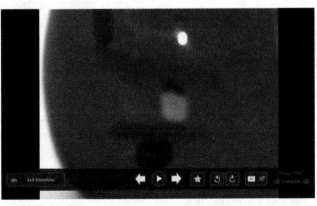

Figure 3. View images at full-screen size to check edits.

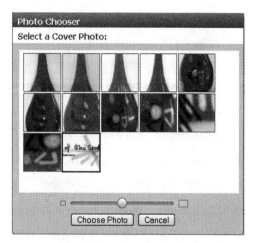

Figure 4. Select an image to use for the album's cover from the uploaded album files.

the Upload Setting, and whether the album is public or unlisted. Jody decides to test the album first, making it unlisted.

5. Click OK to upload the images. The upload process is shown as a display in the Upload Manager dialog box as the files are being transferred.

6. Click View Online in the Upload Manager when the files are uploaded to open the album in a browser window.

Configure the Finished Album

So far, Jody has imported a collection of images from a folder on her hard drive, selected and edited those she wants to include in the album, and organized and uploaded the images. Her last Picasa task is to organize the Web Album, as shown here.

She also wants to make an album cover, and edit the captions she added as reminders when editing the images.

Select an Album Cover Click Choose Album Cover from the links at the left of the window to open the Photo Chooser (Figure 4). Click to select the image for the cover and click Choose Photo to close the dialog box.

Rearrange the Order of the Images Next, Jody needs to reorder the images so the full images and close-ups

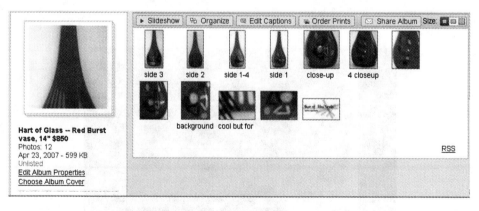

The files are uploaded in the order they are listed in the Picasa folder, but Jody wants to change this.

are in sequence. Click Organize from the tools above the album's thumbnails to display the Rearrange

Album window. Drag the thumbnails to reorder the list, and then click Delete to remove images from the album. Jody deletes two images, leaving the final ten in the order shown here.

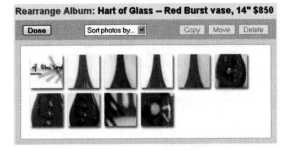

Revise the Captions The original captions were added as a reference while Jody was editing, to make sure she had representative images of the entire piece. To change the captions, click Edit Captions from the buttons above the thumbnails to open the Edit Captions dialog box. Scroll through the list and replace or change the text as necessary. As shown in Figure 5, PicasaWeb automatically saves the changes. Click Done to return to the main window.

Finally, Jody can test the slideshow by clicking the Slideshow button above the images' thumbnails. **Save the Album's Code for Later** Jody plans to insert her slideshow into her blog. Google conveniently offers a link to automatically generate the code for her page.

Click Link to This Album at the left of the Picasa Web Album browser window to open two text fields, as shown here.

Copy the content below the Paste HTML to Embed in Website field and paste it into Notepad or another text file program to save for inserting into the blog.

Jody is finished with her first task. She has some logo images for use in the blog and as placemarks, but they don't need editing or uploading at the present.

Design and Post a Blog

Jody needs an online presence, and decided she wants to use a blog for its convenience, ease of updating, and ability to quickly communicate with her clients and other artists.

Create and Name the Blog Site

Jody is building her blog in Blogger, and opens the site at www2.blogger.com.

> **NOTE**
>
> Read about using Blogger to create and manage a blog in Chapter 14. Starting the blog is described in the section Start Your Blog; read about using templates in the section Define Your Blog's Layout; learn about blog posts in the section Make Your First Blog Post; refer to Create and Publish the Post Content for information about publishing the blog. Read about Google Account in Chapter 8.

Figure 5. Modify the captions for the images as desired.

Follow these steps to create the blog site using the Blogger wizard:

1. Click Create Your Blog Now to open the Create Account window, and log in with a Google Account. Enter a display name, password, and accept the Terms of Service.

2. Click Continue to display the Name your Blog page (Figure 6).

3. Type a name for the blog, such as **Hart of Glass Studio** and check for an address, such as hartofglassstudio. Type the verification characters and then click Continue to open the Template page.

4. Select a template from the choices shown on the page. Jody chooses the default Minima template. Click Continue to complete the creation process.

5. In the final pane of the wizard, click Start Posting.

The blog is up and running! Now Jody is going to add some content and customize the appearance to suit her business' color scheme.

Write the First Post to Introduce the Blog Site

The Blogger site displays, showing the Create window of the Posting tab. To get things started, type an

Figure 6. Choose a name and URL for the blog.

introduction to the blog, like the example shown here. Blogger will save the content every few minutes.

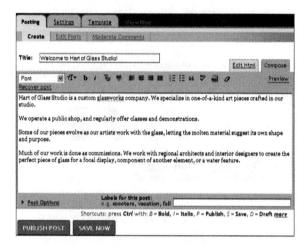

Once the content is typed, click Save Now to store the first post. Jody wants to modify the template next, and will come back to the posting to edit it.

Apply and Customize a Template to Reflect the Business Brand

The blog uses the default template. Jody likes its simplicity, but wants to modify the color scheme and fonts, following these steps:

1. Click the Template tab to display the pages; click Fonts and Colors to open a list of color elements and swatches.

2. Scroll through the color list and select an item to change. The colors can be from the blog, other colors that match, more colors shown in the right color swatch panel, or by typing the value of the number (Figure 7).

3. Jody is matching the colors to the colors used in her business logo, and types the color hex code values in the field, such as #972BC6 to match the lavender color in her logo.

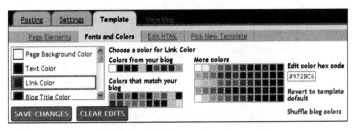

Figure 7. Select an item and change its color in the window.

4. Scroll through the font list and select an item to change. When a text item is selected the options change to Font Family, Font Style, and Font Size, as you see here.

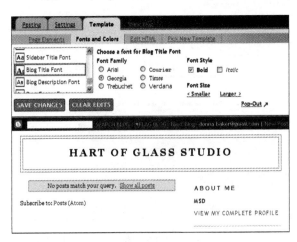

5. Choose optional font changes, and check the changes in the preview area at the bottom of the page.

6. When you are finished, click Save Changes to store the styles in the blog's template.

Edit the Post

Now back to the original post to do some edits. Jody follows these steps to modify some text and add an image to finish up the post:

1. Click Posting to display the tab's contents and then click Edit Posts. The first post is listed as a draft (Figure 8).

2. Click Edit to reopen the post in the Edit Posts view of the Posting tab. Configure text changes as desired, such as adding bold text.

3. To insert an image on the page, position the cursor in the appropriate location on the page.

4. Click the Add Image button on the toolbar to open the Add an Image From Your Computer pop-up window (Figure 9).

5. Choose the image features, including:

   ■ Click Browse to locate and select the image on the hard drive.

   ■ Click an option to choose the image's location on the page.

   ■ Choose an Image size.

   ■ Select or deselect the option to Use This Layout Every Time.

Figure 8. Select the original post for some edits.

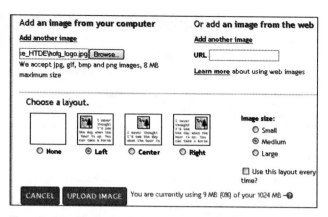

Figure 9. Select the features for the image to be inserted on the page.

6. Click Upload Image to store the image in the blog's storage area at Blogger.

7. Click Done to close the pop-up window and return to the Blogger page.

Publish the Blog for the World

The post is almost complete. Click Preview at the upper right of the Edit Posts window to show how the finished page will appear online. Make any further adjustments and click Publish Post, as shown here, to publish the page.

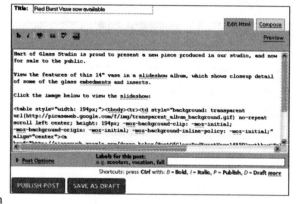

Figure 10. Insert the custom HTML for the Web Album on the page.

Build a Post for the Web Album

One page down and one to go. Jody stored the HTML code for the Picasa Web Album she created

to showcase one of her pieces, because she's going to publish the album in a separate post.

Follow these steps to insert HTML into a page and publish the post:

1. Click Create in the Posting tab to open a new blank page.

2. Type a title for the post, such as **Red Burst Vase Now Available**.

3. Add text to the page as desired, such as an introduction to the Web Album.

4. Click Edit HTML to display the window shown in Figure 10. Copy the HTML code saved from the Picasa Web Album and then paste it on to the page.

5. Click Preview to check out the page's appearance.

6. Make any necessary adjustments, and click Publish Post. The page is now published, and the window displays a link to view the blog post.

7. Click the link to open the blog in a new window. As you see here, an attractive link to the slideshow is included on the page.

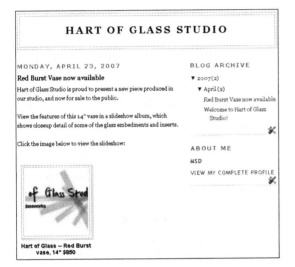

Jody has completed her blog, and now has an online presence for her company. Blogger allowed her to match the colors in the blog pages with her business color scheme, and she can easily update the content as new pieces are available.

Use Google Tools to Work and Communicate Online

T here are a number of existing and upcoming services that let you conduct much of your day-to-day business online, as Jody discovers.

Google Tools offers several common applications that you can use online, including document processing and spreadsheet applications.

One common way to promote a product or company is through use of a custom e-mail signature, which Jody can use in Gmail. To promote Hart of Glass Studio further, she's discovered that Google Calendar lets her create and post custom calendars that can be searched publicly.

Build a Form in Google Spreadsheets to Store Inventory Data

One of Jody's business issues is discovering a simple way to handle inventory and project deadlines with her subcontractors. She can use Google Spreadsheets to display her product data (Figure 11). Not only that, but she can allow her subcontractors to use the same spreadsheet, and even chat online to communicate issues and ideas.

Inventory List June 2007	Hart of Glass Studio		
Type	**Name**	**Artist**	**Quantity in Stock**
Chandelier	Sparky	Jody Hart	1
	Spider sense	Tom Franks	1
Candlesticks	monolith series	Jody Hart	2
	Confetti	Sally Wilson	4
Plate 6" or less	Summer daze	Tom Franks	14
	Big blue skies	Tom Franks	7
	Confetti	Sally Wilson	3
Plate 10" or less	Summer daze	Tom Franks	6
	Confetti	Sally Wilson	12
Vase 8" or less	Monolith series	Jody Hart	3
	Juniper berry	Sally Wilson	1
	Wild thang	Tom Franks	1
Vase 9" or more	Red burst	Jody Hart	1
	To the top	Jody Hart	1

Figure 11. Upload spreadsheets from your computer to use online.

Upload a Spreadsheet for Work Online

Google Spreadsheets can be created online in the program or can be uploaded from your computer. Jody uploads a current inventory spreadsheet from her computer, following these steps:

1. Log into your Google Account and select the Docs & Spreadsheets link from your Google product and service list.

2. In the Google Docs & Spreadsheets home page, click Upload (Figure 12).

3. In the resulting form, click Browse to locate the file on your computer. You can also specify a name for the file, or use the default which is the original file's name. Click Upload File.

4. The file is uploaded to the Google Docs & Spreadsheet storage area, and displayed in the file list.

5. Click the spreadsheet's name to open it in Google Spreadsheets. The spreadsheet

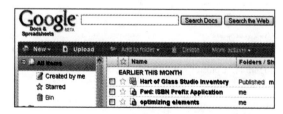

Figure 12. Upload an existing spreadsheet from this homepage.

displays in the program window, using the same color scheme, text, and cell arrangement as the original .xls spreadsheet file.

Share with Subcontractors

Each uploaded file is assigned a storage URL at Google. Jody can share that file location with her colleagues so that they can update inventory as they finish new pieces, and she can update inventory as pieces are sold.

Follow these steps to add collaborators to the spreadsheet:

1. Click the Share tab at the upper right of the Spreadsheets toolbar to display the invitation form, as shown here.

2. Select an option for the invitees. They can either be invited as collaborators, which gives them rights to make changes to the spreadsheet, or as viewers who can look at the spreadsheet but can't make changes.

3. Type the names of those you want to add as collaborators and click Invite Collaborators.

4. In the resulting pop-up window, add a message to the default information, which explains the document sharing process and offers a link to the spreadsheet.

5. Click Send Invitation to close the pop-up window and send the e-mail message.

6. The new collaborators are listed at the right of the Share tab as shown here.

> **This document is currently shared.**
>
> **Collaborators (2)** - remove all
> Collaborators may edit the document and invite more people.
>
> sallyw@wizerdworks.com - Remove
> tom.franks@wizerdworks.com - Remove
> ✉ Email collaborators
>
> **Viewers (0)**
> Viewers may see the document but not edit it

7. Add more collaborators, or click Remove to remove an existing collaborator. Assign the right to invite additional people by selecting the Collaborators Can Invite Others checkbox at the left of the Share tab.

Jody's colleagues can make changes as they occur. They can also chat online if they like via the Discuss tab. The Google Spreadsheets program is a convenient way to stay on top of a collaborative effort, such as Hart of Glass Studio in this example.

NOTE

Keep your content restricted: Don't select the Anyone Can View This Document checkbox on the Share tab, or Publish Now on the Publish tab as both those actions make the spreadsheet available for public searching and access.

NOTE

Read about creating and using custom signatures in Gmail in the section Adjust the Program Settings to Suit Yourself in Chapter 10.

The spreadsheet access and content is restricted to those listed as owners and collaborators.

Create Custom Signatures to Use in Gmail

Jody needs to keep her business information private. At the same time, she wants to make her business known to the public in as many ways as possible. She can extend her corporate branding to e-mail by creating and using a custom signature for Gmail.

Jody follows these steps to construct a custom signature for the e-mail she sends from Gmail:

1. Click the Settings link at the upper right of the Gmail homepage to display the Settings window.

2. Scroll down the page to the Signature area.

3. Type the content in the field for the signature (Figure 13).

4. Click Save Changes at the bottom of the window to store the signature changes and close the Settings window, returning to the Gmail homepage.

Figure 13. Customize the signature appended to outgoing e-mail messages.

5. As new e-mail messages are sent, the content appears at the end of the message, as you see here.

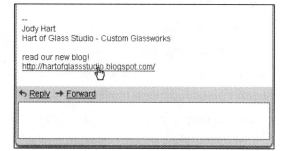

Design and Publish a Calendar in Google Calendar

One of the neatest features Jody decides to add to her online exposure arsenal is a custom Google Calendar. She will create a calendar listing her studio's class and demonstration schedule that can be searched publicly.

Create the New Calendar

To create a custom Google Calendar, follow these steps:

1. Click Calendar from your list of installed programs and features, such as at the top of the Gmail homepage, to display the Google Calendar homepage.

2. Click Manage Calendars at the lower left of the window to display the Calendar Settings window and click the Calendars tab.

3. Click Create New Calendar to display the Create New Calendar window (Figure 14).

4. Add information to describe the calendar, including a name, description, and a general location.

5. Check other features as required, such as the time zone and how to share the calendar. For public use, choose Share All Information on This Calendar With Everyone.

6. Scroll to the bottom of the page and click Create Calendar.

7. A prompt opens to ask if you are sure you want to share the calendar, click Yes to return to the Google Calendar homepage.

Enter Dates on the Calendar

The calendar is ready for use. Jody has planned an open house for June 24. She's also created a blog posting that she can link to from the calendar. How convenient! To add content to the calendar, follow these steps:

1. On the Google Calendar homepage, select the calendar to work with in the Calendars list at the left of the page.

Create New Calendar

Calendar Details

Calendar Name:	Hart of Glass Studio -- custom glassworks
Description:	Online schedule of glass fusing classes, demonstration days at Hart of Glass Studio
Location:	Gimli, MB Canada
	e.g. "San Francisco" or "New York" or "USA." Specifying a general location will help people find events on your calendar (if it's public)

Calendar Time Zone:

Please first select a country to select the right set of timezones. To see all timezones, check the box instead.

Country: United States

(choose a different country to see other timezones)

Now select a timezone: (GMT-06:00) Central Time

☐ Display all timezones

Share with everyone:
Learn more

○ Do not share with everyone
◉ Share all information on this calendar with everyone
○ Share only my free / busy information (hide details)

Figure 14. Specify the settings for the new calendar.

2. Use the controls above the calendar to display the appropriate month, such as June 2007.

3. Click the event's date cell to open a pop-up balloon (Figure 15).

4. Enter basic information in the balloon, or click Edit Event Details to display the larger form that lets you add more details. You can specify the time frame, and add a description.

5. Click Save to close the event details form and return to the Calendar homepage.

6. Click the link on the page to show the event information in a pop-up balloon. Notice the balloon includes a map link, which opens Google Map when clicked (Figure 16).

Sun, June 24, 2007 ☒

What: "Behind the Flames" demonstration
e.g., 7pm Dinner at Pancho's

Which Calendar: Hart of Glass Studio --

[Create Event] edit event details »

| 24 | 25 | 26 |

Figure 15. Quickly add an event in the pop-up balloon.

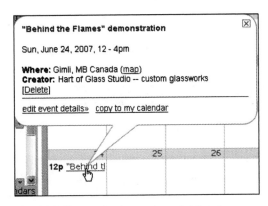

"Behind the Flames" demonstration ☒

Sun, June 24, 2007, 12 - 4pm

Where: Gimli, MB Canada (map)
Creator: Hart of Glass Studio -- custom glassworks
[Delete]

edit event details»   copy to my calendar

| | 25 | 26 |
| 12p "Behind tl | | |

Figure 16. The completed event shows details in the pop-up balloon.

NOTE

Read about catalogs for public use in the section Catalog Shopping. Learn about customized searches for products in the section Track Down Products with Google Product Search in Chapter 2.

Jody's Place in the World

Jody has created a variety of online features and avenues for promoting her business. She also decides to list her business with Google so it can be included in search results. She's going to round off her efforts by adding a custom placemark that viewers can see in Google Maps and Google Earth.

List a Business for Google Maps

As part of Google's mapping and directory system, Jody can list her business in the Google Local Business Center.

Follow these steps to apply for a Google business listing and configure the details of the listing:

1. Open the site at http://tinyurl.com/37yute and click Add New Listing to display the entry form shown here.

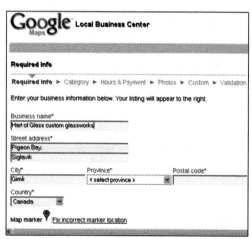

2. Type the basic contact information for your business, such as its location and e-mail and web address information. Required fields are indicated by an asterisk (*).

3. Click Fix Incorrect Marker Location to activate the map on the page and then place the marker correctly if necessary.

4. Click Next at the bottom of the page to progress through several screens:

   ■ Select terms for your business on the Category page in the Category and Sub-category fields. Jody chooses options for two categories, shown here.

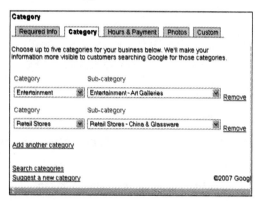

   ■ Choose additional attributes to use in the business description on the Hours & Payment page if you like.

   ■ Locate and select images you'd like to show in Google Maps. You can use up to ten images, but they must be <1MB in size. Select images from locations online or upload them from your computer.

   ■ Add additional information such as a cross street or the number of years the business has operated on the Custom page.

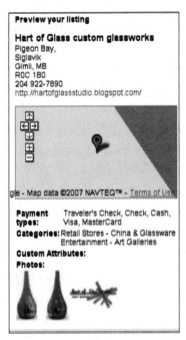

Preview your listing

Hart of Glass custom glassworks
Pigeon Bay,
Siglavik
Gimli, MB
R0C 1B0
204 922-7890
http://hartofglassstudio.blogspot.com/

gle - Map data ©2007 NAVTEQ™ - Terms of Use

Payment types: Traveler's Check, Check, Cash, Visa, MasterCard
Categories: Retail Stores - China & Glassware Entertainment - Art Galleries

Custom Attributes:
Photos:

Figure 17. Check the details for the listing and make necessary changes.

5. As you add information your listing is shown as a preview at the right of the page (Figure 17). To make changes at any time, click one of the tab labels at the top of the page.

6. Click Finish to display the Validation page. Choose a verification method from the postcard by mail, telephone, or SMS options.

NOTE

Read about using Google Earth in Chapter 4. For specifics on adding a placemark, turn to the section Save Places for Future Reference. Chapter 3 offers more discussion on placemarks in the section Add Custom Content to Personalize Your Map.

7. Click Finish. Google will generate a postcard to send by mail or an automated telephone message to provide a PIN to enter at a later date. Once the listing is confirmed by the PIN, it can be included in Google Local Maps searches.

Add a Google Earth Placemark

Google Earth and Google Maps share many types of content. The Google Local Maps process will generate a Google Maps listing for Hart of Glass Studio, but Jody can also make a placemark for use in either or both programs. She starts in Picasa.

Start with the Image in Picasa

To add a custom placemark for use in Google Earth, follow these steps using Picasa:

1. Locate and select the image in Picasa that you want to use within Google Earth.

2. Choose Tools | Geotag | Export to Google Earth File. Picasa will attach tags to the file, and then open a dialog box in Google Earth.

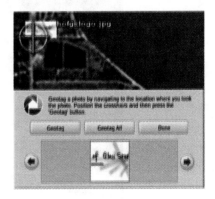

3. Position the crosshairs over the tagging location.

4. Click Geotag to attach the image to the map location.

5. Click Done to close the dialog box and return to Picasa.

6. You see a Save As dialog box to save the image data in the KMZ format used by Google Earth. Name the file and click Save.

7. Close Picasa.

Now it's back to Google Earth for some final edits to the placemark.

End with the Placemark in Google Earth

The placemark is added as part of the Picasa-Google Earth connection. In Google Earth, the tagged image is listed in the Temporary Places in the Places panel (Figure 18).

The name isn't very interesting, and the default information accompanying the placemark doesn't help Jody sell Hart of Glass Studio's products.

Figure 18. The image from Picasa is listed in the Google Earth Places panel.

To reconfigure the placemark, follow these steps:

1. Right-click/CONTROL-click the listing in the Places panel (or the placemark on the map) to display the shortcut menu and choose Properties to open the Google Earth - Edit Placemark dialog box.

2. Revise the information for the placemark as desired, such as its name and description, as shown here.

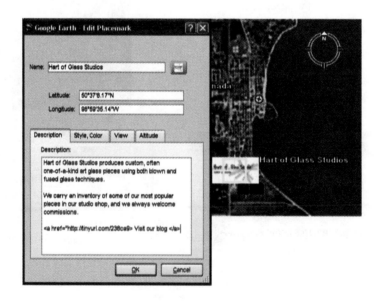

NOTE

The original image placed from Picasa is still listed in the Picasa Link folder of the Places panel. You can delete the temporary place as it has been replaced by the custom placemark.

3. Click OK to close the dialog box and finish the placemark.

4. Right-click/CONTROL-click the listing in the Places panel to display the shortcut menu and choose Save to My Places.

5. The placemark is transferred to a permanent location. Click the placemark on the map and view the information about Hart of Glass Studio (Figure 19).

Summary

This Spotlight project outlined some of the ways a business person can take advantage of free Google tools and services to promote their business and products online. First Jody assembled images in Picasa. To prepare the images for use online she edited and cropped them, and then uploaded a collection to PicasaWeb to store in a Web Album.

Next she turned to Blogger to create a blog for Hart of Glass Studio, which she customized with her own choice of colors and template. She added and published new posts, including a link to her Web Album.

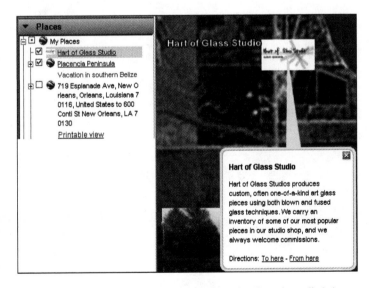

Figure 19. The finished placemark contains information about the studio in its pop-up balloon.

N O T E

Hart of Glass Studio is live at Blogger. Check it out at http://hartofglassstudio.blogspot.com.

To keep track of her inventory and communicate with her subcontractors she uploaded her inventory spreadsheet to Google Spreadsheets and invited her subcontractors to collaborate on the spreadsheet.

She also added a custom signature in Gmail and designed a calendar she published publicly to spread the word of her studio's open house.

Jody then turned to Google Maps for local business and created a presence for her business, pending validation by Google. Finally, Jody put Hart of Glass Studio on the map—literally—by tagging her logo image and creating a placemark for it in Google Earth.

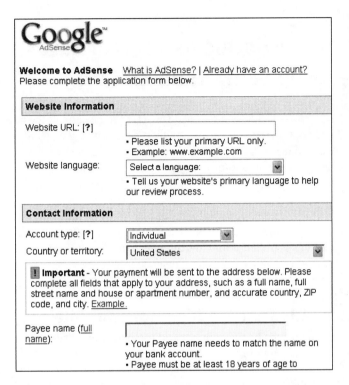

3. Select the checkboxes to acknowledge compliance with program policies.

NOTE   *The policies prohibit clicking your own ads and offering people incentives to click on your ads. They also state that you can indeed receive checks as the payee, that you won't use the ads on sites containing pornography, and that you have read the AdSense Program Policies, located at http://tinyurl.com/29eypp.*

4. Click Submit Information.

5. Your information is transferred to Google for review.

6. When you receive an introductory e-mail, in 2-3 days, you can log into AdSense and start building your ads.

Generating Ads for Your Site

Once you have been approved for the program, you can log into AdSense and create your ads.

TIP   *This chapter's discussion starts with the AdSense setup, describes the My Account features, and then returns to the Reports section—it's simpler to understand what the reports mean when you know how the ads are constructed!*

Advertisements Prevent Pages from Being Valid XHTML

A web page containing Google ads won't validate as XHTML because of the ad structure. The ads use the JavaScript `document.write` method, deprecated in XHTML.

The workaround is rather sophisticated, and involves placing the AdSense code in a separate file and then serving it as text/html using the `object` element.

Google AdSense offers a range of different ad structures and layouts to use on different areas of your site. You can use AdSense for Content, which displays ads using links, AdSense for Search, which shows a search box and allows general Google or site-specific searches, and Referrals, which lets you add content to products such as Firefox or Picasa.

Design Content Ads That Are Right for Your Site

To log into your account, type the e-mail address used for the account and set a password from the AdSense homepage. Click Sign In.

The Overview Reports page is displayed. On this page, choose from the Reports, AdSense Setup, and My Account tabs, each of which allows access to different features and settings, shown here.

To create your first AdSense for Content ad, follow these steps:

1. Click the AdSense Setup tab to display the options as four links.

2. Click Products to display the page. The process for building an ad can be done using the default your page wizard, or you can click Single page to combine all the selections on the same web page.

3. In the first section, select an option to define whether to create an Ad unit or Link unit (Figure 7-2).

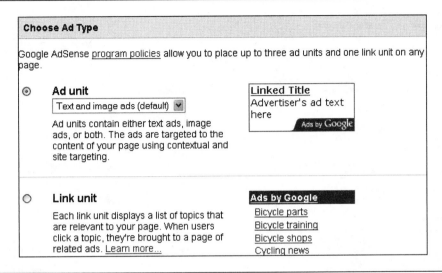

Choose Ad Type

Google AdSense program policies allow you to place up to three ad units and one link unit on any page.

⊙ **Ad unit**

[Text and image ads (default) ▾]

Ad units contain either text ads, image ads, or both. The ads are targeted to the content of your page using contextual and site targeting.

┌─────────────────────────┐
│ **Linked Title**   │
│ Advertiser's ad text   │
│ here   │
│   Ads by Google│
└─────────────────────────┘

○ **Link unit**

Each link unit displays a list of topics that are relevant to your page. When users click a topic, they're brought to a page of related ads. Learn more...

Ads by Google
Bicycle parts
Bicycle training
Bicycle shops
Cycling news

FIGURE 7-2   Select the type of unit, either ad or link, from the page.

4. Choose a Format from the drop-down list on the Choose Ad Format and Colors section of the page. You can choose from horizontal leaderboard or banner ads, vertical ads, rectangles and boxes, or buttons.

> **TIP** *Read about formats and see examples of them at http://tinyurl.com/3dbour. For information on the best-selling ad formats, read the sidebar "Did You Know: Some Ad Formats Work Better Than Others?"*

5. Select the colors for the ads from the Colors section of the page (Figure 7-3). You can choose an existing palette from the Palettes drop-down list, change individual elements of the existing palettes, or save a set of colors that matches your site.

> **TIP** *Refer to the sidebar "How To: Decrease Ad Blindness By Making Clever Color Choices" for a discussion of ad color choices.*

6. Choose an option to display when ads aren't available on your site. The default shows public service ads; you can also show ads from another location or fill the space with solid color.

> **NOTE** *The next part of the page is used to define custom channels to track the effectiveness of ads in different areas of your site. See the upcoming section "Test Your Success with Channels" to learn about using channels.*

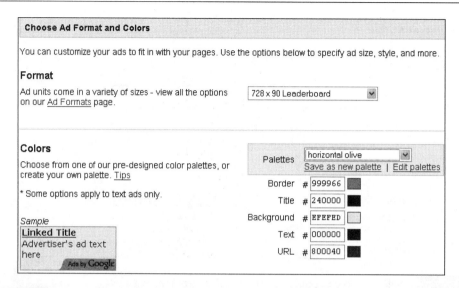

FIGURE 7-3   Choose an existing color palette or modify the swatches and save your own color scheme.

7. Click anywhere in the code shown in the Get Ad Code section of the page to select the content and copy it.

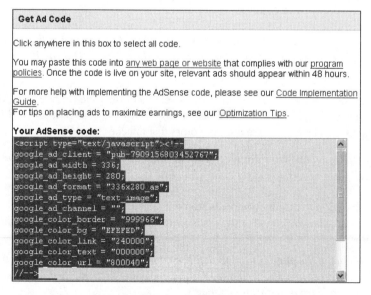

8. Paste the code into your web page's code and then post the page. You'll see targeted ads on your site in approximately 48 hours.

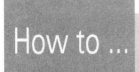 **Decrease Ad Blindness by Making Clever Color Choices**

Viewers to your site may suffer from *ad blindness*, a state where users ignore everything that's not the main content on the page. You don't want ads on your site to blend into the site, making them appear as content, but you do want to have your viewers click on ads of interest.

 *Check out the Google tips for choosing color at http://tinyurl.com/3ysege.*

Start with General Color Ideas

Match the overall appearance of the ads to the overall appearance of your site. If you use a fresh pastel color scheme, users may find ads designed in primary colors against a black background too startling, even offensive.

On the other hand, if your site is a kaleidoscope of color and content, unless your ads are designed in similar fashion your viewers won't notice them.

Match the Color Scheme to Your Site

The appearance of the ads has a direct impact on their visibility. The color schemes break down into three categories:

Ads That Blend Into the Page   Ads that blend into the page are useful where you don't want the content to stand out dramatically, just to be ignored by the viewer. A blended ad block uses the same background and border color as your page's background.

 *If you have a white background and don't want to spend a lot of time customizing the appearance of the ads, consider the default Open Air palette.*

Ads That Complement the Site's Color Scheme   A complementary ad block uses the colors you work with on your site, but don't match borders and backgrounds. For example, if you use hunter green as a link or accent color, you could use the same green as the border for the ads.

Similarly, a pale yellow used as a background for a heading style can be used as a background for your ad blocks.

Ads That Contrast with the Site's Color Scheme   Contrasting ads use colors that stand out against the page's background, and are most commonly seen on sites with dark backgrounds, such as a pale yellow ad background against a black page, or a white ad background against a dark blue page.

Use Multiple Color Palettes for the Same Ads

Some sites have visitors that return frequently. To attract their attention to the ads, you can have your ads automatically rotate among several color palettes.

In the Choose Ad Format and Colors page, follow these steps:

1. Click the Palettes drop-down arrow to open the list and choose Use Multiple Palettes. The page layout is reconfigured to allow you to choose multiple selections.

2. Press CTRL/COMMAND and select the palettes from the list. You can choose up to four palettes

3. View a sample of each palette as you select it (Figure 7-4).

4. Once you have made your selections, continue on with the rest of your ad design.

Choose the Best Page Placement for Your Ads

The best location to insert Google ads on your web page varies, depending on the page's content. The goal is to integrate ads that the reader will notice without making them too intrusive.

Google offers suggestions and information about matching location and value of your ads at http://tinyurl.com/y9fj7l.

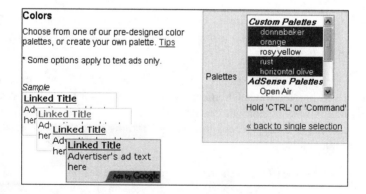

FIGURE 7-4   Select multiple color palettes to rotate on your site pages.

Google describes ad placement locations on a "heat map," laid out as in this example. The darkest areas represent the best ad performance; the lightest represent the worst ad performance.

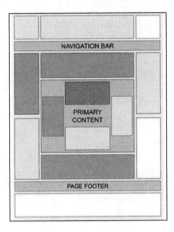

The best locations for ads vary according to the page content and where the user's attentions are focused. For example, ads close to navigation units and rich content such as video usually do well as the user is focused on that area of the page. In the same way, ads placed at the end of an article perform well as they give the viewer something to do when they finish reading the article.

In general, wider ad formats are easier to read than tall formats that wrap text every few words. The best performing ad sizes, according to Google, include:

- 336×280 pixel large rectangle
- 300×250 pixel inline rectangle
- 160×600 pixel wide skyscraper

Insert Multiple Ad Units to Increase Performance

The AdSense Terms of Service let you include up to three ad units, one link unit, and two referral units per page. Consider using multiple ad units when the reader has to scroll down the page, such as a page with a lot of text content, or one containing forum or message board content.

Google offers tips and ideas for placing multiple ad units on forums and other text-heavy pages at http://tinyurl.com/yubszk. Also at this site, look for a heat map showing the best producing ad placements for forum sites (Figure 7-5).

Here are some tips for using multiple ad units on a forum site's pages:

- The best position seems to be a skyscraper ad above the fold at the left side of the page; other than the one skyscraper location, horizontal ads are the best-producing format

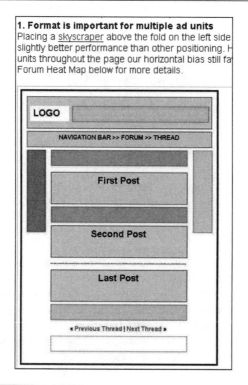

1. Format is important for multiple ad units
Placing a skyscraper above the fold on the left side
slightly better performance than other positioning. H
units throughout the page our horizontal bias still fa
Forum Heat Map below for more details.

LOGO

NAVIGATION BAR >> FORUM >> THREAD

First Post

Second Post

Last Post

‹ Previous Thread | Next Thread ›

FIGURE 7-5 Optimize ad placement on forum pages according to performance.

■ Horizontal link units can be placed on the page just below the header and offer readers a
list of relevant topics, like the list shown here:

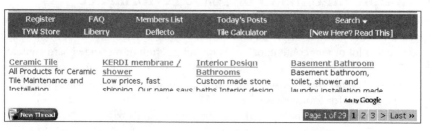

■ Place an ad unit above or below the first post rather than the page heading as readers
usually skip headings and view the posts directly

■ Add a leaderboard after the last post to give the reader a place to go, but before the page
footer as forum visitors often don't view the footer.

How to ...   **Enhance Your Ad Income**

Many sites use AdSense to monetize their content. Here are some tips for maximizing AdSense income on your website:

- Methods used to drive traffic to your site, such as links in your e-mail signatures, and postings you make on forums, enhance the potential for making money with AdSense

- Valuable and regularly updated content on your site attracts AdSense ads paying higher rates

- If you have multiple ad units on the page, make sure the unit with the best page placement is listed first in the page's code—the ads that placed highest in the page's auction and generate the most revenue for your site are assigned to the first instance of the code in the page.

- You can use terms such as "Advertisements" or "Sponsored Links" to increase click rates. Google doesn't allow overt requests such as "Be sure to click my AdSense ad."

NOTE *Google also offers AdSense for RSS and Atom feeds, although the program isn't currently taking new applicants. Images are inserted into a feed. When the viewer displays the feed, Google writes the ad content into the image based on the content surrounding the image. Read more about AdSense for RSS feeds at http://tinyurl.com/2k5gs5.*

Use Specialized Ads for More Impact

In addition to the varying combinations, colors, sizes, and arrangements of regular AdSense ads, Google offers a few specialized features you can consider for your site. You can add a search box to your site, add Referrals, and have your sitemap listed at Google.

Search the Web from Your Site

AdSense includes a search feature, called AdSense for Search, which lets you place a Google search box on your site for your users to search either your site or the Web at large. Your income is derived from clicks users make on search results pages. To maintain your site branding, the search results page can coordinate with your site's overall theme.

NOTE *Find details about the program in the AdSense for Search help files at http://tinyurl .com/2fhz8g.*

Follow these steps to customize the search feature for your site:

1. Log into AdSense using your login information at www.google.com/adsense.

2. Select the AdSense Setup tab, and click AdSense for Search to open the AdSense for Search configuration wizard.

> **TIP** *You can choose either the three-pane wizard, or click Single page to display all configuration options on a single page, used in this example.*

3. Specify the search type and locations. You can choose either Google WebSearch alone, or in conjunction with SiteSearch. As shown here, type up to three URLs to include in the search feature.

4. Choose features for the search box's appearance, such as whether to show the Google logo, where to place the search button, and text color (Figure 7-6).

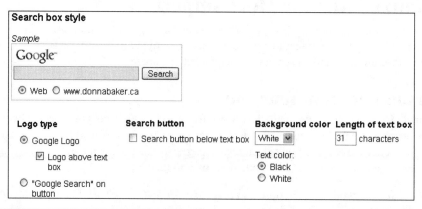

FIGURE 7-6   Specify the appearance of the AdSense for Search search box.

5. Select other features, including the site language, whether to open results in a new window or the same window, and the page encoding.

6. Specify the appearance for the search results page. You can include a logo image, as well as a link from the logo to your web page. Select different colors for the search returns page to coordinate with your website's color scheme, as shown here.

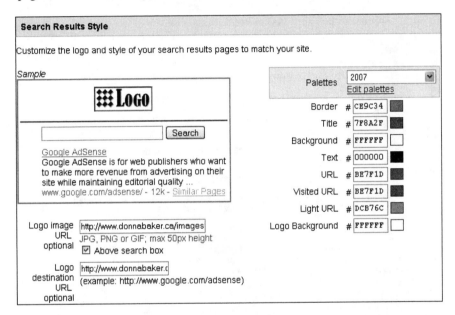

7. Choose more options from the lower section of the configuration page. You can:

   ■ Select a domain to use for searching if you prefer not to use the default United States

   ■ Choose the Use SafeSearch option to exclude adult-themed returns

   ■ Specify a custom channel to track the results (read about channels in the section "Produce Site Reports to Keep on Top of Your Advertising Efforts")

8. Click in the search box code frame to select the text and copy it. Paste it into the web page for your site where you want to see the search box (Figure 7-7).

FIGURE 7-7   The new search box is displayed on the page, ready for use.

9. Test the site's search. The results are shown in a web page, using the custom color palette, as seen here.

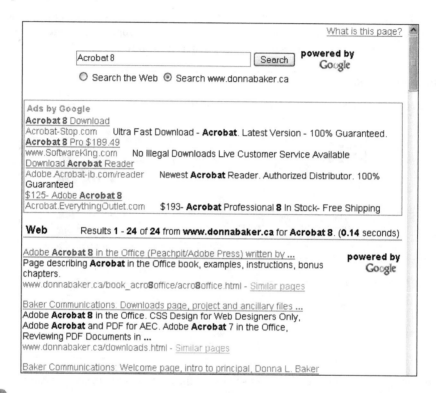

You can use two search boxes on a single web page.

Increase Your Revenues Using Referrals

Referrals is the third type of AdSense service. You can direct users to interesting products including AdSense, AdWords, Firefox, and Google Pack.

Your referral generates income based on the type of referral made, and other criteria. Read more at http//tinyurl.com/2ahsg3.

Follow these steps to add a Referral to your site:

1. Log into your AdSense account. Click AdSense Setup to display the Products page, and click Referrals.

2. On the Referrals configuration page, follow the wizard, or click Single page to display the settings in one page.

FIGURE 7-8 Insert Referral links or buttons on your web page for different Google products.

3. Choose a product from the Google referrals list. Your choices include Google AdSense, Google AdWords, Firefox/Google Toolbar, and Google Pack.

4. Scroll through the lists of options to select a referral product. You can choose text links, or various sized and colored buttons.

5. Copy the code from the code box at the bottom of the page and paste it into your web page's code.

6. Post the page and check the referral links (Figure 7-8).

NOTE   *You can customize text links using your website's HTML font tags. Read more about optimizing and using Referrals at http://tinyurl.com/2zf38u.*

How to ... Use Sitemaps to Get Your Site Included in Google's Search Results

The key to success with AdSense, and your site in general—is traffic. Google offers Webmaster Guidelines you can read to maximize your site's potential.

Read the Webmaster Guidelines for Advice

The guidelines are available at http://tinyurl.com/36zoxp. You can read about:

- Technical aspects of site construction, such as freedom for search bots and pages without session IDs or arguments

- Design and content guidelines, such as a site hierarchy and links

- Quality guidelines, such as designing for humans (not search engines), and avoiding hidden links and text

Include Your Site at Google Sitemaps for Improved Recognition

Google offers a way to improve your website's exposure to the public and improve your search rankings. You can submit your site's URLs to Google Sitemaps via the Webmaster Tools Dashboard, shown here.

Open the page at http://tinyurl.com/y27von and enter your site's information. Once it has been verified by Google, you can check out different features of the site, such as the settings used by Googlebot, types of errors found, and other details (Figure 7-9).

Test Your Success with Channels

Once you have gone to the effort of applying for and being accepted into the AdSense program, customized your ads and placed their code on different pages of your site, you can test to see how effective different ads are by using channels. Google AdSense lets you have up to 200 custom and URL channels.

Specify Channels to Evaluate Changes Effectively

Channels are used to track your activity, and have no effect on how the ads are targeted to your site, or your earnings. Use channels to evaluate changes you make to your site, or your advertising. The Google AdSense reports include a breakdown of activity based on your channels, described in the upcoming section "Create Custom Reports to Simplify the Returns and Save Time."

Choose the Type of Channel to Use

AdSense offers two types of channels—based on the page URL or a custom description:

FIGURE 7-9   Read how your site is indexed and evaluated by Googlebot.

URL Channels   A URL channel is based on your site's pages, and available only for the AdSense for Content program. Use a URL channel to identify the success of individual pages on your site.

Find Specifics Using Custom Channels   Custom channels are used on your site to track specific ad units across a number of pages. You might use custom channels to track the success of a new ad placement or type, such as a leaderboard across the top of your main site pages for example. Custom channels can be used with AdSense for Content, AdSense for Search, and Referrals programs.

NOTE   *Read in-depth information in the Optimizing with Channels article at AdSense, located at http://tinyurl.com/39uzlb.*

You Can Create Ad Placements from Custom Channels

In addition to tracking information for your own use with custom channels they can also be defined as an ad placement. Ad placements are offered to advertisers as a specialized type of ad. The custom channel code contains additional information such as the location of the ad and the type of page which is offered to advertisers when they are using targeted ads.

Read about using custom channels at http://tinyurl.com/3ajeqk.

Create a URL Channel for Your Site

Both URL and custom channels are assigned from the same location in AdSense. Log into your AdSense account, and follow these steps:

1. Choose **AdSense Setup | Channels** to display the page.

2. Click the AdSense for Content button, and click URL channels to display the form. Click Add New URL Channels to open the fields shown here.

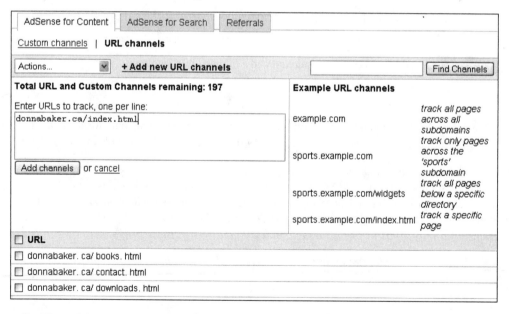

3. Type the name of the URL you wish to track, but don't include the protocol prefix, such as **http** or **ftp**. You can add several channels at the same time by entering each address on a separate line.

4. Click Add channels. The new URL(s) display in the URL list at the bottom of the page.

Read about optimizing your site using channels in the Google AdSense Help files at http://www.tinyurl.com/2df7qd.

How to ...   Understand the AdSense and AdWords Lingo

Here are some simple definitions of the common terms you encounter when working with AdSense and AdWords:

Keyword   A keyword is a term or phrase you assign to target your ads for potential customers. A keyword can contain more than one word, such as **metal garden shed**.

Keyword Matching Options   Keyword matching comes in four varieties to use for targeting your ads on Google search pages. The options include:

- The default option is broad matching which includes general keywords or phrases. The ad can appear when a user searches for your keywords in any order, with or without additional terms. For example, if you sell garden sheds, and use the terms **garden** and **sheds** as the broad matching option, your ads may display if a user uses a range of search terms such as **garden, potting,** or **outdoor sheds**.

- The exact matching option requires the users to search for the specific phrase in the order you specify, such as **[garden shed]** enclosed in braces and without any other search terms.

- Use phrase matching for user searches where the keyword search is a phrase using your terms in the same order, with or without additional terms, written as **"garden shed."** A user may see your ad if they search for **outdoor garden shed** or **vinyl garden shed**.

- To limit the ads to searches for relevant keywords, use a negative keyword option. As in Google searches, use a (-) before the keyword you don't want to use. For example, a keyword written as **garden shed -greenhouse** won't appear if the user searches for **garden greenhouse**.

Cost-per-click (CPC)   Each time a user clicks on your ad, it is registered. The CPC is the maximum amount you pay in a keyword-targeted ad campaign each time the ad is clicked.

Impression   An impression is a view of an ad on a web page used to calculate a cost-per-thousand price for an ad campaign.

Cost-per-thousand impressions (CPM)   Each view of your ad is an impression; one of two ways of costing AdWords. You specify a maximum amount to pay for each thousand impressions.

Produce Site Reports to Keep on Top of Your Advertising Efforts

In addition to the tools for creating and using different advertising schemes to monetize your website, Google AdSense provides an equally expansive set of tools to monitor your efforts and produce generic and custom reports.

Review Reports on Your AdSense Advertising

Log into your AdSense account to view your reports in the Reports tab, shown by default. Check out the basic report information on the Overview tab.

View Default Reports for Quick Info

You see your day's earnings first, followed by a breakdown of the AdSense products by Content, Search, and Referral, shown here.

Reports	AdSense Setup	My Account			
Overview	Advanced Reports	Report Manager	Site Diagnostics		

Today's Earnings: $0.00
View payment history

TIP Are you ready to be paid? Read our Payment guide to learn the steps you need to take to prepare your account for payment.

View: last month - April

	Page impressions	Clicks	Page CTR	Page eCPM [?]	Earnings
AdSense for Content ▾ top channels	1,319	2	0.15%	$0.77	$1.02
donnabaker. ca/ contact. html	6	0	0.00%	$0.00	$0.00
donnabaker. ca/ index. html	42	0	0.00%	$0.00	$0.00
donnabaker. ca/ books. html	12	0	0.00%	$0.00	$0.00
donnabaker. ca/ downloads. html	103	0	0.00%	$0.00	$0.00
view all AdSense for Content channels »					

	Queries	Clicks	CTR	eCPM [?]	Earnings
AdSense for Search	17	3	17.65%	$41.70	$0.71

	Clicks	CTR	Sign-ups	Conversions [?]	Earnings
Referrals ▸ products	0	0.00%	0	0	$0.00

You can read an overview for a different time frame by selecting an option from the View drop-down list, such as the last week, or month, or since the last payment date.

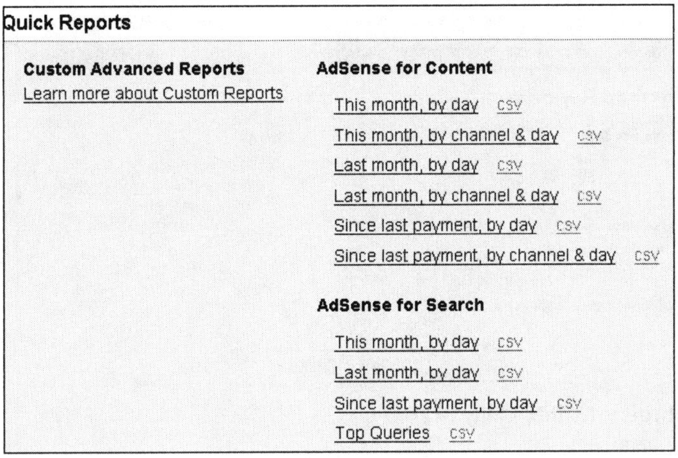

FIGURE 7-10   Download reports in formats suitable for viewing in a spreadsheet program.

Download Reports for Viewing Offline

Scroll down the page to find a set of links for downloading reports on different products and time frames in CSV (comma separated values) format you can open in a spreadsheet program (Figure 7-10).

Improve Your Site Using AdSense for Search Queries Reports

If you use AdSense for Search on your site, you can view the reports, including a list of the top 25 searches performed using your search box.

Follow these steps to view a query report:

1. To open a report, click the Top Queries link in the Quick Reports part of the AdSense Reports page, shown in Figure 7-10. The Advanced Report page of the Reports tab opens.

NOTE   *You can also click the Advanced Reports link to open the page and choose a product directly.*

2. Choose a product from the Choose Product drop-down list; AdSense for Search is shown as it was selected in the previous step.

3. Choose a date range from the drop-down list, or type the range of dates.

4. Click Report to display the results, shown here.

The top queries report find out two different types of useful information:

- What users are looking for on your site, which you can use to emphasize your site's contents
- What users can't find on your site, which you can use to expand and enhance your site's contents

Create Custom Reports to View Specific Activity

If you work with numerous channels, or want to track your activity closely, look at making custom reports. You can specify the contents of the report and select features such as the date range or types of views.

Specify Features for a Custom Report

To create a custom report, follow these steps:

1. Click the Reports tab, and choose the Advanced Reports link to display the Advanced Reports page.

2. Choose a product from the Choose Product drop-down list, such as AdSense for Content.

3. Choose a date range from the drop-down list, or type the range of dates.

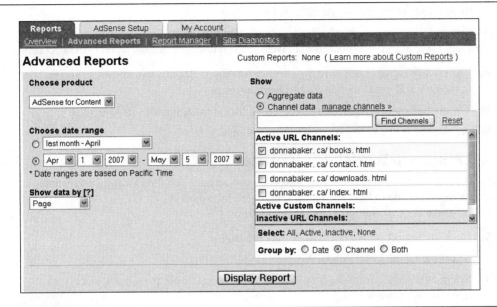

FIGURE 7-11   Choose features for a custom report from the page options.

4. Choose an option to view data from the Show Data By drop-down list. Your choices include:

■ Choose Page to count a page impression every time a user views a page containing an ad regardless of how many ads are shown on the page

■ Choose Ad Unit to count an impression for each ad on a page every time a user views a page

■ Choose Individual Ad to count an impression for each unit of each ad on a page

5. Choose what data to show in the report by selecting either the Aggregate Data or Channel Data buttons. As shown in Figure 7-11, the Channel data option and one of the custom channels is selected.

6. Click Display Report.

7. The results are shown at the bottom of the page. To save the format for a custom report type a name in the Save As Custom Report field, such as **books channel**, shown here, and click Save.

April 1, 2007 - May 5, 2007   Save as Custom Report: books channel   [Save]   CSV

Channel ▲	Page impressions	Clicks	Page CTR	Page eCPM [?]	Earnings
donnabaker. ca/ books. html	29	1	3.45%	$30.48	$0.88
Totals	29	1	3.45%	$30.48	$0.88
Averages	29	1			$0.88

Ways to Access Your Custom Reports

Rather than repeating the option selections, your custom report can show you the information automatically. Once the report is created and saved, you can find your custom report in these locations:

- The custom report is added to the Custom Advanced Reports list, shown in Figure 7-10 in the Quick Reports section of the Overview page
- The custom report is added to a drop-down list on the Advanced Reports page
- A custom report can be e-mailed to you automatically

E-mail Reports to Yourself to Save Time

Save some time: instead of logging into your AdSense account and then locating and running a report, set up a schedule to have the report sent to you by e-mail.

Follow these steps to configure automatic mailing:

1. Click the Report Manager tab to display the page.

2. Select the report name's checkbox.

3. Select a frequency from the drop-down list. You can choose from daily, weekly, or monthly report frequencies.

4. Select an e-mail address if you have more than one address associated with your AdSense account.

5. Choose a format from the drop-down list. You can use either CSV or CSV-Excel format.

6. Click Save Changes (Figure 7-12). Monthly reports are sent on the first day of the month; weekly reports are sent on Monday.

NOTE *The AdSense Reports pages also include Site Diagnostics to check for URLs that the Google AdSense crawlers can't read. Find out more about blocked URLs at http://tinyurl.com/32x5wz.*

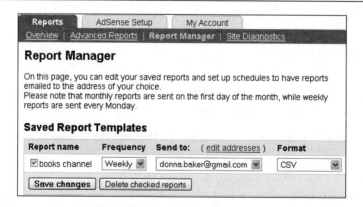

FIGURE 7-12   Choose settings to have your reports e-mailed to you automatically.

How to ... Analyze Site Traffic in Depth with Google Analytics

Regardless of the type of site or business you conduct online, knowing about your visitors, and how they found and interact with your site are vital to your business' financial success. Google Analytics tracks all online campaigns, from e-mails to keywords, regardless of search engine or referral source.

NOTE   *Find help for Google Analytics at http://tinyurl.com/2qc4y7.*

About Google Analytics

Log into Google Analytics using your Google Account to display the Analytics Settings page of the site, shown here. Click the Edit Analytics Account link to open a form where you input information about the site you want to analyze.

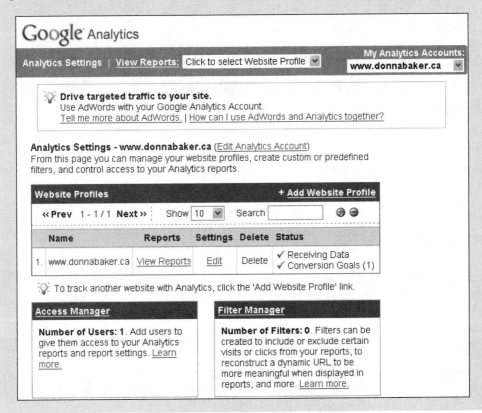

Google Analytics tells you about how your visitors found you and how they interact with your site. Using Google Analytics, you can evaluate your advertising efforts and determine the effectiveness of your keywords in attracting business prospects.

Google Analytics is available in multiple languages, and can be integrated with AdWords. Check out Google Analytics Conversion University at http://tinyurl.com/lsnys for articles on driving traffic to your site, converting visitors, tracking and testing your plan, and understanding how analytics functions.

 *At the time of writing Google Analytics was in transition from one beta format to another beta format. Your page views may look different from those shown in this chapter depending on the status of the Analytics program when you view the site.*

Overview of the Analytics System

The Google Analytics program works by defining *goals*, such as user purchases, registrations, or downloads. You can define a *funnel*, which is a path through your site's pages leading to the goal.

To establish goals for the site, click the Settings Edit link, shown on the Analytics Settings page, to display the Profile Settings window. Fill in fields for your site's URLs as indicated. Your site's goals are listed in the settings as shown here.

Conversion Goals and Funnel 🛈

Select up to 4 conversion goals for this profile, and define the funnel pages leading up to each goal.

	Goal Name	URL	Active Goal	Settings
G1	downloads	www.donnabaker.ca/downloads	On	Edit
G2	(Goal not configured)		Off	Edit
G3	(Goal not configured)		Off	Edit
G4	(Goal not configured)		Off	Edit

View Reports

Google Analytics contains a huge amount of information. To see the basic report, select the site you want to view from the View Reports drop-down list at the top of the Google Analytics homepage. The first page of reports shows summaries of the various types of data collected (Figure 7-13).

 *Read about setting goals and funnel pages at http://tinyurl.com/2fodoe.*

You'll see several reports in the Analytics home page, as listed in Table 7-1.

There are literally dozens of reports you can view in four categories. The Saved Reports list opens links to the content shown in Figure 7-13.

Choose an option from the Dashboard list at the left of the Analytics page shown in Figure 7-13.

Check Out the Overview Reports   Rather than hunting for a specific report based on a category, choose one of the overview options from the Saved Reports list in the Dashboard to show a particular segment of the Analytics home page, such as the Visitors Overview or Map Overlay.

Learn About Visitors   Click the Visitors link in the Dashboard to display a list of reports you can use to learn details about your visitors such as whether they are new or returning visitors, the browsers they use, and details such as screen resolutions. For example, a report showing Browser & OS used by the viewers, shown here, helps to determine how much customization the site's CSS requires to accommodate visitors using different browsers.

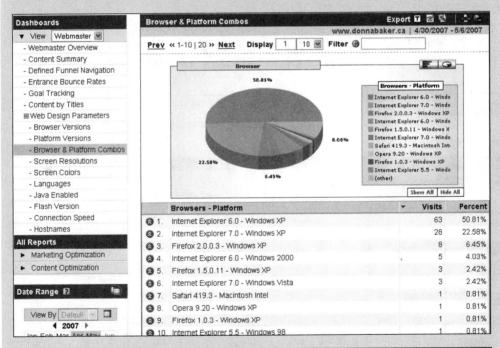

In addition, you can see where users interact with your site in the Site Overlay report. As shown here, the links display a bar indicating how the users interact with the link, such as the number of times the link is clicked.

Learn About Your Site's Traffic   Click the Traffic Sources link in the Dashboard to display a list of reports designed to show you where and how visitors were brought to your site—useful information to increase your site traffic. The reports are shown based on sources and keywords, in addition to being shown graphically.

Learn What Content Visitors View on Your Site   Click Content in the Dashboard to open a series of links to reports about what your viewers are seeing. You can see content by titles or entrance paths. You can see where users interact with your site in the Site Overlay report. The links display a bar indicating how the users interact with the link, such as the number of times the link is clicked, or what percentage of viewers leave the site after visiting a specific page (Figure 7-14).

Evaluate Your Site Goals   Click Goals in the Dashboard to display a list of links to reports on your site's goals. You can find detailed information for each established goal, as well conversions, funnels, and goal value reports.

> **NOTE**   *Finding a particular report can be tricky when there are several dozen to choose from. Click Report Finder in the Help Resources list at the bottom left of the Analytics homepage for help.*

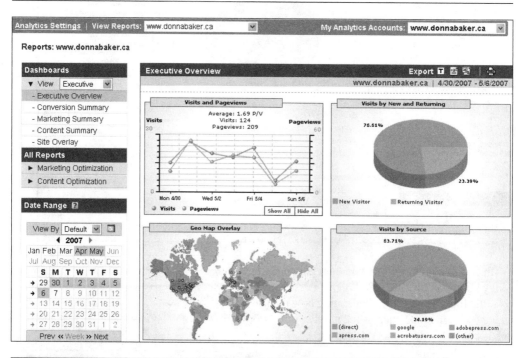

FIGURE 7-13   The reports shows overview graphs of different types of information.

Report Name	What It Shows
Site Usage	Links from the Site Usage report open further graphs showing numbers of visits, visitors, how many pages were viewed during each visit, and so on. For example, in Figure 7-13, over 77% of visitors were new to the site.
Visitors Overview	The total number of visitors to the site on a daily basis.
Map Overlay	The map overlay shows you where the visitors to your site are located; the darker the color, the higher the concentration of visitor locations.
Traffic Sources Overview	The referring site is shown. In the example, nearly 62% visit my site directly, while another 27% visit as a result of using a search engine.
Content Overview	The pages viewed are listed in order of ranking. For example, nearly 57% of visitors viewed my download.html page
Goals Overview	Establishing a goal displays a graph of how many times a viewer visited or purchased a product from a particular page.

TABLE 7-1   Google Analytics generates different types of reports.

Advertise Your Business with the AdWords Program

The days of banner ads and annoying popup windows are over—thank goodness. As Google has largely redefined the Web as a massive search/results tool, they have also redefined advertising online. Instead of indiscriminate advertising, Google AdWords displays text-only ads adjacent to search results that are relevant to the keywords used and displayed in the search process (Figure 7-15).

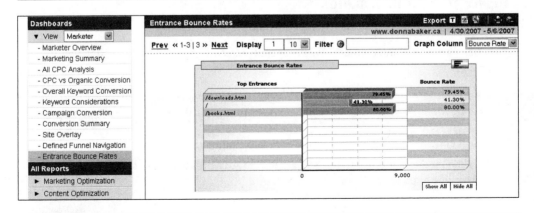

FIGURE 7-14   Show the activity of individual links on a page using the Site Overlay report.

FIGURE 7-15   Ads based on keywords display on the search results page.

List Your Business with AdWords

To get started with AdWords you need to create an account, as with AdSense. Open the site at http://tinyurl.com/m4ocu, and login with your Google Account.

Configure Your Ad Information

Follow these steps to get your account up and running:

1. Click Create Account on the AdWords opening page to display the page listing your options.

TIP   *If you have an AdSense account, you'll see a notification asking if you logged into the wrong program. If you want to use both AdSense and AdWords, click Create Account.*

2. Select either the Starter Edition or the Standard Edition option shown next:

   ■ Choose the Starter Edition if you are new to AdWords and want to advertise a single service or product

■ Choose the Standard Edition if you want to create a more complex campaign, including multiple products, advanced bidding options, tracking, and other features

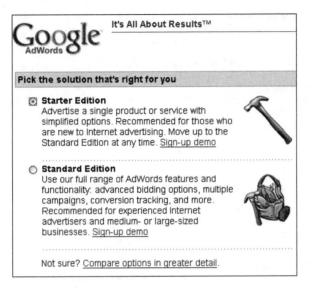

3. For either package, click Sign-up Demo to display a Flash movie showing how the process works.

4. Click Continue to open the Signup Wizard. On this page, define the specifics for the ad you want to place in the AdWords system.

5. To change the country where the ads are displayed, click the select a different country or territory link shown here. Select a country for displaying the ads from the drop-down box that displays. Target the ads locally by specifying a city or region and then choose the language for displaying your ads if required.

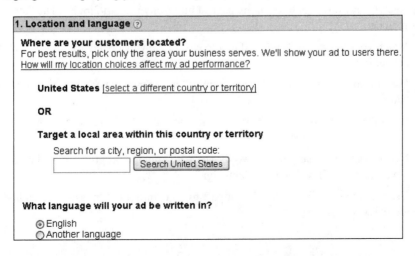

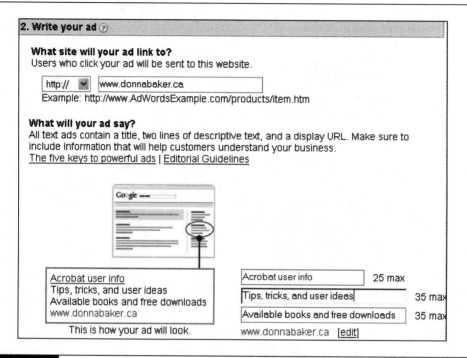

FIGURE 7-16   Write the ad copy and specify the link address.

6. Write the content for your ad next. Type the website address, a headline, and up to two lines of additional text (Figure 7-16).

7. Decide on the keywords to associate with your ads. If you aren't sure what to use, click Top Secret Keyword Tips to open the page at http://tinyurl.com/2l6u8p. The "top secret" tips include:

    ■ Match your keywords to your ad text to ensure the viewers are looking for what you are selling

    ■ Use specific terms such as "beagle puppies" rather than generic, broad terms such as "dogs"

    ■ Limit the number of keywords to 20 or less to focus the search results that match your product or service

    ■ Experiment with changing keywords as your campaign progresses (read more in the next section "Follow Your Ad Campaign")

    ■ Use the Keyword Tool located at http://tinyurl.com/qkfuh for assistance in finding logical words to use

8. Select your keywords from the matching categories shown on the wizard, or add other words to find related keywords, shown here. As you find appropriate keywords, click Add to include them in the keyword list shown here.

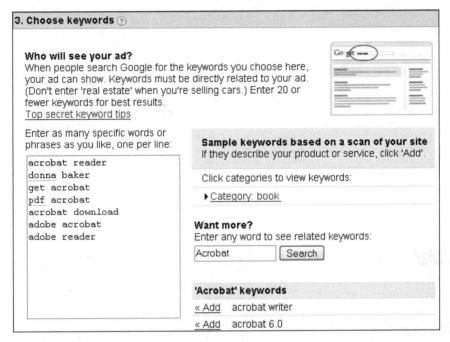

9. Choose your currency and specify the amount you want to spend monthly (Figure 7-17). For your budget amount, choose one of the listed amounts, or type a value for a custom amount. You won't be charged more than your monthly limit, but may be charged less than the monthly budgeted amount.

10. By default, the final step of the wizard offers announcements about improving your ad performance as well as newsletters. Deselect a checkbox if you don't want to receive the information.

11. Click Continue. Your keywords and the information you provided are processed.

NOTE

One issue that publishers need to monitor is called click fraud. *This is a situation where one company's employees click on their rivals' ads to increase ad costs, or when a site owner clicks on ads hosted on their own sites. There are a number of commercial click tracking programs that can display information about the origin of ad clicks; check out the open source AdLogger program for access to a free script at http://www.adlogger.org. Read more about click fraud at http://en.wikipedia.org/wiki/Click_fraud.*

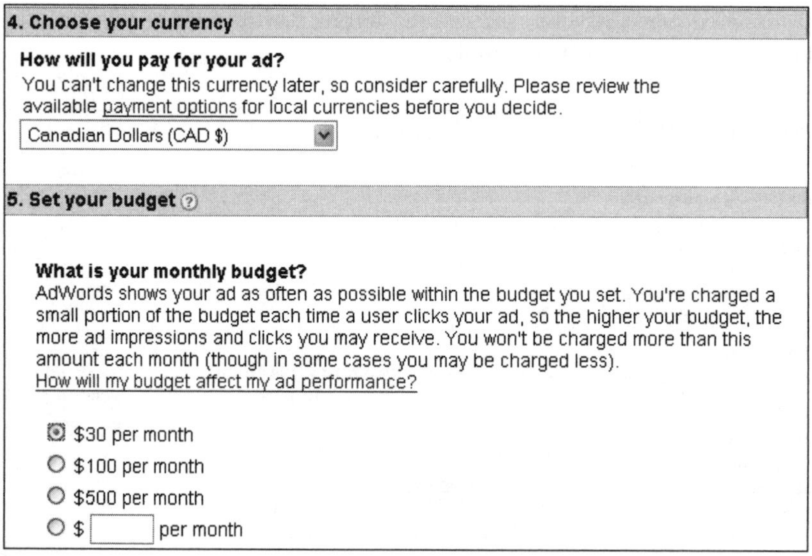

4. Choose your currency

How will you pay for your ad?
You can't change this currency later, so consider carefully. Please review the available payment options for local currencies before you decide.

Canadian Dollars (CAD $)

5. Set your budget ⓘ

What is your monthly budget?
AdWords shows your ad as often as possible within the budget you set. You're charged a small portion of the budget each time a user clicks your ad, so the higher your budget, the more ad impressions and clicks you may receive. You won't be charged more than this amount each month (though in some cases you may be charged less).
How will my budget affect my ad performance?

◉ $30 per month
○ $100 per month
○ $500 per month
○ $ [____] per month

FIGURE 7-17 Choose your currency and the amount of your monthly budget.

How to ... Figure Out the AdWords Fee Structure

Advertisers pay Google to have their ads appear next to search results based on search keywords. AdWords advertisers list keywords or search queries they want their ads associated with and then Google includes the best matches as it generates search result pages. Advertisements are not sold on a fixed-cost basis. Instead, ad space is sold through a bidding process where the most sought-after keywords for advertisers produce the highest bids.

Although the bidding process is complex, you don't need to spend a lot of money to have your products and services included in AdWords ads. AdWords charges per user click, not per page display. If a hundred people view a page and none click your ad, you don't owe any fees.

Google watches for ads that don't perform well, automatically remove an underperforming ad from the keyword rotation, and ask you to change your keywords or modify the ad text.

Set Up the Payment Account

Once Google has processed your information the AdWords page shows an Account Set Up window. Follow these steps to complete the ad campaign setup.

1. First, choose whether you have an existing Google services account, and if you would like to combine AdWords with your other account. If you choose to use your basic Google Account, log into your account.

2. Your personalized Google AdWords page opens (Figure 7-18). You see a copy of the ad you created in the wizard shown on the page. On this page, click Enter Billing Information And Activate Ad.

3. The My Account tab displays, showing the Account Setup form. Follow through the form, adding your location, form of payment, terms, and billing details.

4. Once you have completed the forms, click Save And Activate.

5. As soon as your account is activated, you can start using the program. Google will send you e-mail information about your account.

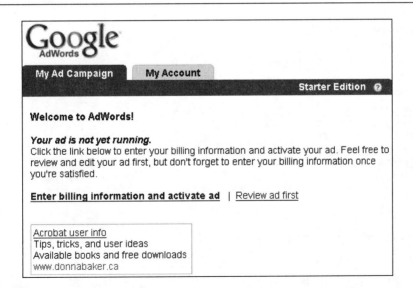

FIGURE 7-18   Check over the ad you created and enter the billing window from this page.

Keep an Eye On Your Ads

Log into your AdWords account at any time to check the status of your campaign. The My Ad Campaign window is shown here.

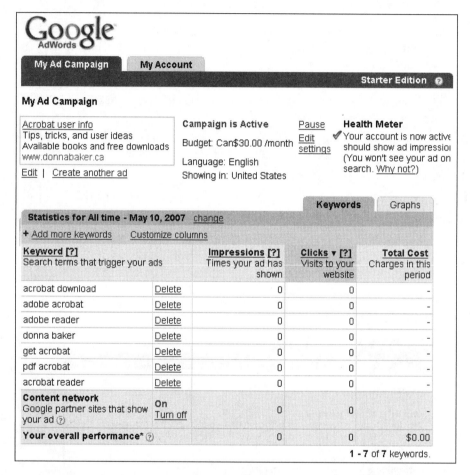

From this page, you can:

- Edit your existing ad, or create a different ad
- Monitor your budget and change the budget settings
- Add or remove keywords
- View impressions of each keyword, how many times the keywords resulted in a visit to your website, and your charges

Did you know?

There Is a Special Type of Site Called a "Zombie" Site

Have you ever come across a link that is a web page full of nothing but a long list of links? These sites are designed to make money from clicks, and contain very little content.

You may see a limited amount of content copied from the Open Directory Project (www.dmoz.org), Wikipedia (www.wikipedia.org), or other sources of online content included as the content for the zombie site. You can report these sites to Google as they are considered search engine spam. Report spam sites to Google at http://tinyurl.com/3y97s.

Summary

This chapter describes the business side of Google. You saw how Google AdSense can be used by a site publisher to monetize their site content by receiving payments for advertising activity. Google AdSense offers a great deal of customization to make the advertisements you place on your pages appropriate for your site. AdSense offers three programs, including AdSense for Content, AdSense for Search, and Referrals. Channels are a way to evaluate the effectiveness of your advertising, and track any changes you make to your ads and pages. Along with customized ads, AdSense offers a range of reporting mechanisms to evaluate your efforts. If that's not enough reporting for you, Google Analytics offers a wealth of information on your site and how visitors interact with it. If you have a product or service to sell, Google AdWords helps to construct, manage, and evaluate an advertising program.

The next section takes a look at building an online office using Google products. First, see how to customize your Google search program, and add other customization features and services.

Part III

Construct a Mobile Office

What does the term "mobile office" suggest to you? Until recently, a mobile office meant you carried your programs and files around on a laptop. In this section, you'll see how the mobile office is changing from a portable contained unit, to a freely available service that allows you to access files and programs from anywhere you have an Internet connection.

Chapter 8

Make Your Web Interface Your Own

How to...

- ■ Personalize your home page using iGoogle
- ■ Add gadgets of all sorts
- ■ Use notes to keep track of online information
- ■ Speed up your online work using Web Accelerator
- ■ Add Google Desktop to expand searching and content management

You need to be able to get to your tools, files, and other "stuff" quickly and efficiently. You might work online and offline in a static location. Your work might be more mobile, and you may be using computers at work or school as well as at home or other locations such as libraries and airports. Google Labs offers some tools that let you organize your desktop and your browser interface to make it simpler and more efficient to find what you need.

Some Google Lab tools are designed to make browsing and online work simpler and more efficient. You can check out Google Notebook for storing snippets of information and other data for future reference. You can speed up your search and page loading using the Web Accelerator, and use Google Desktop to combine online and offline work and searching seamlessly.

Personalize Your Google Homepage for Convenience

It's easy to make your Google Homepage (now called iGoogle) a virtual desktop. Rather than showing a simple window used to access Google Searches, check out the hundreds of neat little plug-ins, add-ins, widgets, and gadgets that you can use to enhance your work day or just amuse yourself.

The Google interface starts out in its default classic form, shown in the following illustration.

Now look at the personalized iGoogle page version shown in Figure 8-1. It's clear that the intent of the site remains focused around search, although there are additional features to allow

Open Google sites　　Organize using tabs　　　　　　Choose a theme　Locate modules

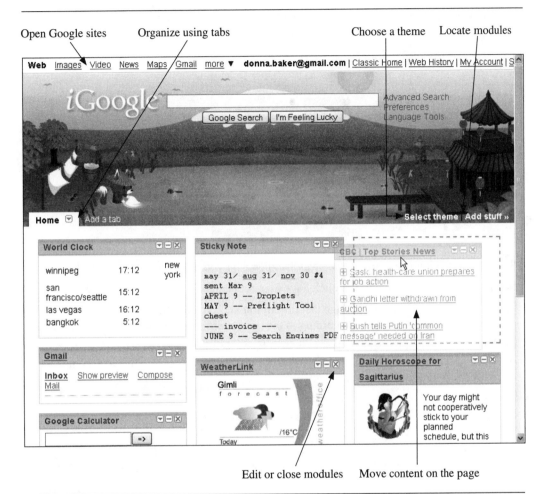

Edit or close modules　　Move content on the page

FIGURE 8-1　A personalized iGoogle home page

access to Google Account programs and information. You can even choose a theme for the page, which changes according to your local time.

Choose a Theme

The classic Google home page is functional, but if you want to perk it up visually you can apply a theme. Follow these steps:

1. Sign into your Google Account.

2. Click iGoogle at the top-right corner of the page to open a version of your home page for customizing.

3. Click Select Theme to display the panel on the iGoogle page shown here.

4. Click an option from the list to display the theme on your iGoogle page.

5. When you've chosen a theme, click Save to close the list.

6. Read the Enter Location message that displays next. The message explains how the theme dynamically changes according to the time of day. Your location is shown, as well as a Change link. Click it to choose another location instead.

7. Click OK to close the Enter Location message and return to the iGoogle page, complete with new theme.

Locate Content to Customize the Homepage

To add content to your home page, follow these steps:

1. Click iGoogle at the top-right corner of the page to open a version of your search page for customizing.

2. Click Add Stuff to open the Homepage Content Directory where you can find modules and gadgets to add to your homepage (Figure 8-2).

> NOTE *If you haven't used iGoogle before, you'll see a message box asking you to "Choose from a sampling of content to get started" when you first open the page. Click Show My Page.*

3. There are a few ways to locate the content you want to insert on your homepage:

- Type the name of the gadget in the Search field and then click Search.
- Choose a category from the list at the left of the browser window to display the available modules; scroll through the list to find the gadget to insert.
- Click More to display further modules.

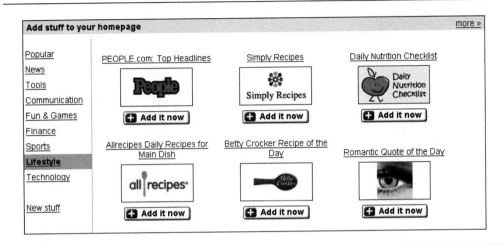

FIGURE 8-2   Homepage content directory

4. Click Add it Now below the gadget's thumbnail, as shown here, to insert it on your homepage.

TIP   *You might see a dialog box explaining that the object is from a third-party source, and asking if you want to proceed. Gadgets created by external developers show the dialog box. Click Yes to acknowledge the dialog box and install the gadget.*

If you want to find out more about a gadget before adding it to your page, click its name to open a dialog box explaining how the feature works (Figure 8-3). Click Add It Now to insert the gadget and return to your iGoogle home page.

Modify the Gadget's Appearance on the Page

Modify a gadget on your iGoogle home page in different ways, depending on its characteristics, such as:

- ■ Click Edit to open a dialog box to adjust the configuration options for the gadget (if they exist). A weather gadget, for example, will let you choose a location, whereas the Quote of the Day doesn't have any user controls.

- ■ Some gadgets, such as Gmail or News headline gadgets, let you open or collapse their display to save space on your homepage.

- ■ Drag a section to move it on the page; you can see an example of this in Figure 8-1.

Add stuff to your homepage

Daily Nutrition Checklist   edit ⊠

You should be eating about 2200 calories a day.

Limit extra fats & sugars to 290 calories.

Grains (1 oz each)   ☐ ☐ ☐ ☐ ☐ ☐ ☐
Vegetables (½ cup each)   ☐ ☐ ☐ ☐ ☐ ☐
Fruits (½ cup each)   ☐ ☐ ☐ ☐
Milk (1 cup each)   ☐ ☐ ☐
Meat & Beans (1 oz each)   ☐ ☐ ☐ ☐ ☐ ☐
Oils (1 tsp each)   ☐ ☐ ☐ ☐ ☐
Water (1 cup each)   ☐ ☐ ☐ ☐ ☐ ☐ ☐ ☐

                    Clear All

Daily Nutrition Checklist

Categories: Tools, Lifestyle

Track your healthy eating with a checklist based on the USDA food pyramid.

Rachel G. - Mountain View, CA

➕ Add it now

Contact the developer - View source »

FIGURE 8-3   Description and use of a gadget explained

Your personalized preferences are stored in your Google Account so you can access them from any computer by signing in. If you are sharing your computer and want to maintain your home page's privacy, be sure to sign out of your Google Account when you are finished.

Add More Tabs for Storage

If you are the sort of person that likes to work with large numbers of icons on the desktop, you can replicate that feat of organizational prowess on your iGoogle homepage.

Rather than trying to fit what you want to use on one page, you can add additional tabs to the interface. You can use up to six tabs in your iGoogle homepage to hold all the gadgets you'd like, and you can sort them for different purposes. For example, you might have one tab with gadgets for work, another with gadgets related to a hobby or personal interests, one tab with headlines from different news aggregators or sources, and so on.

Click Add a Tab on the iGoogle homepage to add another tab. The default label Name that Tab is active—type a custom name for the new tab as shown here. To remove a tab, click the label to show the Delete command to the right of the label and then click Delete to remove the tab.

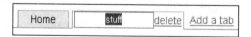

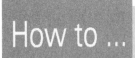

Find Google Widgets for Mac OS X

A number of widgets are available for the Mac OS X system. Users install the widgets to an interface named Dashboard. The Google widgets include Blogger, Gmail, and a Search History function.

TIP

To move a gadget from one tab to another, drag it to the tab label where you want to place it and release the mouse.

Keep Track of Online Content in Google Notebook

Where do you save information you find online? You might keep bookmarks for different tasks or topics, such as parts for your garden railroad or business insurance price lists. Maybe you copy and paste content from web pages to files you save on your computer. Or perhaps you go the old-fashioned route, and scribble details and URLs on scraps of paper or post-it notes that you save until the glue dries up or the paper scraps float into the trash (doesn't that sound familiar?)

Regardless of your method, Google Notebook provides an easier way. By using it, you can safely and simply store and organize information you find online.

Install Google Notebook

Google Notebook is a browser extension that you download and install before use. Log into your Google Account and then follow these steps:

1. Open the page at www.google.com/notebook.

2. Read the Terms of Service information. Click Agree and Download if you are using Firefox. For Internet Explorer, click the Internet Explorer Version Available Here link to locate and download the extension.

3. Close your browser and then reopen it to install the extension. You will see an icon and an Open Notebook label displayed at the lower-right edge of the browser window on the status bar.

Add Clippings

You add content, called *clippings,* to the Notebook in two ways. These include

- Right-clicking the text, image, or link you want to clip, and choosing Note This (Google Notebook) as shown here.

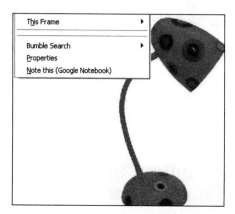

- After searching, right-clicking a link, image, or other search result in the browser window and then choosing Note This (Google Notebook).

Store Clippings for Safekeeping

Clippings are stored in the mini Google Notebook window, shown in Figure 8-4. The window opens automatically when you add a clipping, or you can click Open Notebook on the status bar.

Use the icons at the upper right of the window to change the placement of the window on screen. Collapse the window, or click the arrow to pop out the window into a separate browser window you can then position or resize.

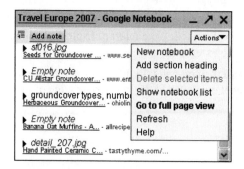

FIGURE 8-4 The mini Google Notebook window and Actions menu

Organize and Share Results with Others

The mini Google Notebook window offers commands that allow you to add or delete content, and even start new Notebooks. The small pop-up window is great for storing and selecting clippings, but it's easier to manage the contents with the Notebook in a full-page view.

View a Full-Page Notebook

There are two ways to open a Notebook in a full browser window, including:

- Click Actions | Go to Full Page View from the mini Google Notebook window.
- Log in to your notebook at www.google.com/notebook.

You organize, modify, sort, and share your clippings in the full page view, shown in Figure 8-5.

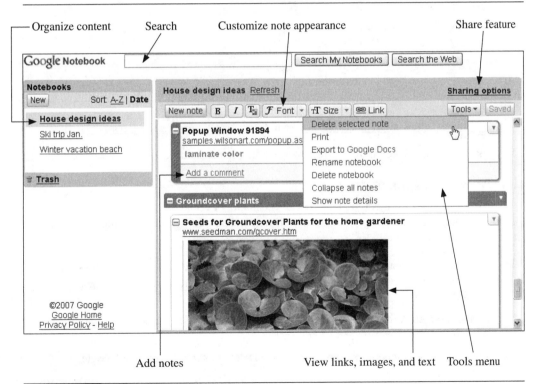

Organize content   Search   Customize note appearance   Share feature

Add notes   View links, images, and text   Tools menu

FIGURE 8-5   Main Google Notebook window

Add Section Headings

All contents are initially collected into a single group. To add more sections, select the notebook from the frame at the left of the Google Notebook window. Type a name for the new heading in the text field at the top of the right frame, and click off the field or press ENTER to add the heading.

Rename the Notebook

The default name for a notebook is My Notebook, which is true, but not very descriptive. In the full page Notebook view, choose Tools I Rename Notebook. Type the new name in the displayed text entry field, and press ENTER to rename the notebook.

Reorganize Content

Drag a clipping among headings in full page view to sort them into logical groups. You see a hatched line and faint outline of the clipping's contents as shown here.

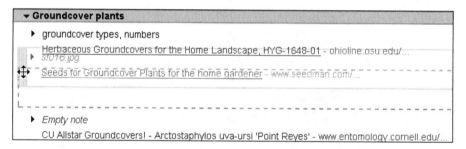

When the clipping is listed in the correct section, release the mouse.

Delete Notebook Information

When you have finished a project, bought your new camera, or booked your vacation, delete the clippings you collected during your research. Delete notes, URLs, sections, clippings, or an entire notebook, such as:

- For an individual note, click the drop-down arrow and then choose to delete the entire clipping or the title and URL—you can also select a note and choose Tools I Delete Selected Note.

- For a section, click the section's drop-down arrow and choose to delete the section header or the entire section and its contents.

- Delete an entire notebook by choosing Tools I Delete Notebook from the Google Notebook menu.

TIP *Anything you delete is stored in your Google Notebook Trash. You have up to 30 days to retrieve it before it is permanently deleted.*

How to ...   **Share Your Google Notebook Online**

Some Google programs let you collaborate with others online, and Google Notebook is one of these. You can invite others to share in your Notebooks, or publish them for the world to see. A shared Notebook is a super tool to use for planning a group vacation, organizing a family activity, or sourcing ideas for your workgroup.

Here's what you do:

1. Organize the content you want to share. You can only share an entire Notebook, so make sure to move other content, unless your collaborators won't mind reading about your searches for the perfect kitchen curtains.

2. Click Sharing options, shown in Figure 8-5. The sharing options settings for the current Notebook open in the same browser window, as you see here.

```
House design ideas: sharing options

This notebook is not currently shared.
⅓ Tip: this icon will appear next to a shared notebook.

Invite Collaborators:
Collaborators may view and edit this notebook. If you
add someone who does not have a Google account,
we'll help them set one up.

Separate email addresses with commas.
┌─────────────────────────────────┐
│ hazel@housekeepers.com,         │
│ glenda@goodwitch.com,           │
│ mickey@rodent.com,              │
│ george@curiousjungle.com,       │
└─────────────────────────────────┘

Publish this notebook (make a public web page)
⦿ No   ○ Yes...

« Back to notebook   [ Save Settings ]   [ Cancel ]
```

3. Type the e-mail addresses of those you'd like to share the notebook in the Invite Collaborators area, separating the addresses with commas.

4. Select Yes or No to Publish the notebook to a public web page.

5. Click Save Settings to open a dialog box for you to type an invitation. Click OK to send the invitations and a link to the Notebook to your addressees. You return to the Notebook's main page.

Other collaborative products include Google Docs & Spreadsheets, described in Chapters 11 and 12, and Google Calendar, discussed in Chapter 10.

 Don't publish a notebook as a web page if you want to share it with just a limited number of people. Once it is a web page, it is public. You can search public notebooks from the Google Notebooks main page.

Browse Faster with Web Accelerator

Use Google's network to make pages load faster when you install Google Web Accelerator. Download the file from http://webaccelerator.google.com. Depending on the type and version of browser you use, the file may install itself. If not, locate the file in your download location and install it.

After Web Accelerator is installed, look for a new toolbar on the browser window or your system tray, like the one shown in Figure 8-6. The toolbar shows a speedometer icon when it is active.

Manage Settings for Custom Performance

The Web Accelerator can be adjusted for different sites or different pages on a site. Click the drop-down arrow on the Web Accelerator toolbar to open the menu shown in Figure 8-6 and choose an operation from the list.

Stop Google Web Accelerator   Choose Stop Google Web Accelerator from the drop-down menu to stop the feature from operating altogether. When the program is stopped, the icon shows as a pale gray circle without a speedometer indicator.

View Performance Data   Choose the Performance Data command from the Web Accelerator's drop-down menu to open a page displaying the Web Accelerator cache data, shown in Figure 8-7. Click Reset to clear the stored time history, which is saved as files on your hard drive.

Set Preferences   Click to open a web page to specify how pages are cached and prefetched, and to list sites to exclude from the Web Accelerator function. For example, a page used for downloading streaming video or audio is unaffected by the Web Accelerator—running the program wastes resources. The speedometer icon for the Web Accelerator is shown as grayscale when it isn't operating.

FIGURE 8-6   The Google Web Accelerator increases browsing speed.

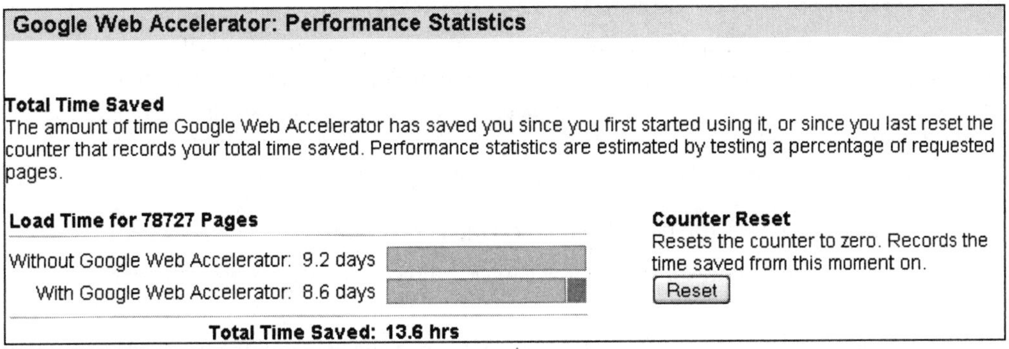

Google Web Accelerator: Performance Statistics

Total Time Saved
The amount of time Google Web Accelerator has saved you since you first started using it, or since you last reset the counter that records your total time saved. Performance statistics are estimated by testing a percentage of requested pages.

Load Time for 78727 Pages	Counter Reset
	Resets the counter to zero. Records the time saved from this moment on.
Without Google Web Accelerator: 9.2 days	
With Google Web Accelerator: 8.6 days	Reset
Total Time Saved: 13.6 hrs	

FIGURE 8-7   View an estimate of the time saved.

Clear History   Clear the Web Accelerator cache when you want to restart your tracking. You may want to clear the cache to see how efficient your browsing is if you change service providers or tweak your computer settings, for example.

TIP   *To find the Web Accelerator in your browser program, choose View | Toolbars | Google Web Accelerator in Internet Explorer or Tools | Add-ons in Firefox.*

Did you know?

The Web Accelerator Tool Stores Files on Your Hard Drive

The Google Web Accelerator has to create a cache on your hard drive, and works in many ways like an ISP (Internet Service Provider). The feature will:

- Manage your Internet connection to reduce delays.
- Send page requests through servers dedicated to Web Accelerator traffic.
- Store copies of frequently used pages. When you call for a page, only updates to the cached page are compressed and downloaded.
- Prefetch pages from a site in advance.

Don't expect miracles: there's no difference in downloading for dialup users, for HTPPS pages due to their security requirements, or for some media files like streaming video or MP3 files.

Manage Content with Google Desktop

The Google Desktop brings searching to your desktop. Once the program is installed, the content on your computer is indexed and ready for searching. The Desktop search includes web pages you have viewed, e-mail, files, and multimedia such as music, photos, and video, like the example shown in Figure 8-8.

Follow these steps to install Google Desktop to your computer:

1. Open the Google Desktop page at http://desktop.google.com.

2. To begin the file download, click Agree and Download. The file is stored on your hard drive.

3. Locate and double-click the GoogleDesktopSetup.exe file to install the program. Program elements are downloaded, and a progress screen displays on your desktop.

Display Google Desktop in Different Ways

There are several ways in which you can display Google Desktop, depending on how often you use the features to how much room you have (or don't have!) on the desktop. To choose an option, click the Google Desktop icon installed on the task bar to open the menu, shown in Figure 8-9.

The Google Desktop can be shown in one of these three ways:

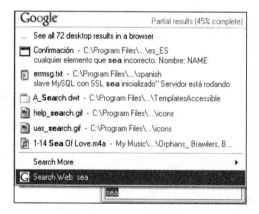

FIGURE 8-8   Search content from your computer.

FIGURE 8-9   Choose a display option.

Show Google Desktop as a Sidebar   The sidebar view is convenient in that it can be resized, and docked on either the left or right side of the display, like the example shown in Figure 8-10. Drag from the top or bottom of the sidebar to reposition it at either side of the desktop.

> **TIP**   *You might find the most convenient way to use the sidebar is to use the AutoHide command, from the sidebar's Options menu. The sidebar slides into view when your mouse is near the edge of the sidebar, and disappears when the mouse moves away from the sidebar's edge.*

Show a Toolbar   If you prefer a small display, choose Deskbar from the Google Desktop menu. The sidebar is replaced by a single text field with a drop-down arrow. Click the drop-down arrow to open the Google Toolbar menu.

Float the Toolbar on Your Desktop   The third display option lets you float the toolbar anywhere on your desktop. The appearance is identical to that of the Deskbar.

Add and Remove Gadgets

The Google Desktop uses Google Gadgets, just as those used in a personalized Google Homepage, described earlier in the chapter. On your Google Desktop display, move your mouse over a gadget to display a small toolbar and a drop-down menu, like the one shown in Figure 8-11.

Each gadget you add to the sidebar offers the same commands. You can:

- Click Collapse to display only the name, saving space on your desktop.
- Click Options to open configuration settings for the gadget if it offers custom settings.
- Click About to read how the gadget works.
- Click Undock from Sidebar to let you float and position the gadget anywhere on your desktop, which is handy if you want to see one gadget but not in the sidebar position.
- Click Remove to delete the gadget from the sidebar.

FIGURE 8-10 Dock the configurable sidebar on the desktop.

| FIGURE 8-11 | Each gadget has a toolbar and commands. |

Let Google Make Recommendations Based on Your Activity

Suppose you are searching for a new car, or checking the weather a few times a day. Google
Desktop will show an information window listing gadget recommendations, like the ones you see
here. Not only can you install new gadgets to match your activity, but Google will also create a
personalized homepage if you like, using your most popular subjects.

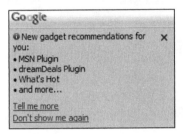

If you aren't interested, and prefer to look for gadgets when and if you want to use them,
click Don't Show Me Again.

Summary

Google offers an ever-expanding range of tools and features to make your browser an easy-to-
customize tool, configured for the way you work, and more like your desktop. You learned how
small programs called gadgets are located and installed. You saw a simple way to collect online
clippings for storing in a Google Notebook. We also went behind the scenes to see how the Web
Accelerator works to speed up your performance. Finally, you saw how the Google Desktop
makes your desktop more like your browser.

Coming up, see how Gmail works, and how it can become part of your online mobile office.

Chapter 9

Manage E-Mail with Gmail

How to...

- Create and manage a Gmail account
- Send and receive e-mail
- Use and maintain Contact Lists
- Customize program settings

Google's Gmail offers a great e-mail solution, whether you are at home or away. You can route messages to and from other e-mail accounts to Gmail and never lose another e-mail message. Setting up a Gmail account is simple, and you can even import contact lists from other programs.

Create a New Gmail Account

In the earliest days of Gmail, the only way to have an account was to be invited by an existing Gmail account holder. One Gmail account holder could invite five others to get their own Gmail addresses. Later, the number of invitations rose to 100 per Gmail user, and new accounts were based on either an invitation, or directly for Google mobile users. Now, anyone can have a Gmail account.

> NOTE   *You can have a Gmail account—using the same Gmail interface as online—for your mobile phone. Read more on Gmail mobile in Chapter 6.*

Open a New Account

Sign up for a Gmail account at http://mail.google.com/mail/signup. The signup window asks for your name, a desired Google Login Name, and then a password. You supply a security question, and a secondary e-mail address (if you have one), which can be used to communicate with Gmail if you lose your password or have other problems using Gmail.

Sign into Gmail at mail.google.com, using your Google Account.

Locate Features in the Program

When Gmail launches, you see the Inbox window (Figure 9-1).

Here are some points on using the program features shown in Figure 9-1:

- Many commands are shown in two or more places. For example, the row of buttons and actions starting with the Archive button are duplicated at the bottom of the page.
- The time or date that the most recent message in a conversation has arrived is displayed on the far right of a conversation line. Dates appear when messages are older than 24 hours.

Selection choices   Search feature

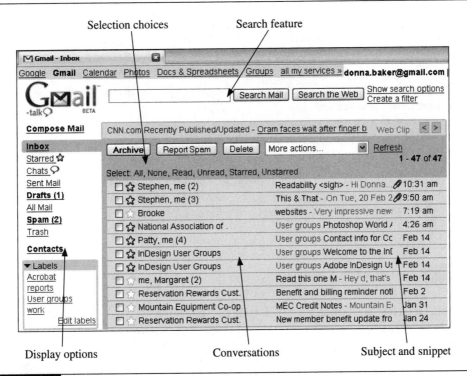

Display options   Conversations   Subject and snippet

FIGURE 9-1   Gmail offers a range of e-mail services.

TIP

Messages are stamped with your operating system clock's date and time. If your messages are displaying an incorrect time, check your calendar properties.

■ Type a search term in the field at the top of the window shown in Figure 9-1. Click Search Mail to look in your Gmail folders, or click Search the Web to move the search outside the program. See how to conduct specialized e-mail searches using Gmail filters in Chapter 10.

NOTE

You will see snippets of different news headlines, web feeds, sponsored links, and other content at the top of the Inbox and Message windows. Customize these messages, called Web Clips, using the method described in the sidebar "How To: Read Web Clips" in Chapter 10.

View and Manage Incoming E-Mail

The Inbox is the heart of the Gmail program. In the Inbox window you receive new e-mails, and are able to organize, read, and reply to messages and conversations. Gmail refers to a single communication as a *message,* whereas follow-up replies and responses are part of a *conversation.*

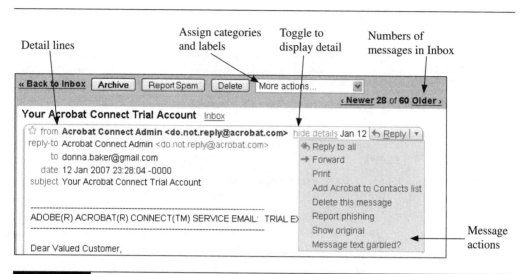

FIGURE 9-2   A typical e-mail message

Read Incoming Messages or Conversations

Click a message listing in the Inbox to display the message window, shown in Figure 9-2.
In the e-mail message, you can:

- Toggle the Show Details/Hide Details command to collapse the heading, leaving only the From line visible. The message heading details are shown in Figure 9-2.

- Click the Reply drop-down arrow to display a list of actions you can apply to the message.

- Move forward or backward chronologically in the list of e-mail messages by clicking Newer or Older at the upper right of the window. The number of current e-mails as well as the number of the e-mail being viewed is shown for reference.

Specify Whether to Show Images

When you receive an e-mail from an unknown address, Gmail disables the images to protect you against spammers. If you recognize the address and want to see the images, click Display Images Below. As you see here, the options are shown above the e-mail message.

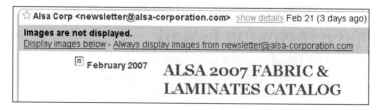

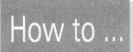 **Play MP3 Files in Gmail**

If an MP3 file is attached to a message, you will see a Play link next to the attachment icon. Click Play to launch the Flash player in a new window, complete with Volume and Pause functions. Click Download to download the file to your computer.

Download the latest Adobe Flash Player at http://tinyurl.com/zgkz2.

If you receive newsletters or flyers regularly via e-mail and want to view the images automatically, click Always Display Images From [name@address].

TIP   *If you choose to always display images from a sender, you can change the setting at any time to remove the display. Open the message, click Show Details at the top of the message window, and then click Don't Display from Now On.*

Check Out the File Attachments

One or more files may be attached to a Gmail conversation. You have several alternatives for viewing the attachment. The options include:

View the File in its Native Format   Click Download at the bottom of the message window to open a dialog box, shown here.

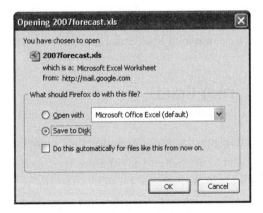

Choose Open to display the file in a new browser window. Select Save the File to open a dialog box and then download and save the file to your computer.

View the File in HTML Format If you'd like the contents of your attachment to appear in a new browser window without having to download the file, view the attachment as HTML. Click View as HTML at the bottom of the message, as shown here.

The attachment opens in a separate browser window. When you've read the attachment, close the browser window and return to Gmail.

There are numerous file formats you can view in a browser window. Some are common types, such as .doc and .pdf, while others are formats used by Open Office and Star Office. These include:

.doc	.sdc	.sxi
.pdf	.sdd	.sxw
.ppt	.sdw	.wml
.rtf	.sxc	.xls

NOTE *An attachment in a spreadsheet format also offers a choice to open the file in Google spreadsheets program. Read about using Google spreadsheets in Chapter 12.*

Send E-mail from Gmail

Next you'll learn how to send a new e-mail from Gmail, respond to an incoming e-mail message in a conversation, or respond to a previous message in a conversation.

Send a New E-mail from Gmail

Gmail lets you send e-mail to one or many contacts at the click of a button. Follow these steps:

1. Click Contacts at the left side of the page to display the Contact window.

2. Select the check box next to the contact you want to e-mail; to e-mail a number of people, select multiple contacts.

3. Click Compose to open the Composition window as a separate browser window, shown in Figure 9-3.

4. Type your message and click Send.

How to ... Troubleshoot Working with Gmail

There are a few common problems that can prevent you getting up to speed in Gmail. Loading issues are usually caused by your browser's settings or by security software that conflicts with Gmail.

Here are a few tips to help you on your way:

- If you are outside the USA, accessing Gmail can be a problem because of proxy issues. If you can't log into Gmail directly, try logging into your account at https://mail.google.com.

> **TIP** *Be sure to type the "s" in https, as it indicates that you are logging into a secure site.*

- Be sure to have JavaScript and cookies enabled in your browser. Read about configuring browser settings in Chapter 8.

- Use the Gmail troubleshooter page for assistance, located at http://tinyurl.com/ 34xvbn. An error message tracking example is shown here.

	Step 1. Many Internet security, firewall and anti-virus applications can prevent Gmail from working correctly. Please select all of the listed applications you have installed on your computer and follow the instructions provided. If you're still having trouble after following these instructions, please proceed to the next step.
I get a 007 error when I try to send › I get a 008 error when I try to send ›	☐ Norton ☐ ZoneAlarm Pro ☐ McAfee ☐ Freedom Privacy and Security ☐ eTrust EZ Firewall ☐ Kerio ☐ Proxomitron ☐ Telus ☐ BellSouth Internet Security ☐ None of the above

> **TIP** *Instead of using the Contacts list, type the first few letters of a name or Contact Group in the To field. Gmail gives you a list of possible addresses and groups from which to choose the correct recipient.*

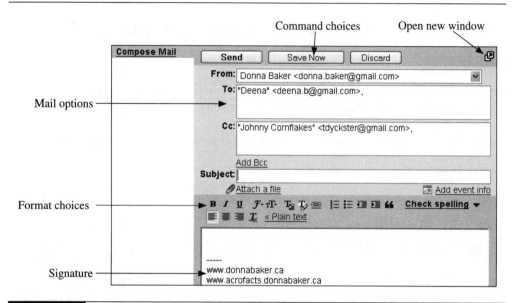

FIGURE 9-3 Composition window for creating e-mail

Respond to an Existing E-mail

As you correspond with someone the messages are collected into a conversation. Your messages are stacked in a cascade, displaying the names and subject lines from oldest to newest (Figure 9-4). The newest message is always the top of the stack.

> **TIP** *If you are working in Windows using either Internet Explorer or Firefox browsers, press <TAB> then <ENTER> to send a message from the Compose window.*

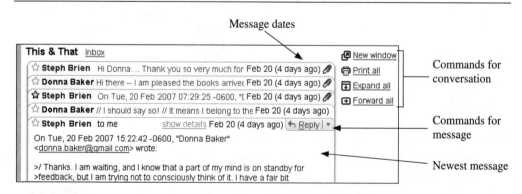

FIGURE 9-4 Messages stack chronologically in a conversation.

Tips for Sending Messages

To respond to a message, click Reply at the upper right of the message window to add a blank message to the thread, like the example shown in Figure 9-3. Keep these tips in mind when responding to a message:

Select a Message in a Conversation   Click any message in the conversation to open it. You can reply to any message in a conversation, not only the newest. Suppose you have an ongoing conversation about a project at work. After some discussion, you want to summarize what you've decided. Instead of repeating yourself, open the previous message listing your action items, and respond again to the list with your new information.

Expand the Conversation's Messages   If you are looking for something in a conversation, aren't sure where it is located, and can't remember the exact term to use for Gmail Search, you can open the entire conversation. Click Expand All from the commands to the right of the Message window, shown in Figure 9-4 to view the entire conversation, letting you scroll through the conversation to find the content. The available command changes to Collapse All; click this to close the messages again.

If you have opened a few messages in a long conversation but want to collapse them and look in other messages, don't close them one by one. Instead, click Expand All; when the command changes to Collapse All, click it again to close the conversation.

Send an Organized Forwarded Message   If you want to forward the conversation to someone else, click Forward All to the right of the Message window, as shown in Figure 9-5 if you have

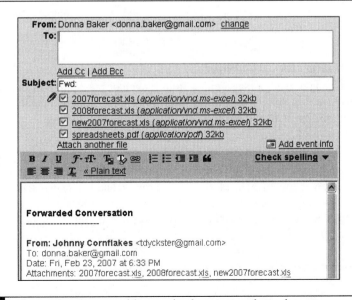

FIGURE 9-5   Forward messages with organized content and attachments.

multiple messages. You'll see that Gmail provides an organized message, as shown in Figure 9-5. All attachments are included, and the message starts with the label "Forwarded Conversation". The existing content is shown in gray.

NOTE *The labels for the commands vary according to the message you are forwarding. When there is a single message, the command is Forward, rather than Forward All. The new message starts with Forwarded Message, rather than Forwarded Conversation.*

Save a Draft Message for Later Use   Sometimes you might not be able to finish writing a message. Click Save Now at the bottom of the message to save a draft. Later, when you are ready to continue, click Drafts to open a window and select the message. The number of Draft messages are shown at the left of the Gmail screen, as you can see here.

Send Messages to Multiple Contacts   If you are working with a group you may find that some messages in a thread should be circulated to the entire group, while others are best addressed only to a subset of the group. In either case, use the Reply to All command, located in the Reply drop-down menu at the upper right of the message window, as shown in Figure 9-2. Delete the addresses for those you don't want to send the message to.

Pick the Recipient Status   By default, a message is sent using an address in the To field. Click Add Cc or Add Bcc below the To field shown here to display the additional fields.

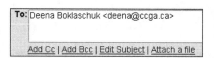

Send copies to additional people by typing their addresses in the Cc field. You can include Bcc recipients as well, which means their addresses are hidden from others—even themselves. That is, if you receive an e-mail where you have been defined as a Bcc recipient, your e-mail address isn't shown in the heading of the message.

Finish Preparing the Message

Once you have written an e-mail message, either from scratch or in response to an existing message or conversation, use other program features to enhance the mail. Gmail lets you add attachments, format the appearance of the text, and even check your spelling.

Attach Files to an E-mail

Gmail uploads files and attaches them to your e-mail for sending. Click Attach a File below the To field in the Message window to open a field. Click Browse, and locate and select the file you want to attach to the e-mail message. You can't send an executable file such as an .exe format file via Gmail, even if it is in a zipped file format such as .zip or .tar. If you attempt to send the files they are bounced back to the sender.

TIP   *The restriction is used as a security measure against potential viruses.*

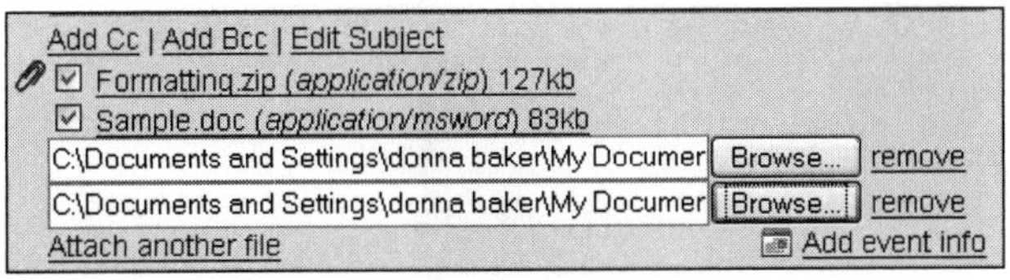

```
Add Cc | Add Bcc | Edit Subject
☑ Formatting.zip (application/zip) 127kb
☑ Sample.doc (application/msword) 83kb
C:\Documents and Settings\donna baker\My Documer [ Browse... ]  remove
C:\Documents and Settings\donna baker\My Documer [ Browse... ]  remove
Attach another file                                      Add event info
```

FIGURE 9-6   Multiple files attached to an e-mail message

You can add multiple files to a single e-mail. As shown in Figure 9-6, the information about attachments can look different on the message window.

The attachments show different types of information and can be managed in a number of ways, such as:

- If the attachment has been saved with the e-mail draft, you will see the name of the attachment in italics.

- Deselect the check box for saved attachments to remove them from the list of attachments.

- Click Remove following the Browse button for any attachment, in order to remove it from the list of attachments.

- Click Attach Another File to open another field and the Browse button to add more files.

- Gmail lets you send and receive attachments totaling 10MB in size. If the attachment is too large, you see a warning stating the file is too large to send.

CAUTION   *Take care using files over 6MB in size, as they may not be allowed. When you add an attachment, transport encodings are added that let the message be safely read and sent. A message may increase dramatically in size when the encodings are added.*

Configure the E-mail Appearance

Gmail offers a toolbar of formatting commands that you can apply to the content of your e-mail messages. In the Compose window, look for the toolbar above the message entry field. If you don't see the tools, you are working in a plain text window. Click Rich Formatting to display the Formatting toolbar, shown in Figure 9-7.

Many of the commands are self-explanatory. Both the Text Color and Highlight Color offer the same color swatches, as shown in Figure 9-7. Select the text you want to modify and click the formatting button to apply the text appearance.

NOTE   *Don't bother using HTML tags in the message—Gmail doesn't recognize them.*

You can read about and see many of the formatting features in the text of the e-mail shown in Figure 9-8.

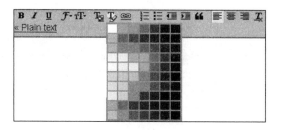

FIGURE 9-7   Format e-mail messages with rich text settings.

If you want to remove formatting, click the Remove Formatting icon—it shows a "T" overlaid with an "x". Many people prefer to have plain text messages, or use their e-mail program to convert content to plain text. If you want to return to a basic format, click the Plain Text link shown below the Formatting toolbar.

Spell Check for Accuracy

Before sending an e-mail, especially when you have to make a good impression, take a minute and check your spelling. The message is tested using the same language you selected for the program.

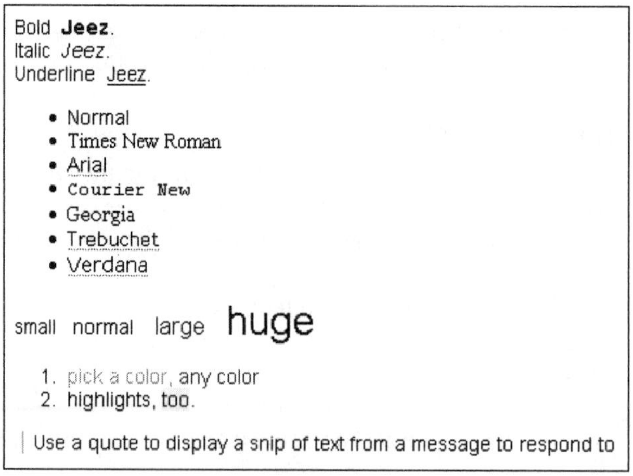

Bold **Jeez**.
Italic *Jeez*.
Underline Jeez.

- Normal
- Times New Roman
- Arial
- Courier New
- Georgia
- Trebuchet
- Verdana

small normal large huge

1. pick a color, any color
2. highlights, too.

| Use a quote to display a snip of text from a message to respond to

---

FIGURE 9-8   Text using formatting features

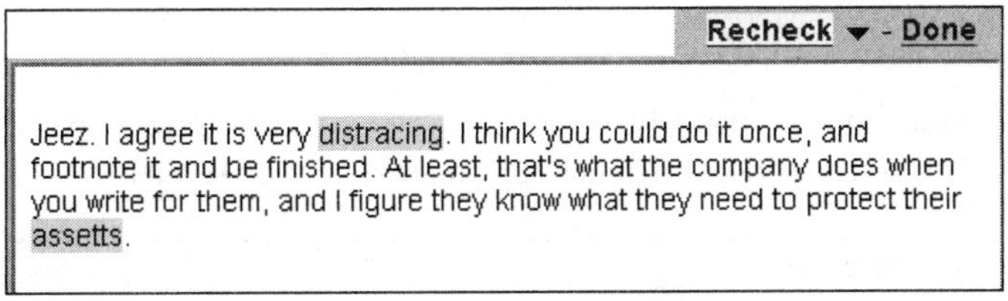

Recheck ▼ - **Done**

Jeez. I agree it is very distracing. I think you could do it once, and footnote it and be finished. At least, that's what the company does when you write for them, and I figure they know what they need to protect their assetts.

FIGURE 9-9   Spelling errors highlighted on the message

TIP
If you type a message in another language, click the Check Spelling drop-down arrow to open a list and choose the appropriate language.

Follow these steps:

1. Click Check Spelling at the top of the message. The message is reviewed, and words not found in Gmail's dictionary are highlighted in yellow. In the image shown in Figure 9-9, you see the highlight as light gray.

2. Click the misspelled word to display a list of suggested words.

3. Click to select a replacement.

4. Continue through the list and make corrections. Click Done to remove highlighting; click Send to send the e-mail.

Use the Contacts List for Easy Addressing

Gmail uses the Contacts List as an address book for storing information about your e-mail contacts. In some cases, the e-mail address is automatically added to the Contacts List. A new contact is added automatically if you choose the Reply, Reply to All, or Forward commands from the menu in the e-mail message window, or unmark a Spam message. If you like, you can add additional contacts manually.

TIP
Refer to the section "Manage Spam Automatically" in Chapter 10 for information on how Gmail handles spam messages.

Choose a Method for Adding Contacts

In addition to automatically adding contacts, Gmail offers a few ways to add people to your Contacts List manually.

Type a New Contact   Add a new contact at any time by following these steps:

1. Click Contacts at the left side of the browser window to open the Contacts window.

2. Click Add Contact to open the Add a Contact window. Add information about your contact. You can add as little or as much information as you like, as you can see here.

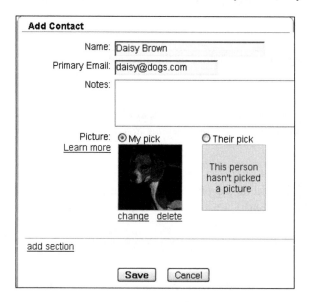

3. Click Save to add the newest member to your Contacts list.

Add Contacts from a Message   When you receive an e-mail message from someone new to Gmail, they are added to the Contacts list as soon as you click Reply. If you receive an e-mail message from someone you'd like to add to your Contacts list, but don't need to respond to their e-mail, click the drop-down arrow next to Reply on the message window. Click Add Sender to Contacts List.

Import and Export Contact Lists to Save Time

Most e-mail programs produce contact information files in formats that can be read by other programs. You can export contacts from Gmail that you can use on a home computer, for example. If you are starting with Gmail, you may want to import your contacts into Gmail from another e-mail client.

NOTE   *Whether importing or exporting, you use the same comma-separated value (CSV) file format.*

Reuse a Contacts List in Gmail

Instead of having to type and save new contacts in Gmail, you can simply import the contacts file. Follow the directions in your e-mail client to export the contacts list in CSV format. In Gmail, Click Contacts to display the Contacts window, and click Import at the upper right of the window. In the resulting Browse window, locate and select the file you want to import, as shown in this example.

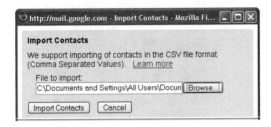

Click Import Contacts to close the dialog box and import your contact information into Gmail.

Export Contacts to a Downloadable File for Transfer

To put your contacts into a downloadable file that you can save to a disk for safekeeping or install on another computer, follow these steps:

1. Click Contacts to open the Contacts List.

2. Click Export at the top right of the Contacts List window.

3. Choose either Gmail CSV or Outlook CSV format for exporting the file and click Export Contacts.

4. Select a location to save your file, and click OK.

Gmail automatically encodes the information using Unicode language encoding format; if you intend to use Outlook, be sure to specify the UTF-8 format instead. When you import your contacts into Outlook, some content may appear garbled if it contains characters that aren't part of the character set used.

Edit Contact Information to Keep It Current

Whenever you get a notification from a contact of a new address or telephone number, take a few seconds and update the Contacts List. Follow these steps:

1. Click Contacts, located on the left side of a Gmail page, in order to display the Contacts List.

2. Click the name of the contact and then click Edit Contact Information to display the information window.

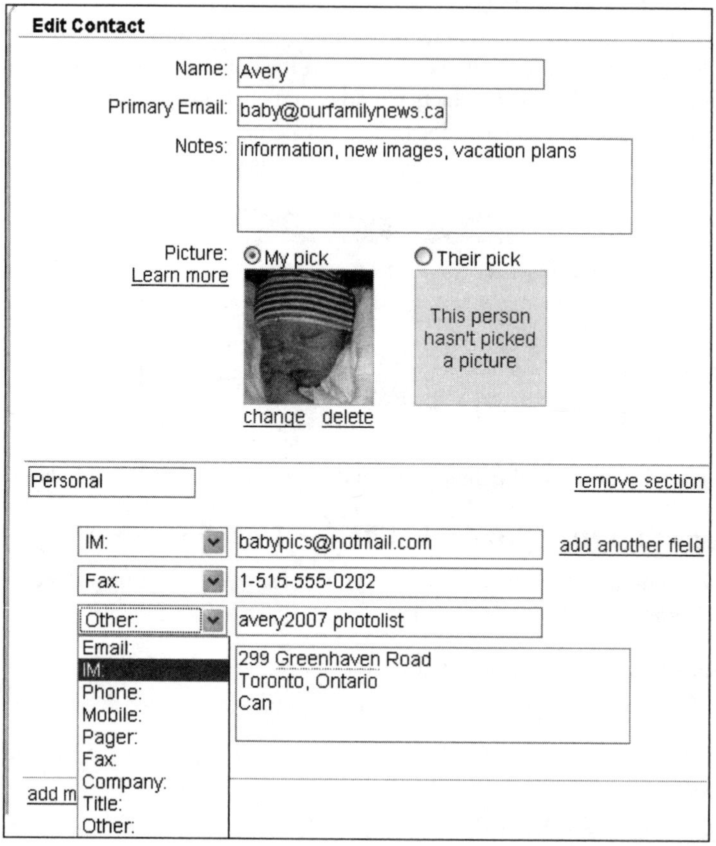

```
┌─────────────────────────────────────────────────────────────────┐
│ Edit Contact                                                      │
│                                                                   │
│              Name:  Avery                                         │
│     Primary Email:  baby@ourfamilynews.ca                         │
│             Notes:  information, new images, vacation plans       │
│                                                                   │
│           Picture:  ⦿ My pick          ○ Their pick               │
│       Learn more                                                  │
│                                           This person             │
│                                           hasn't picked           │
│                                           a picture               │
│                                                                   │
│                     change   delete                               │
│                                                                   │
│ Personal                                          remove section  │
│                                                                   │
│         IM:        ▾   babypics@hotmail.com       add another field│
│         Fax:       ▾   1-515-555-0202                             │
│         Other:     ▾   avery2007 photolist                        │
│         Email:                                                    │
│         IM:            299 Greenhaven Road                        │
│         Phone:         Toronto, Ontario                           │
│         Mobile:        Can                                        │
│         Pager:                                                    │
│         Fax:                                                      │
│         Company:                                                  │
│  add m  Title:                                                    │
│         Other:                                                    │
└─────────────────────────────────────────────────────────────────┘
```

FIGURE 9-10   Use additional sections for complete contact information.

3. Make the edits as required in the appropriate fields, shown in Figure 9-10.

4. Click Add More Sections (partially hidden by the drop-down menu in Figure 9-10) to add an additional section to the contact; click add another field to open the drop-down list shown in the figure, and then pick a heading.

5. Click Save.

TIP   *A selected contact shows a list of recent conversations below the information entry area on the window. Click a listing to view the conversation.*

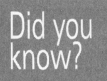

You Can Search for Contacts Using Gmail Search

For those of you with hundreds of contacts, it's nice to know the Google Search feature is offered in Gmail! Follow these steps:

1. Click Contacts along the left side of the page.

2. Type the name or address into the search box like the example shown here.

3. Click Search Contacts.

If you are having problems searching for contacts, try one of these ideas:

■ Use a contact's first or last name only

■ Search by the domain name, such as @gmail.com for contacts using Gmail

■ Enter the username only to find a contact

Create Groups for Easy E-mailing

Many of you regularly e-mail correspondence to groups, whether that group is a gang you play softball with on the weekend, a project workgroup, or family members. Take advantage of Gmail's Groups feature to easily address messages to a number of contacts at one time.

Create a Contact Group

There are two ways to create a Contact Group. Follow these steps to use an auto-complete method for starting a Contact Group:

1. Click Contacts at the left side of a Gmail page to display the Contacts window.

2. Select the Groups tab and click Create Group.

FIGURE 9-11   Select addresses from an auto-complete list.

3. Enter your contact group's name in the Group Name field.

4. Type contacts in the Add Contacts field, separating each address with a comma. As you type, the auto-complete feature suggests addresses from your Contacts list (Figure 9-11). Scroll up or down using the arrow keys; click the desired address, or press <TAB> to select a contact.

5. Click Create Group.

The second method for creating a group lets you choose addresses visually by following these steps:

1. Click Contacts along the left side of a Gmail page to open the Contacts window.

2. Select the Frequently Mailed or All Contacts tab to display the addresses.

3. Select the check boxes next to the names of the contacts you want to include in the group.

4. Click the Add Contact To drop-down arrow to open its menu, as in the following example, and choose New group.

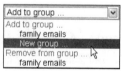

5. Type a name for the new Contact Group, and click OK.

Edit an Existing Contact Group

In the Contact list, look for Contact Group names next to the contacts' listings, like the example shown in Figure 9-12.

☑ **Deena**	deena.b@gmail.com Acrobat pals, family emails

FIGURE 9-12   Contact listings include Group Contact names.

Select the check box next to the name of a contact that you want to edit, and then:

■ Click the Add to Group drop-down arrow to open the menu and then choose the name of the group to which you'd like to add your contact.

■ Click the Add to Group drop-down arrow to open the menu and then choose the name of the group from which you want to remove the contact, as shown here.

TIP

Save time starting an e-mail to a group. Click Contacts to open the window and select the Groups tab to display your list of groups. Select the check box for the group you want to e-mail. Click Compose at the top of the window.

Adjust the Program Settings to Suit Yourself

There are many ways to configure Gmail, from choosing a language to using mail forwarding. Click Settings at the upper right of the browser window to open the collection of tabs, shown in Figure 9-13.

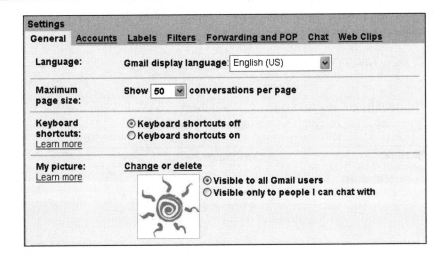

FIGURE 9-13   Customize program features in the Settings window.

NOTE   *The Settings are made up of a number of tabs. In this chapter, we'll look at the General tab. See how the settings on the other tabs are used to configure more advanced options and features in Chapter 10.*

Choose common features for all aspects of your Gmail program in the General tab. Your choices include:

Language   Choose your language from the drop-down list. Gmail supports many common and popular languages and alphabets.

Page Size   Click the Show drop-down arrow and choose to display 25, 50, or 100 messages per page.

Keyboard Shortcuts   Select either to turn the shortcuts feature on or off; Off is the default value. There are many keyboard shortcuts you can use in Gmail. In the Inbox window, try some easy-to-remember shortcuts for moving through different categories of mail, like the ones listed next. In each shortcut, press G (for Go) and then a letter corresponding with the view, including:

G then A	Go to All Mail
G then S	Go to Starred
G then C	Go to Contacts
G then D	Go to Drafts
G then I	Go to Inbox

My Picture and My Contacts' Pictures   Choose a picture to display in your e-mail messages. Specify whether all Gmail users can see the picture, or only those using Gmail Chat. For your *contacts,* those you exchange e-mails with, choose whether to show all pictures, or only those that you've chosen for your contacts.

NOTE   *Read about Gmail Chat in Chapter 5.*

Signature   The default choice is No Signature; select the option to add a signature and type the information you want to see on outgoing messages, as shown next:

Signature: (appended at the end of all outgoing messages)	○ **No Signature** ⦿ "Harry the Hound" - read it now! We are at the Westchester Invitational. Don't miss it!

The signature is shown at the bottom of the outgoing message, separated from your message with two dashes. You can't specify formatting to apply each time the signature is placed in an e-mail. If you like, add formatting to the signature in the e-mail message.

TIP *Select and delete the text to remove the signature when you don't want to send a message displaying the signature content.*

Personal Level Indicators   The default is to use No Indicators; select Show Indicators to display arrows of different types for different message types. A single arrow (>) is found next to a message sent to you and others; a double arrow (>>) when a message is sent to you alone; no arrows when a message is sent to a mailing list.

Snippets   Gmail displays *snippets,* or lines of text showing the first few words of the most recent message. The default is to Show Snippets, like the one shown here. If you prefer, select No Snippets to display only the e-mail subject.

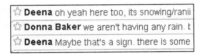

Vacation Responder   Set a vacation responder to automatically reply to incoming e-mail. Gmail sends a reminder vacation response to any subsequent messages received from the sender after four days following the first message.

Follow these steps to configure the Vacation Responder:

1.   Type the message contents in the Subject and Message fields (Figure 9-14).

2.   Specify whether to send responses only to those people listed in your Contacts, or in response to all your e-mail.

3.   Click Save Changes.

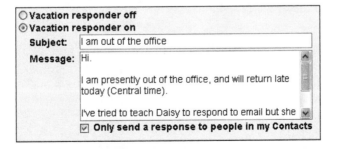

FIGURE 9-14   Type a vacation responder message

Notification of vacation responder on program window

NOTE   *If you have a personalized signature, it is attached to the end of the vacation response.*

When a Vacation Responder is active, you see a banner across the top of the window (Figure 9-15). The banner shows the subject of the vacation response. As you see in the figure, the response can be cancelled by clicking End Now. If you want to retain the response but change it, click Vacation Settings to reopen the Settings window.

Outgoing Message Encoding   Choose one of two methods for encoding messages, either the default text or Unicode (UTF-8) for outgoing messages. Gmail automatically selects the appropriate encoding text based on the language of the e-mail. If your contacts are having trouble viewing messages, switch to UTF-8, which is another type of encoding text.

Summary

In this chapter you checked out Gmail, which is a terrific e-mail client and is accessible anywhere you can make an online connection. Gmail offers a range of e-mail activities such as sending and receiving e-mail and managing contacts. You also learned how most program features in Gmail—from your signature to the appearance of the text on the page—can be customized.

In the next chapter, learn more about using sorting and filtering features in Gmail, as well as how to integrate Google Calendar with Gmail.

Chapter 10

Do Way More than Just E-Mail with Gmail

How to...

- Sort your Gmail using different features
- Use filters to automate e-mail handling
- Keep a current schedule with Google Calendar
- Share calendar events publicly

Everyone uses e-mail, but not everyone understands or uses their e-mail program to its full potential. Along with holding existing messages, and receiving and sending messages, you can use the program to manage the information contained in the e-mail.

Gmail offers the power of Google to search, filter, and organize the content of your e-mail. You can also integrate other Google tools into Gmail, such as Google Chat and Google Calendar to extend the program's function.

Sort Your Mail

All new Gmail messages arrive in the Inbox. You are likely to find that keeping all your mail in the Inbox isn't convenient, nor is it easy to find a particular conversation that way.

Sort into Categories

There are several Select links, found at both at the top and bottom of the Inbox, which let you move the content into groups (Figure 10-1).

The Select links are listed below, and include:

All	This selects all the messages in the Inbox
None	This deselects any selected messages
Read	This selects all the messages that have been read
Unread	This selects any unread messages
Starred	This is used to select those messages you have flagged with a star
Unstarred	This is used to select messages not sporting a star

Along with the Select links, Gmail lets you use two other features for sorting and organizing.

Archive Messages Select a message or messages in the Inbox and click Archive, shown in Figure 10-1. The files are moved to a long term storage area, where they are still available for searching, but no longer listed in the Inbox.

Add Stars Select a conversation or conversations and then click the Star icon next to the check box, shown here.

FIGURE 10-1   Use the default selection options to sort the mail.

Stars are a discretionary sort feature in that you can use them to identify whatever messages you wish. You might want to assign stars to messages about a project you are working on, and then remove the stars when the project is completed.

Sort into Folders

Although all the mail comes into the Gmail Inbox, there are several other folders that can hold content (Figure 10-2).

For the most part, the contents of the other mail folders result from specific actions. For example:

- The Inbox holds all new mail messages that aren't defined as Spam.
- Conversations you have defined with stars are held in the Inbox, unless you also select the message and click Archive. Select the Starred link to show only those messages and conversations that you have applied stars to.
- Chats stores conversations you have held with others using Google Chat.
- Sent Mail holds copies of all the messages you have sent from Gmail.
- The Drafts category holds incomplete messages. If you are writing an e-mail and need more information, or decide to come back to it when you have more time, don't worry—the draft of the e-mail is saved every few seconds. If you want to save the draft yourself, click Save Now when the button is active.
- Click All Mail to show items that are listed in the Inbox, as well as Starred messages.

FIGURE 10-2   Mail is assigned to different folders.

■ The Spam folder holds content that is considered spam messages. Read about training spam filters in the section "Manage Spam Automatically" later in the chapter.

■ Trash holds unwanted messages and conversations. Content deleted from the Spam folder is sent to Trash, as are any messages you select in any other window and define as Trash.

> **TIP** *Messages that you have listed in the Spam and Trash folders are automatically culled by Gmail. Any message over 30 days old is deleted permanently.*

Create Labels for Organizing Messages

Labels work in the same way as the personalized mail folders you may have used in other e-mail clients. The difference is that you can assign multiple labels to the same message in Gmail. Use labels to organize your messages, or as a search term.

Create a New Label

Follow these steps to create a new label in Gmail:

1. Select the check boxes next to the message or messages you want to label.
2. Click the More Actions drop-down arrow to open the menu shown here and choose New Label.
3. Type the name for the new label in the field.
4. Click OK to create the new label and apply it to the messages.

More actions... ▾
More actions...
Mark as read
Mark as unread
Add star
Remove star

Apply label:
Acrobat
reports
User groups
work
New label...

Delete Message Labels

You may start out with a few labels, and then find over time that some aren't being used, or that other labels aren't named correctly.

Follow these steps to remove a label from your list:

1. Click Edit Labels at the bottom of the Labels box.
2. Click Remove Label next to the label you want to delete (Figure 10-3).
3. Click OK to confirm the deletion and remove the label.

> **TIP** *Deleting the label doesn't affect the messages that used the label.*

Rename a Label

To rename a label, click Rename next to the label to be edited. Type the new name into the displayed text entry field and click OK. Messages previously labeled with the old name are now categorized with the new label.

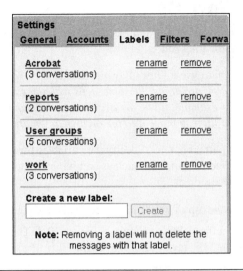

FIGURE 10-3   Labels are listed in a block for easy access and modification.

You Can Check Your Mail from Your Desktop

The Gmail Notifier is a downloadable application that alerts you whenever you have new Gmail messages.

NOTE   *Download and install the Notifier from http://tinyurl.com/g5pcy.*

After you download the Notifier, an icon like this displays in your system tray so you don't have to open a browser to let you know if you have unread Gmail messages.

The Notifier plays a sound to notify you when mail arrives, and shows you bits of text from up to 30 new messages.

Construct Filters to Sort Mail

Filters are a convenient way to organize your mail as it arrives. It takes a few minutes to set up a filter, but saves a lot of time in the long run.

TIP   *How do you know when to use a filter? Pay attention to how you deal with incoming e-mail—if you realize you are doing the same steps with the same mail, building a filter will save you time. For example, if you always store e-mail from the same senders as archived mail, set up a filter to move it to the archive automatically.*

Filters are designed in two parts: First you specify the variables for the filter, such as keywords or senders. Next, define the outcome such as archiving or adding a label.

Set up a filter following these steps:

1. Click Create a Filter at the top of any Gmail page to display the filter form fields.

2. Type the filter criteria in the fields, as shown in Figure 10-4. The more fields you use, the more precise the filter and the fewer returned results.

3. Click Test Search to apply your filter and show your results. If necessary, change the criteria and test again.

4. When your results are satisfactory, click Next Step to display a list of actions.

5. Select the action or actions from the list shown in Figure 10-5 that you want applied to the e-mails.

6. Click Create Filter.

TIP   *You can apply a filter to messages already filtered in your Gmail. In the Create a Filter dialog box, select the Also apply filter to x number of conversations below the check box.*

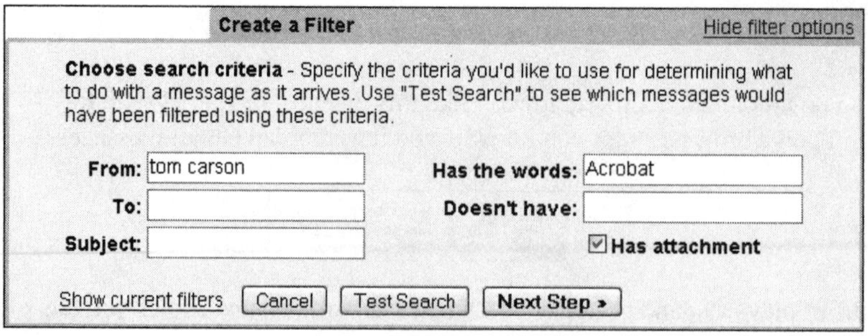

FIGURE 10-4   Specify the criteria to use for constructing a filter.

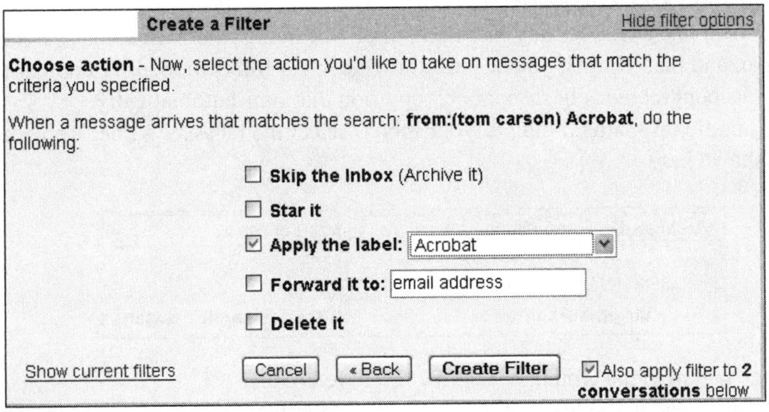

Create a Filter   Hide filter options

Choose action - Now, select the action you'd like to take on messages that match the criteria you specified.

When a message arrives that matches the search: **from:(tom carson) Acrobat**, do the following:

☐ **Skip the Inbox** (Archive it)

☐ **Star it**

☑ **Apply the label:** Acrobat

☐ **Forward it to:** email address

☐ **Delete it**

Show current filters   Cancel   « Back   **Create Filter**   ☑ Also apply filter to **2 conversations** below

FIGURE 10-5   Select actions to apply to the filtered e-mail messages.

Filter Messages from Different Addresses

You can adjust your existing filters to accommodate e-mail arriving from different e-mail addresses. Follow these steps to set up the filter:

1. Click Create a Filter at the top of the Gmail page.

2. Type the e-mail addresses in the From: field. Separate the addresses by typing OR, and add parentheses around the content in the From: field, shown in Figure 10-4.

3. Add the message criteria for the rest of the filter. Click Next Step.

4. Specify the action or actions by clicking the appropriate check boxes, shown in Figure 10-5.

5. Click Create Filter.

Manage Your Filter Collection

Take care of your Gmail filters in the Settings window, following these steps:

1. Click Settings at the top right of a Gmail page.

2. Click Filters to display your list of filters.

3. Locate the filter you want to modify and make the changes:

    ■ Click Delete to remove the filter from your settings.

    ■ Click Edit and change the criteria for your filter. Click Next Step, and finally click Update Filter.

Manage Spam Automatically

Gmail handles spam just as it does any incoming mail—by using filters. In some systems, and with some e-mail and mail clients, you have to train the spam filters to identify content as spam. In Gmail, your account includes basic spam recognition that runs automatically.

If you find additional spam landing in your Inbox, select the message's check box and click Report Spam, shown here.

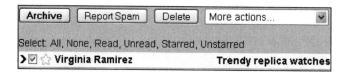

The message is sent to the Gmail system for future reference.

If you find a message in the Spam window that is a legitimate message, select the message's check box in the Spam window and click Not Spam at the top of the message. The label is removed, and the message is moved to your Inbox.

How to ...   Read Web Clips

Gmail includes a display of updated information from news services, blogs, RSS and Atom feeds, and other sources found at the top of the Gmail inbox and messages. By default, a number of Web Clips are displayed in the program.

Follow these steps to customize your Web Clips display:

1. Click Settings at the top of a Gmail page to open the Settings window; select the Web Clips tab.

2. Select a topic link at the left of the window.

> TIP   *Search for feeds by typing topics of interest or feed URLs.*

3. Click Add next to the clips you want to use in your Gmail account.

A clip displays its source, when it was published, and a link to the page. Scroll through clips by clicking the left or right arrows shown in Figure 10-6.

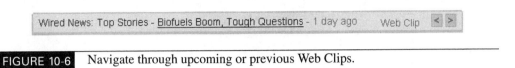

FIGURE 10-6   Navigate through upcoming or previous Web Clips.

Organize Your Schedule with Google Calendar

Google Calendar has become a functional and easy to use calendar that integrates neatly with other Google tools such as Gmail. Along with the default calendar, you can create as many custom calendars as you need to keep track of activities, hobbies, groups, work projects, and so on. Your calendars can be privately held, shared with a select group of people, or offered for searching and public use.

If you have a Google Account, visit the Google Calendar homepage at http://calendar.google.com. Enter your Google Account name and password, and click Sign in.

TIP   *You don't need a Gmail account to use Google Calendar, but there are Calendar features only available in Gmail, such as sending event invitations via Gmail or adding events from Gmail messages to the calendar.*

Getting Around in Google Calendar

You can view content in Google Calendar in a number of ways, depending on what you are doing or looking for. For example, if you have several appointments on the same day, zoom in to see the single day; if you are trying to decide if you can squeeze in a few days of vacation, you'll want to see the full month.

Viewing options include:

- Select a day or click and drag to select a range of dates in the mini-calendar (Figure 10-7).

- Use the arrow buttons at the upper left of the window to move forward or backward from the visible date or select a tab at the upper-right corner of the page. Tabs include Day, Next 4 Days (Customizable), Week, Month, and Agenda.

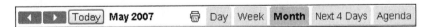

- Select the calendar from the Calendars list at the left side of the page—read about creating new calendars and importing calendars later in the chapter. Select the check boxes next to the calendars' names to toggle their visibility.

FIGURE 10-7 Specify the date range in the mini-calendar.

TIP *You can print any calendar view you like. Click the printer button at the left of the calendar's view tabs. Then, click Print in the Adobe Reader or Acrobat browser window, and then click OK to close the dialog box and print the calendar.*

Setting the Calendar's Appearance

Click Settings at the top of any Google Calendar page to open the settings window, shown next.

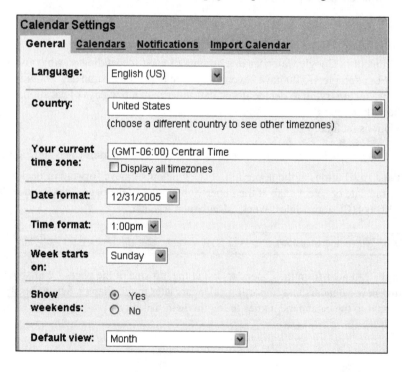

Take a few minutes to configure how you want to view the default calendar in the General settings. If you always want to view the month, for example, set the default to show the month. The options you can configure are listed here.

- Language
- Country
- Your current time zone
- Date format
- Time format
- Start date for week
- Show weekends
- Default view
- Custom view (day and week options)
- Location (only if country selected is United States)
- Show weather (only if country selected is United States)
- Show events you have declined
- Add invitations to the calendar automatically

Create New Calendar Events

There are several ways in which you can add new events to your calendar. The option you choose depends on your workflow and personal preferences. For example, a visual person may want to drag to include several days in the calendar to block off for vacation, while someone else may prefer to type the dates in a dialog box. Regardless of your approach, you'll produce the same scheduling results.

Add an Event and Invite Others

To create a new event and configure its settings, follow these steps:

1. Click Create Event at the left of the Google Calendar page to display the event forms.

2. Add information about the event, such as its location, time, date, a description, and so on (Figure 10-8).

TIP   *Access time and calendar drop-down features by clicking either a time field (as shown in Figure 10-8) or a date field; type in a time that isn't on the list, such as 9:15.*

3. Select a calendar from the Calendar drop-down list.

What	dinner party
When	5/13/2007 6:00pm to
	9:00pm 5/13/2007 ☐ All day

9:00pm (3 hrs)
9:30pm (3.5 hrs)
10:00pm (4 hrs)   repeat
10:30pm (4.5 hrs)
11:00pm (5 hrs)
11:30pm (5.5 hrs)

Where	
Calendar	
Description	

FIGURE 10-8   Add details of the event in the appropriate fields.

4. To invite others, start to type the names in the Guests field; or select your invitees from the names that pop up, as you see here. If your invitees aren't on the contacts list, type their addresses in full.

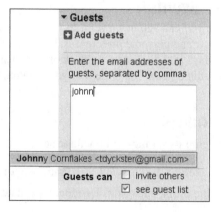

5. Specify whether guests can invite others or see the guest list.

6. Choose other options, including:

   ■ Click the Reminder drop-down arrow and choose a reminder time.

   ■ Specify whether the calendar is to show you as Available or Busy.

   ■ Select a Privacy setting for the event.

7. Click Save to save the event.

8. If you have invited others, click Send or Don't Send in the Send Invitations pop-up dialog box to save the event and return to the main Calendar page.

Other Ways to Create Events

There are ways to add events that are even quicker than the previous method. For example, if you have both Gmail and Google Calendar, when you receive an e-mail message in your Inbox that possibly contains an event, Google Calendar automatically offers the option to add it to your calendar.

In all cases, you can access the same dialog box as that shown in Figure 10-8 to add additional information and invitations.

Open Google Calendar and choose from these options:

■ Click the date when you want to add an event to display an Event dialog box shown here. Type the title and event time and click Create Event to publish the event to the calendar.

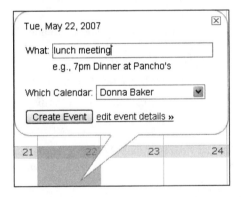

■ Click the Day tab and choose the day; click the time block for the event and add the information, such as "Dentist at 10:00 am."

■ Click Quick Add or type the shortcut Q to open the Quick Add field. Type the information for the event and click (+) to add the event to the calendar.

■ Use SMS to send a text message to the shortcode GVENT (48368). Include event details, such as "Pick up dress Saturday 10 am Fluff 'n' Go" in the message. Google Calendar will interpret your message and put it into your calendar.

TIP *To use SMS, in Google calendar choose Settings | Notifications and complete the information. You need to provide the cell number, carrier, and a verification code that Google sends to your cell phone.*

Migrate Events

You can bring calendar events from Outlook, Yahoo! Calendar, or Apple iCal into Google Calendar. Each program offers different methods for exporting the file, but all use the same import process in Google Calendar.

Outlook In Outlook, choose Export | Export to a File. Select Comma Separated Values (Windows) as the export format; choose the calendar you want to export and its storage location. Click Finished.

Apple iCal In Apple iCal, select the calendar from the list of calendars in the iCal window. Choose File | Export to open the Export dialog box. Name the calendar and click Save.

Yahoo! Calendar Sign in to your Yahoo! Calendar account. Choose Options | Import/Export. Click Export in the Export to Outlook section. Name and save the file to a storage location.

CAUTION *In order to use the calendar file, you have to add hard returns before the beginning quote on each event in a text program such as Notepad.*

Once your calendar file is exported, follow these steps in Google Calendar to import the file:

1. In Google Calendar, choose Settings | Import Calendar.
2. Click Browse and select the calendar file. Click Open.
3. From the drop-down menu, select the calendar to use for displaying the imported events.
4. Click Import.

CAUTION *Files exported from Yahoo! Calendar and Outlook don't include recurring events; instances of the event that fall between the selected dates are included.*

Share Your Calendars

You can share your calendars in a number of ways. If you want to publicize an event such as a community garden visit, share the calendar publicly. If you are planning a garden tour, share the calendar with those in your garden club.

Follow these steps to share calendars:

1. Click the drop-down arrow next to the calendar you want to distribute and select Share This Calendar to open the settings.
2. Specify a selection option, shown in Figure 10-9:
   - Share all information on this calendar with everyone.
   - Share only my free/busy information (hide details).
   - Type the e-mail address of those you want to receive a copy of the calendar, and choose a permission level.
3. Click Add.

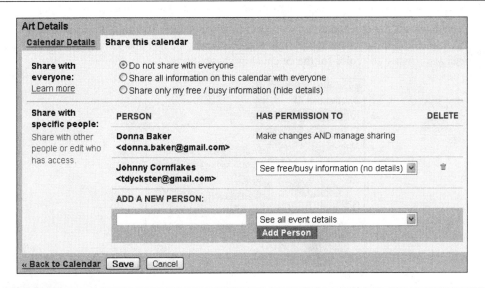

FIGURE 10-9 Calendars can be shared with a select group, or the whole world.

For a public calendar, the information can now be used in Google searches; for a shared calendar, those listed in your recipients list are sent an e-mail invitation to view the calendar.

Add Additional Calendars

Google Calendar offers four types of calendars, including personal, public, friends, and holiday calendars.

Add Personal Calendars for Different Schedules

Google Calendars includes one default personal calendar, but many of us have different activities that are easier to manage if they are on different calendars. For example, a schedule of action items and due dates for work is easier to understand (and achieve!) when separated from orthodontist appointments and piano lessons.

Follow these steps to add another calendar:

1. Choose Settings | Calendars | Create new calendar, or click (+) next to My Calendars to show the Create New Calendar form.

2. Add information about the calendar.

NOTE   *You must name the calendar, but any other settings can be left at default values or blank.*

3. Click Create Calendar to add the new calendar and return to the main Calendar page.

4. The new calendar is listed along with your other calendars. To configure its settings, click the drop-down arrow to the right of the calendar's name and select a command. You can also change the color for the calendar as shown here.

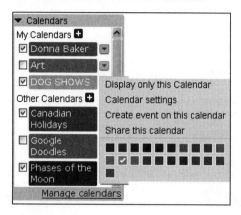

Track Down Public Calendars

Suppose you are an avid theatre-goer or like to attend gallery openings. Check to see if your favorite venues offer public calendars that you can add to Google Calendars.

To find and add public calendars to Google Calendars, follow these steps:

1. Click the (+) button following Other Calendars in your Calendars list to open the Add Other Calendar form.

2. On the default Search Public Calendars tab, enter keywords or other data as search terms. You can

- Use a keyword as a search term.
- Type a URL for the calendar.
- Enter an e-mail address in the search box.

3. Click Search. The results are shown in a list view by default, select one of the tabs to view the results on a calendar page.

NOTE *You may not find results for a calendar. If not, Google asks if you want to search for events. Check out the next section to see how that's done.*

4. Look through the results for the correct calendar. Select the calendar and click Add Calendar, as shown next.

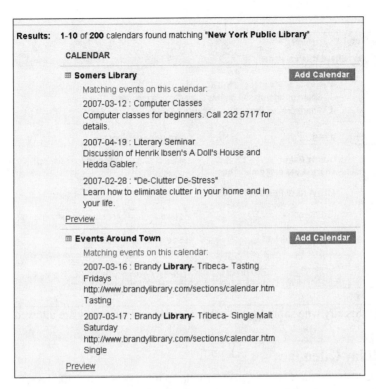

5. The dialog box closes, and the new calendar is listed under Other Calendars on the left side of the window.

TIP

If you have a calendar in iCal or XML format, type the file name in the Public Calendar Address tab and click Add to load the file.

Share Friends' Calendars

You can share a calendar with your friend—whether a fishing buddy or a second cousin helping you organize your family reunion.

Follow these steps:

1. In Google Calendar, click the drop-down arrow next to the appropriate calendar to display the list of options and then choose Share this calendar.

2. Type the names of the e-mail addresses for recipients in the Share with Specific Users section, select a permission level, and then click Add User (Figure 10-10).

3. Once the calendar is specified as shared, notices are sent to those whose e-mail addresses were entered in the previous step.

The calendar displays automatically in the recipients' Google Calendar in the Other Calendars listing.

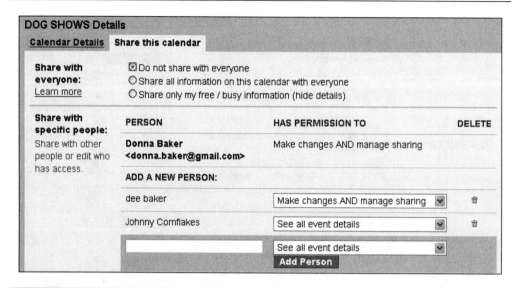

FIGURE 10-10 Specify who should share your calendar, and what they are allowed to do.

Include Holiday Calendars

Add holiday calendars to your Google Calendar to keep track of national holidays, both for your country's holidays, and for other countries, where you have contacts or conduct business. If your calendar shows that the Thai New Year, Songkran, is celebrated this year from April 12 to April 15, you won't bother trying to reach business contacts on those days.

To add a holiday calendar, click (+) next to Other Calendars to open the settings. Select the Browse Calendars tab. Scroll through the list to find the appropriate calendar and click Add Calendar. The calendar is included in the Calendars list, and dates are color-coded on your calendar (Figure 10-11).

FIGURE 10-11   Calendar events are added automatically for holidays or other events.

You can move events from one calendar to another. Select the event on the calendar that you want to move, and choose Edit Event Details. Click the drop-down menu in the Calendar section and choose the calendar where you want to display the event. Click Save.

Add Events from the Web

Use Google Calendar to search for events you want to attend or view, and add them to your Google Calendar.

For example, to find a list of blues festivals in August, follow these steps:

1. Type an event and a location in the Search field on Google Calendar and click Search Public Events.

2. Select an event listing in the search results, shown in Figure 10-12.

3. Check out the information, including a map of where the venue is located and details of the event.

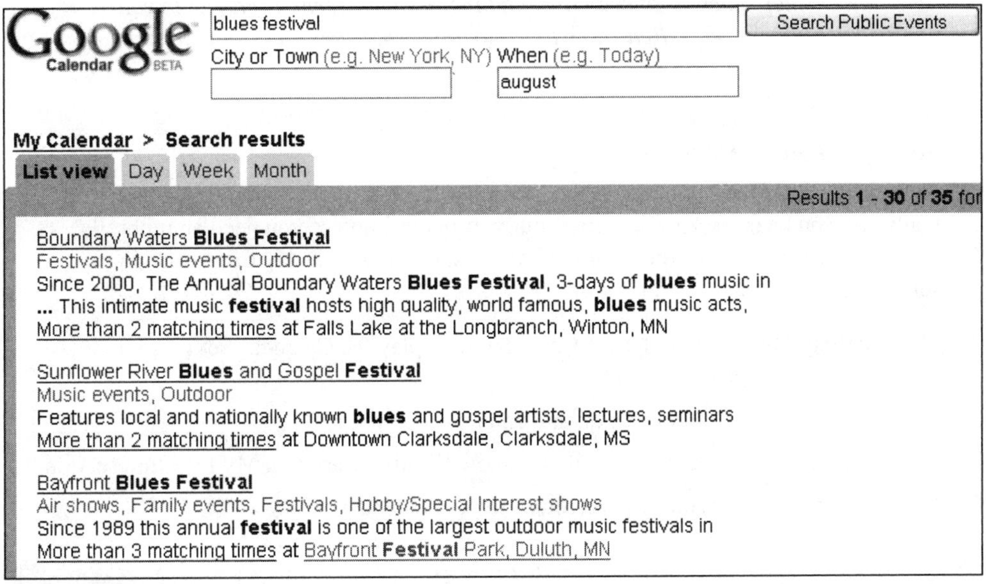

Google Calendar BETA

blues festival   Search Public Events

City or Town (e.g. New York, NY) When (e.g. Today)

                                   august

My Calendar > Search results

List view Day Week Month

Results **1 - 30** of **35** for

Boundary Waters **Blues Festival**
Festivals, Music events, Outdoor
Since 2000, The Annual Boundary Waters **Blues Festival**, 3-days of **blues** music in
... This intimate music **festival** hosts high quality, world famous, **blues** music acts,
More than 2 matching times at Falls Lake at the Longbranch, Winton, MN

Sunflower River **Blues** and Gospel **Festival**
Music events, Outdoor
Features local and nationally known **blues** and gospel artists, lectures, seminars
More than 2 matching times at Downtown Clarksdale, Clarksdale, MS

Bayfront **Blues Festival**
Air shows, Family events, Festivals, Hobby/Special Interest shows
Since 1989 this annual **festival** is one of the largest outdoor music festivals in
More than 3 matching times at Bayfront **Festival** Park, Duluth, MN

FIGURE 10-12 Read about events in the search results.

4. Click on the event time and choose Copy to My Calendar, as shown here.

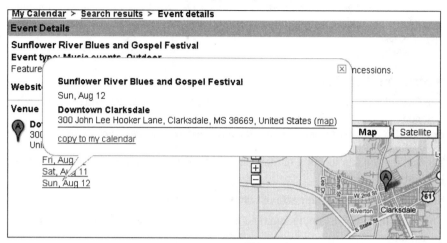

NOTE

Use the mini-calendar gadget for Google Desktop to view your events without opening the browser. The Google Calendar gadget can sit on your desktop or you can dock it in the Desktop Sidebar. You can also add the Google Calendar gadget to your personalized home page. Read how to personalize your homepage and desktop in Chapter 8.

Show Your Weather Forecast

If you live in the United States you can attach a weather forecast to your Google Calendar. That way, not only can you keep track of activities, but you'll also know if you need an umbrella.

Follow these steps to activate the weather feature, showing a four-day forecast and temperature highs and lows:

1. Click Settings at the top of Google Calendar to display the Calendar Settings window; the General tab is selected by default.

2. Scroll down to the Location section and enter your location.

3. Select the temperature scale to use in the Show Weather Based on My Location section.

4. Click Save to store the settings and return to your calendar view.

On your calendar, look for the forecast icon at the upper left of each date's calendar block. Move your mouse over the icon to display the location and temperature high and low for the specific date as you see next.

The weather is available only for US locations. In the General settings, unless United States is selected the location fields aren't available.

Share and Publish Events

Suppose your art group's website offers ongoing and changing art shows, or your baseball team posts its schedule to a common website. Perhaps your business offers client appointments or reservations. If any of these situations apply, there are Google Calendar features you can use on your website.

To make it easier for users to find your events, ensure the title and descriptions are complete and include the full address.

Promote Events to the Public

If you have a public event that you would like to promote, make it accessible to others doing a Google Calendar search.

Follow these steps to specify the calendar's settings as Public:

1. Select the calendar in the Calendars list at the left of the Calendar window, and choose Share This Calendar from the drop-down list.

2. In the Share This Calendar form, shown in Figure 10-13, click Share All Information on this calendar with everyone.

You'll see a Google Calendar button display on the window as shown in Figure 10-13; see how to use it in the next section.

3. Click Save to store the new permissions and return to the main calendar page.

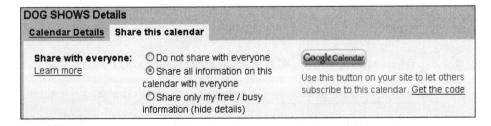

FIGURE 10-13 Specify that a calendar can be shared publicly.

FIGURE 10-14   Copy the selected code to create a button for users to subscribe to your calendar.

Link to a Google Calendar

Instead of leaving your event to be found as a search result, offer your site visitors the option to subscribe to your calendar, or add your calendar as a web page to your site or blog.

Use a Subscription Button

Add a button to your web page that lets the visitor subscribe automatically to your calendar. In the previous section, you saw how a button displays on the Calendar settings when the option is selected to share the calendar. Click the button or "Get the Code" to display a dialog box containing the code (Figure 10-14).

Display a Calendar on Your Site

Each calendar has a unique URL that you can locate and use for sharing.
   Follow these steps to find the address:

1. Click the drop-down arrow to the right of the calendar and choose Calendar settings.

2. In the Calendar Address or Private Address section, click HTML, one of the file format icons, shown here.

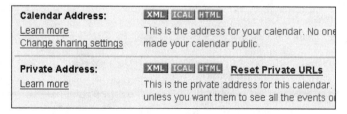

3. View the calendar's URL in the Calendar Address pop up window, shown in Figure 10-15.

Calendar Address

Please use the following address to access your calendar in any web browser.

http://www.google.com/calendar/embed?src=k2i0cb5e68m0qmu9vt4c9a0hjk%40group.calendar.google.com

You can embed Google Calendar in your website or blog. Use our configuration tool to generate the HTML you need.

[OK]

FIGURE 10-15   The URL for the calendar is shown in the window.

4. Click the link for the configuration tool on the pop up box. The Google Embeddable Calendar Helper window will open.

5. Choose settings for the calendar, including a title, the types of controls for the window, its size, color, and so on. Each setting offers a description of your options.

6. Scroll down the page. The code for the calendar is shown in a text frame to copy and paste into your web page.

7. At the bottom of the page, preview the calendar as it will appear on your site (Figure 10-16).

8. Close the browser tab or window. Click OK to close the pop up window showing the page's URL.

FIGURE 10-16   Choose settings and preview the calendar's appearance.

Take care advertising and distributing your calendar publicly—you may find you have more invitations on your calendar than you could possibly imagine. Show only events you've either created or accepted: In the General tab of the Calendar Settings, choose No, Only Show Invitations to Which I Have Responded in the Automatically Add Invitations to My Calendar area. Choose No in the Show Events You Have Declined section.

Summary

In this chapter, you discovered how some of Gmail's features are used to sort, organize, and categorize mail. You learned how to construct filters to help organize yourself even further. From Gmail we looked at using Google Calendar, a separate program that works hand-in-hand with Gmail. There are many ways to configure calendars and add events—you can even add national holidays or phases of the moon automatically. Finally, you learned how to share events for public promotion and searching.

In the next chapter, see how you can work with documents online using Google Docs & Spreadsheets.

Chapter 11

Create and Manage Documents Online

How to...

- Create documents from scratch or use with uploaded files
- Send e-mail invitations to others to edit or view your files
- Publish files as web pages or blog postings
- Save, sort, and manage your files online, including previous versions
- Export documents in a number of different formats

You don't have to spend a lot of money to use programs that perform much of what we do with a document on a regular basis. Instead, you can check out Google's Documents & Spreadsheets program.

NOTE   *You'll learn how to work with the Documents part of the program in this chapter, and will follow up with the Spreadsheets portion in Chapter 12.*

How much work can you do with a program that's free and available online whenever you need to use it? As you'll learn in this chapter—you can do a lot!

Get Ready to Use Docs & Spreadsheets

Make sure your browser is ready to handle the program before you start. You can use Google Docs & Spreadsheets in most browsers, including Firefox, Netscape, Internet Explorer, and Opera. Docs & Spreadsheets is also now supported on Linux. Regardless of the browser you are using, you must have cookies and JavaScript enabled for it to work.

NOTE   *At the time of writing, Google Docs & Spreadsheets wasn't available for Safari browsers. The program works on Mac using Camino 1.0a1 or higher, FireFox 1.0.5 or higher, or Mozilla 1.5 or higher.*

Check Your Browser Settings

Cookies are files stored on your hard drive that contain information on the settings and preferences you use in the Docs & Spreadsheets program. *JavaScript* is a programming language used to run online applications like Google Docs & Spreadsheets. Unless the browser is reading and processing the JavaScript, you won't be able to use the program.

To make sure you have the browser features enabled, check for these settings in your browser of choice:

Check Firefox Settings   Open Firefox and choose Tools | Options | Privacy to open the Privacy tab of the Options dialog box. Ensure that the Accept Cookies from Sites check box is selected. Click Content to display settings for choosing active page features, and choose the Enable JavaScript check box. Click OK to close the dialog box.

Specify IE Settings In either Version 6 or 7 of Internet Explorer, choose Tools | Internet Options | Security to display the Security tab of the Internet Options dialog box. Click Custom Level to display the Security Settings dialog box; scroll down to the Scripting section, shown here (it's a long way down!) and click Enable. Click OK to close the dialog box.

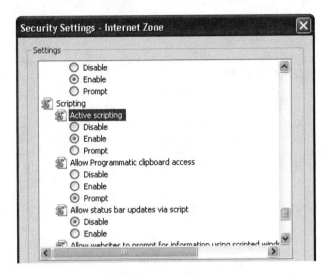

Select Privacy to display options for choosing how cookies are handled, adjust the slider to the Medium setting, and then click OK to close the dialog box.

Check Your Account

Now all you need to start working with Google Docs & Spreadsheets is a Google Account. Sign up for a Google Account at https://www.google.com/accounts/NewAccount.

If you already have a Google Account, go to http://docs.google.com/ and sign in.

TIP   *If you are using Gmail, you already have a Google account.*

Be Aware of File Size and Type

When working with your computer, the numbers and sizes of files are limited only by your software and hardware; however, you do have definite limits working in Google Docs & Spreadsheets. The restrictions for both document and spreadsheets are

- One document can contain up to 500K of formatted text, and can include another 2MB of images. You can keep up to 1000 documents and 1000 images.

- A spreadsheet can't exceed a specific size, which is one of: 20 sheets, 50,000 cells, 10,000 rows, or 256 columns. You can store up to 200 spreadsheets online, and each file you upload can be up to 1MB in size. You can have up to 20 spreadsheets open at one time.

Your Files Have Special Security

Working with a spreadsheet or document online isn't the same as working on your personal desktop. Documents and spreadsheets aren't indexed for searching by robots or spiders unless you publish the file or share them online. In addition, you have to reference the document's URL from another web page in order to have it indexed for searching.

Your Google Account username is used to control access to the files, and you decide whether you want to share the information. Google offers an extensive privacy policy, including a pledge to protect your personal information. Read the privacy policy at http://tinyurl.com/ytfeye.

Many types of files can be used in Google Docs & Spreadsheets. The document formats include:

HTML	TXT	DOC (Microsoft Word)
RTF (Rich Text)	ODT (OpenDocument Text)	SXW (StarOffice)

Spreadsheet files formats include:

XLS (Excel format)	CSV (comma-separated values)	TSV (tab-separated values)
TXT (text)	TSB (tab-separated)	ODS (OpenDocument Spreadsheet)

Check Out the Program and Files

Use the features on the Google Docs & Spreadsheets homepage to manage your document and spreadsheet files, as shown in Figure 11-1.

TIP *In the Docs list, each file shows an icon that identifies it as either a document or a spreadsheet.*

Use Folders to Manage Your Documents

One recent introduction to the Docs & Spreadsheets program is a folder system. You can use the Docs & Spreadsheets folders to organize your work online the same as you do your desktop folder system.

TIP *One file can be stored in multiple folders. You may want to use this feature if you have multiple projects on the go and use a common document for all, such as a cover sheet.*

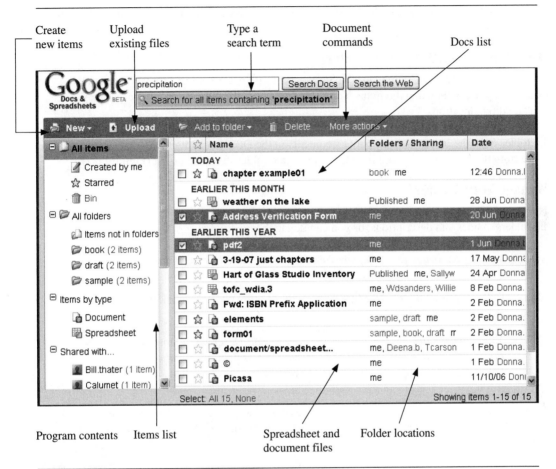

Create new items — Upload existing files — Type a search term — Document commands — Docs list

Program contents — Items list — Spreadsheet and document files — Folder locations

FIGURE 11-1   Home page for the Google Docs & Spreadsheets program.

To add a new folder, follow these steps:

1. Click New on the homepage toolbar to open its drop-down menu, and then choose Folder. A new folder icon displays at the top of the Docs list.

2. Type a name for the folder, such as Example Docs.

3. Click the Add Description/Status link to display a text field where you can type optional information about the folder.

TIP   *You don't need to add a description for the folder. If you are assembling a big project with multiple files and collaborators, you may find using descriptions such as dates or the contributor helps keep you organized.*

Once you have constructed a folder, click its name in the Items list to display the contents in the Docs list.

Move Content Within Your Folders

New items imported into Google Docs & Spreadsheets are not placed in a folder automatically. Instead, they are included in the Items Not In Folders list in the All Folders category. The list acts as a "holding" location.

To move a file from the Items Not In Folders list, or from within one folder to another, select the folder from the Items list to display its contents in the Docs list. Drag the file you want to move from the Docs list and drop it on the appropriate folder in the Items list (Figure 11-2).

Manage Your Folders

The Google Docs & Spreadsheets folders can be managed in a number of ways. You can change the folders' names and descriptions, or you can delete them entirely.

NOTE *Your folder structure is uniquely yours and isn't shared with collaborators.*

Add or Edit Description/Status To edit a folder's description or status, click the existing text to activate a text field and then replace or type new text.

TIP *You can also click Folder Actions and choose Edit Description/Status from the dropdown menu to activate the folder's description text field. Why bother? You can save yourself a couple of steps by simply clicking the text to activate the field.*

Rename Folders If you want to change the name of a folder, select the folder in the Items list to display its contents in the Docs list. Click the existing name of the folder to activate a text field and type a new name.

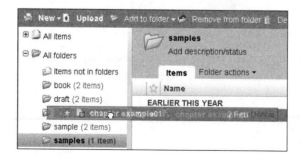

FIGURE 11-2 Drag and drop a file from one folder to another.

Delete Folders   To delete a folder when you no longer need it, click All Folders in the Items list to display the list of folders in the Docs list at the right of the program window. Select the check box to the left of the folder you want to delete. Click Remove Folder on the toolbar, shown here.

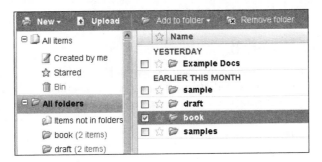

CAUTION   *Be sure to move any of the files you want to keep before deleting a folder. Fortunately, as long as you haven't emptied the trash, you'll be able to recover your files.*

Add and Delete Files

Google Docs & Spreadsheets offers several ways to use files from the program's home page. Your options include:

- Click New | New Document to open a blank document for editing.
- Click New | New Spreadsheet to open a blank spreadsheet for editing (read about spreadsheets in Chapter 12).
- Click Upload to locate and select files to import into your program.

The Editing section later in the chapter shows you how to use new document files, but first, see how you can use existing files from different sources.

Upload a File from Your Computer

You can bring some of your files into Google Docs & Spreadsheets to work with online, when you are away from your own desk, traveling, while you are on vacation…any time can be work time.

To upload files to your Google Docs & Spreadsheet program, follow these steps:

1. Click Upload on the home page to open the Upload a File browser window that offers different choices for uploading files; the first option is locating a file on your computer, as you see here.

2. Click Browse to open your folders to locate and select the file to upload. The Browse dialog box closes, and the name of the file is shown on the browser window.

3. Enter another name for the file in the What Do You Want to Call It? field if you like.

4. Click Upload File to transfer the file from your computer to your program online.

E-mail a File to Yourself

Your Google Account stores a unique e-mail address assigned to your Google Docs & Spreadsheets program. Instead of uploading documents one file at a time through the Upload a File browser window, use your personal e-mail to send one or more files for storage online.

> **NOTE**   *At the time of this writing only documents could be uploaded.*

Once you send an e-mail to Google Docs & Spreadsheets the unique address is stored in your e-mail program's address book. In the future you can address uploads directly from your e-mail program.

Follow these steps:

1. Click Upload on the main Google Docs & Spreadsheet window to open the window that offers different choices for uploading files. Scroll down the page to find the E-mail In Your Documents and Files area.

2. Copy the unique e-mail address shown on the page.

> **NOTE**   *If you look at the e-mail address closely, you'll see the address starts with your public name (I'm MsD, for example) and the files are stored at writely.com. Google Docs & Spreadsheets was developed from a program originally named "Writely."*

3. Open your e-mail program—whether Gmail or another e-mail client—and paste the address into the To field.

4. Attach one or more document files.

5. Send the e-mail.

How to ... Use Even More E-Mail Time-Saving Shortcuts

Suppose you and some colleagues or friends are getting a collection of files together for a group project—work, a school assignment, wedding plans, sports team—anything where a group of people are working on a similar goal. Designate someone in the group to coordinate the information, and share the unique e-mail address for that person's e-mail upload. Anyone in the group can send an e-mail using the storage address and the file is available for all involved.

There are other ways in which you can put the power of your unique e-mail address to good use. Try any or all of these methods:

- Type (or copy and paste) content into a new e-mail message or forward an existing e-mail to the unique e-mail address for your account; the contents of the message become the document and the e-mail message's subject becomes the file's name.

- If you plan to send an e-mail and want a copy as a document in Google Docs & Spreadsheets, include your unique e-mail address in the list of recipients to save time.

- Add as many files as you like to the e-mail before sending it; you will receive a separate confirmation e-mail for each file you upload.

NOTE *When you check the Inbox for the e-mail address you have listed in your Google Account, you'll find an e-mail notice for each item you import into Google Docs & Spreadsheets, along with a link to the new file.*

Delete a File

Are you finished with a file or files? To get rid of old files, follow these steps:

1. Select the check box to the left of a file's name in the Google Docs & Spreadsheets home page.
2. Click the Delete button on the toolbar to move the file to the trash.
3. To empty the trash, click Bin in the Items list to open the list of deleted files, shown in Figure 11-3.
4. If you decide to keep a file, select its check box and click Undelete to restore the file to its previous folder location.

CAUTION *Check over the listed files to be sure you want to delete them—once they are gone, they are gone!*

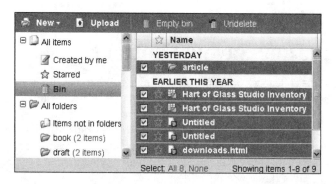

FIGURE 11-3 Deleted files are stored in the Bin.

5. To permanently delete files, select their check boxes and click Empty Trash. If you move a document that is shared to the Trash, it is still available to others with rights to use your files until you actually empty the trash.

> **TIP** *If you have a large number of files to select, click the Select All* n *link below the list of files:* n=*the number of files in your collection.*

Search and Sort Your Google Docs in Different Ways

As you might expect from a tool with "Google" in its name, it's easy to search for content in your files. In addition to searching for content, you can use one of several different features to sort and locate your files.

Search for a Phrase or Term

Perform a search in Google Docs & Spreadsheets just like other types of Google searches, by following these steps:

1. Type a term, phrase, or string of words in the Google search field.

2. Click Search Docs to look for files that contain the search terms in your documents.

3. The files that contain the term or terms are shown in the Docs list.

4. Click a file name to open the document in a separate window.

Use Other Sort Features for Easy File Access

The Docs & Spreadsheets home page offers several other sorting mechanisms. Any file you have stored in the program, regardless of its status or folder location, is shown when you select the All Items heading in the Items list.

Sort in Different Ways

Other sorting functions include:

- Click Created by Me in the Items list to open a list of the files that you created or uploaded in the Docs list. This is useful if you have a number of projects on the go and are working with several collaborators.
- Click Items by Type in the Items list to open the heading and select either the Documents or Spreadsheets item to show a list of the selected type of file in the Docs list.
- Click Shared With to open a list of all the collaborators you have shared your files with; select a name from the list to display the shared files in the Docs list.

Starred Files

Personalize the way your files are sorted using stars. Click the star image between a file's check box and its name in the file list as shown here; click the star image again to deselect the option. To view the starred files in your collection, click Starred in the All Items list, also shown here.

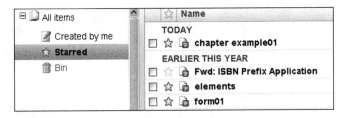

Edit a Document Online

Although documents and spreadsheets are uploaded, deleted, stored, and managed the same way, editing each type of file is different. Regardless of whether you open a document you've imported from elsewhere, or start with a new file, you do the editing in the Editing window. An existing document is shown in Figure 11-4.

Tips for Using Edit Tools

As mentioned, the tools on the Edit toolbar are commonly found in any program that lets you process text. Here are a few pointers to make it simpler to get up to speed:

- Use the Format text tools to apply custom fonts, colors, sizes, and faces to selected text.
- Select a block of text and apply commands such as paragraph justification or indents and outdents.
- Select a block of text and apply commands to generate a bulleted or numbered list.

File commands   Edit toolbar

Handling options   Save options

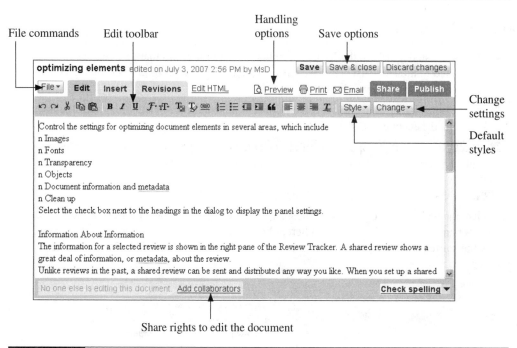

Change settings

Default styles

Share rights to edit the document

FIGURE 11-4 Use common editing tools

■ Apply a blockquote to set off a block of text. Click the Quote button to indent selected text from both left and right sides, and outline it with a faint gray box as you see here.

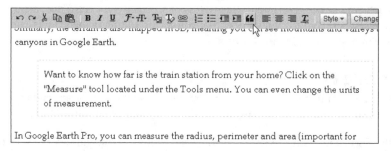

■ Select a block of text on the page and click Remove Formatting to restore the original text.

■ Insert a link from your file to another location, such as a web page or file (read about using links later in the chapter).

Set Styles and Appearances

Google Docs & Spreadsheets uses output for a variety of file formats, ranging from Word documents to web pages. To make these different formats logical, the file is structured using a standard hierarchy of styles.

Apply a Style

To apply a style, select the text on the page. Then, click the Style button on the Edit toolbar to open its menu, and choose a style. As you see, there are several paragraph and text formatting options.

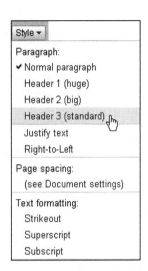

Page spacing, as noted in the menu, is managed in the Document settings dialog box.

 To remove a text formatting style, select the text, and click Remove Formatting on the Edit toolbar rather than opening the menu again.

Define the Document's Settings

New documents use default settings. You can use the defaults, or modify them following these steps:

1. Click the File button and choose Document Settings to open the Document Settings dialog box shown in Figure 11-5.

2. Make your selections in the dialog box. As you change settings you can see the new appearance in the Preview area. You can:

    ■ Click the Font Name drop-down arrow and choose a font from a preconfigured list.

    ■ Click the Size drop-down arrow and choose a text size.

    ■ Click the Line-spacing drop-down arrow and choose a spacing option.

    ■ Select Right-to-Left to use page alignments for writing Hebrew or Arabic.

    ■ Click the Document Background Color number to activate the field and type another hex value to change the color for the page—the default, #ffffff, is a white background.

    ■ Click the Turn Off All Styles radio button to use default Google Docs & Spreadsheets styles.

 *If you find you repeatedly open the Document Settings dialog box and make the same changes, select the check box to make the settings you choose the default for new documents.*

3. Click Save Settings to close the dialog box and return to the program in the browser window. The options selected in the dialog box are applied to the open file.

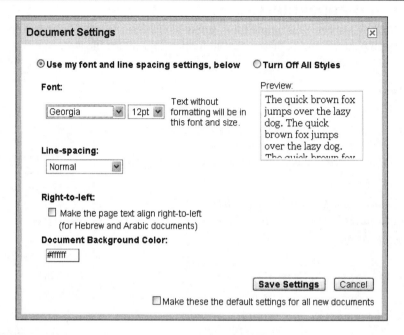

Choose appearance settings for new and existing documents.

Check for Errors

Are you the sort of person that can't imagine finishing a task without checking your spelling? If so, fear not—Google Docs & Spreadsheets has a spell checker. Follow these steps to check your document's contents:

1. Click the Spellcheck command at the bottom right of your document's window. The document is processed, and all misspelled words are highlighted in yellow.

2. Right-click a highlighted word to display a list of suggestions, like the list shown here.

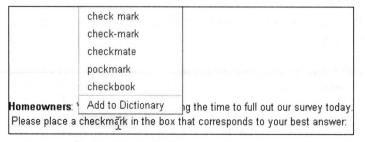

How to ...   **Take a Shortcut**

Like files you work with in programs on your desktop, Google Docs & Spreadsheets offers some common shortcuts to save time as you edit your file. The list includes:

CTRL-A to select all content	CTRL-B to apply bold face	CTRL-C to copy
CTRL-E to center align	CTRL-H to replace	CTRL-I to italicize
CTRL-J to full justify	CTRL-K to insert a link	CTRL-L to left align
CTRL-M to insert a comment	CTRL-P to print the file	CTRL-R to right align a paragraph
CTRL-S to save the file	CTRL-U to underline	CTRL-V to paste content copied to the system clipboard
CTRL-X to cut	CTRL-Y to redo an action	CTRL-Z to undo an action
CTRL-END to go to the end of the document	CTRL-HOME to go to the start of the document	

3. Click the correct spelling, select Add to Dictionary to include your word, or click off the list to close it and type an alternative word.

4. If you decide not to make a change, click Done to remove the yellow highlights.

An initial spell-check is done once in a file. After you have finished the first spell-check, click Recheck to check again at any time.

> **TIP**   *If you need to know the number of words in a document, select File | Count words.*

Insert Special Features

You aren't restricted to using basic text paragraphs and lists in your Google document. Click the Insert tab to display the contents of your document in that window. The Insert tab offers several other tools, shown in Figure 11-6.

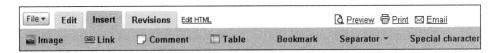

FIGURE 11-6   Include content like images and tables in your document.

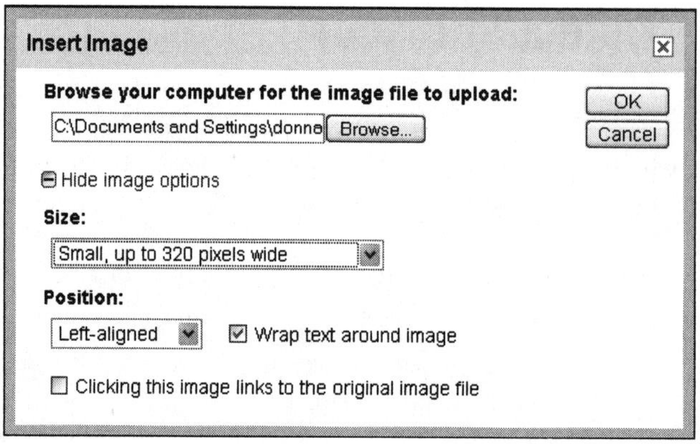

Insert Image   ☒

Browse your computer for the image file to upload: ⬚ OK ⬚
C:\Documents and Settings\donne ⬚ Browse... ⬚   ⬚ Cancel ⬚

⊟ Hide image options

Size:
Small, up to 320 pixels wide   ▾

Position:
Left-aligned   ▾   ☑ Wrap text around image

☐ Clicking this image links to the original image file

FIGURE 11-7   Locate and upload images to insert in a document.

Insert an Image

You can use images of up to 2MB in one document. To upload and insert images into your document files follow these steps:

1. Click the document where you want to position the image.

2. On the Insert tab, click Image to open the dialog box; click More Image Options to expand the dialog box as shown in Figure 11-7.

3. Click Browse to open a dialog box to locate and select an image file from your computer. The file's name is listed on the dialog box.

4. Click More Image Options to display the additional features, and specify these options for the image:

- Click the Size drop-down arrow and choose a setting, ranging from the original file size, to the page width, to a custom width.

- Click the Position drop-down arrow and choose a position for aligning the image on the page.

- If you choose either a Left-Aligned or Right-Aligned placement, you can select the Wrap Text Around Image option to position the image within your text.

- Select Clicking This Image Links To The Original Image File if you want to link the image to its source.

5. Click OK to upload the file and place it on the page according to your chosen settings.

6. To reposition or resize the image, click to display the resize handles, and then drag a corner to resize proportionally, as you see here. Drag a side handle to resize the width or height of the image.

NOTE   *See how to optimize your images for use online using Picasa2 in Chapter 6.*

Link to Other Content

Google Docs & Spreadsheets offers ways to link to a web page, e-mail address, another file, or even a specific location in another file. Follow these steps to insert a link into a document:

1. Click the document location where you want to insert the link. You can either use a blank space or preselect document text.

2. Click Link on either the Edit or Insert tabs' toolbars to display the Link window, shown in Figure 11-8.

3. Select a link type from the Link To options, including the E-mail address option, also shown in Figure 11-8.

4. Type the information in the Link To fields. All types of links let you use the same Link Display options to show both link text and flyover text. The other options vary according to the type of link you are creating.

Link to URL   Type in the URL information, including the http:// or ftp:// prefix. Select the check box Open Link in New Window if you don't want the linked file opening in the same browser window.

Link to Document/Spreadsheet   Click the Document drop-down arrow to open a list of your files. Select the file. Again, select the check box Open Link in New Window if you don't want the linked file opening in the same browser window.

Insert Link   [×]

Link To

○ URL   ○ Document   ○ Bookmark   ⊙ E-mail address

E-mail to: |joe.cook@gmail.com

Link Display

Text: |e-mail
The hyper-linked text, like <u>Click me for the best loan rates!</u>

Flyover: |drop a line and say hi!
The flyover appears when the viewer's mouse cursor is over the link.

[OK] [Cancel]

FIGURE 11-8   Choose settings for a link inserted in the document

Link to Bookmark   Select an existing bookmark from the Bookmark drop-down list in the current document to use as an internal link. If there are no bookmarks in your document, logically you can't select a bookmark.

Follow these steps to add a bookmark link:

1. Type text in the Link Display field; if you selected text before opening the dialog box, the preselected text is shown in the Text field.

2. Type text in the Flyover field if you like. The text is shown when the user moves their mouse over the link.

3. Click OK to close the dialog box and complete the link.

You can't test the link from the Google Docs & Spreadsheets program window. To check out your links, click Preview (found above the toolbar, as shown in Figure 11-4). The file opens in a blank browser window. Now you can test the links and see the flyover text.

Use Bookmark Shortcuts

If you have ever created a table of contents in a document, you have worked with bookmarks. A bookmark is a shortcut to a specific place in a document that saves time scrolling through the document pages looking for a specific topic.

NOTE *Bookmarks in a document aren't the same as the bookmarks (or Favorites in Internet Explorer) that you use to store the location of a web page.*

To create a bookmark in your document, follow these steps:

1. Click the location on the page where you want to place the bookmark.
2. Click Bookmark on the Insert tab to open the dialog box shown here.

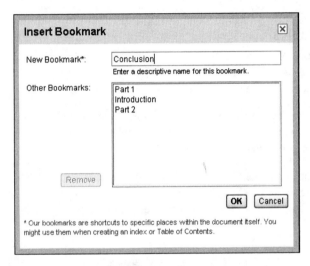

3. Type a name for the bookmark in the New Bookmark field.
4. Click OK to close the dialog box.

Once you have entered your new bookmarks, follow the steps in the section "Link to Other Content" to create links in your document from a specified location to your named bookmark locations by selecting a bookmark from the drop-down list.

Add Text Comments

Use comments to add information about the contents of a document, either for your own benefit, or to share with others. Add a comment following these steps:

1. Click the document page where you want to insert the comment.
2. Click Comment on the Insert tab to add the comment field to the document. As you see, the comment is stamped with the date and username.

> **contact you:** Can we link this contact info to the database? |-MsD 2/1/07 6:11

3. Start typing; click off the field when you are finished.

If you want to change a comment, click it to display a pop-up list. You can change the color, add the text of the comment into your document, or delete the comment. If you change the color, a Comment Settings dialog box opens, asking if you want to use your custom color choice as the new program default, or for all comments in the document. How considerate!

NOTE *Anyone added as a viewer or collaborator can see a document's comments. Comments are only internal to the file. That is, you won't see them when the document is published, printed, or posted to a blog or web page.*

Format Text in Tables

If you want to use data tables in a document, click Table from the Insert tab's toolbar to open the Insert Table dialog box, as shown in Figure 11-9.

Choose these options for the table's appearance:

Size   Type values to specify the size of the table in horizontal rows and vertical columns. Define the width and height based on the cell contents, use the full width of the document page, or define the width in pixels or a percentage of the full width.

Layout   Define the appearance of the table layout by typing values for the Padding and Spacing in pixels. Select an alignment for the cells' contents from the Align drop-down list, and choose Left or Right if you'd like the columns to float to one side of the page.

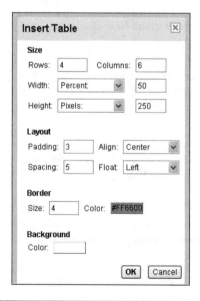

FIGURE 11-9   Configure the structure and appearance of an inserted table

Color   Choose options for the border and background of the table. Type a value in the Border Size field and click the Color field to open a palette of color swatches. Select the color and the palette closes. You'll see the color and its Hex value shown on the dialog box. Add a color for the Background using the same method.

If you want to create the appearance of columns of text on a page, use a table with several columns and one row. Set padding to space out the columns. When the file is published, you don't see any borders—just your tidy column layout.

Once you've chosen the settings, click OK to close the dialog box and display the table in the page, like the one shown in Figure 11-10. If you want to make any changes, click the Change button above the toolbar to open the menu (this is also shown in the figure) and choose from the context-sensitive commands.

SHORTCUT   *As you are making changes to different features in the document, click the Changes button to see what options are displayed. You can also access a shortcut menu by right-clicking an object on the page.*

Separate Content into Sections

Use one of the Separation options to visually space content areas in your document. Click Separator on the Insert toolbar to open a menu. Choose one of two options:

■ Choose Page break to manually start a new page in the document

■ Choose Horizontal line to insert a separator line

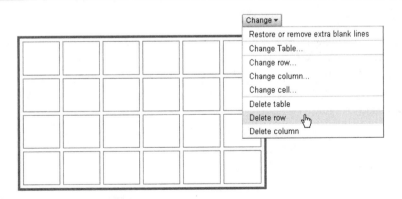

FIGURE 11-10   Adjust the settings used for a table added to a document

Add Special Characters

Add special characters such as punctuation or copyright symbols into your document easily. Click Special Characters on the Insert toolbar to open a dialog box.

Next, choose from special characters, such as accented letters, Asian characters, and Advanced. Select the character to close the dialog box and insert it on the page. The Advanced option lets you enter the Unicode value for a character. Type the value and then click Insert in document to close the dialog box and add the content to the page.

Share Files with Others

One document can be shared among multiple users who can work on the file simultaneously. Two or more people can work from the same document and read or actively edit the content, based on the rights granted.

There are three categories of user for documents.

Owner   An owner has ultimate control over the file. An owner can edit the file and invite collaborators and viewers. The owner can delete the file, removing access for the other categories of users.

Collaborator   A collaborator is given rights to edit a document or spreadsheet. A collaborator can invite more collaborators and viewers.

Viewer   A viewer can read the current version of a file, but can't make changes or edits.

Invite Participants

You don't add collaborators and viewers at the same time. Follow these steps to add collaborators to your editing group, and repeat to add viewers to your editing group:

1. Click the Share tab at the upper right of the program window to display its options. If you prefer, click Add Collaborators at the bottom of the open document window to display the Share tab.

2. Add the e-mail addresses for those you want to invite to collaborate and click Invite Collaborators (Figure 11-11).

3. The addresses display in an e-mail window. Add a personal message in the e-mail if you like, and click Invite Collaborators.

4. Your collaborators are listed in the Share tab.

TIP   *Google can refer to your Gmail contacts list if you click Choose from Contacts. Names from your contacts list will display after you type the first few letters; select the name to autofill the invitation.*

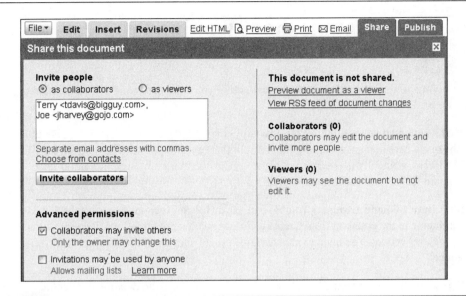

FIGURE 11-11   Invite different levels of participation from others

Here are some tips to keep in mind as you work with collaborators and viewers:

■ If you want to remove yourself from a document's list, open the file, select the Share tab, and click Remove next to your name on the Collaborator's list.

■ If you and a collaborator are editing a document at the same time, you'll see a small box at the bottom of the screen displaying the name of the collaborators or viewers working on the file.

■ Each document can be shared with up to 50 people, including the owner, viewers, and editors.

■ You can see an RSS feed of changes to an individual document by selecting the option on the Share tab's settings. You are taken to a new browser window with two choices: Either add the feed to your iGoogle page, or add it to Google Reader.

■ Choose advanced options, which allow collaborators to invite others, or offer invitations to anyone to use, like a mailing list.

NOTE   *Read more about collaboration at http://tinyurl.com/yv5s9x.*

How to ...   Troubleshoot Viewing Problems

Here are some of the issues that might be preventing you from accessing your document or spreadsheet:

You Are Using E-mail Forwarding   Your invitation may be sent to the original e-mail address, or to the one where you are receiving the mail. In that case, you have to find out which e-mail address is actually invited to participate in the collaboration. Sign into http://docs .google.com with the correct e-mail address.

You Don't Have a Google Account   You have to use a Google Account to access the files and participate in the collaboration. Create a Google Account at https://www.google.com/accounts/NewAccount. You need to use the same e-mail address as that used to send you the invitation.

You Have a Google Account and Multiple E-mail Addresses   Ask the document owner to invite you again using the e-mail address you prefer to use for working with Google Docs & Spreadsheets.

You Have Logged In With a Different Google Account   A collaboration invitation is sent to a particular e-mail address as listed in a particular Google Account. If you can't see the document using one Google Account, log out and then log in using the Google Account used for the invitation.

Publish Documents Online

The Google Docs & Spreadsheets program can automatically produce a web page, including a link, from a document you have been working with. If you like, send the file to your blog. Either way, it's a quick and convenient way to get content online.

Review the Page for Accuracy

Whether you plan to use a document as a web page or a blog entry, you can preview it from the Google Docs & Spreadsheets program. Use either of two methods, depending on your expertise and needs:

View as HTML   Each document and spreadsheet has an HTML counterpart. Click the Edit HTML tab to view the page's code, like the sample shown here.

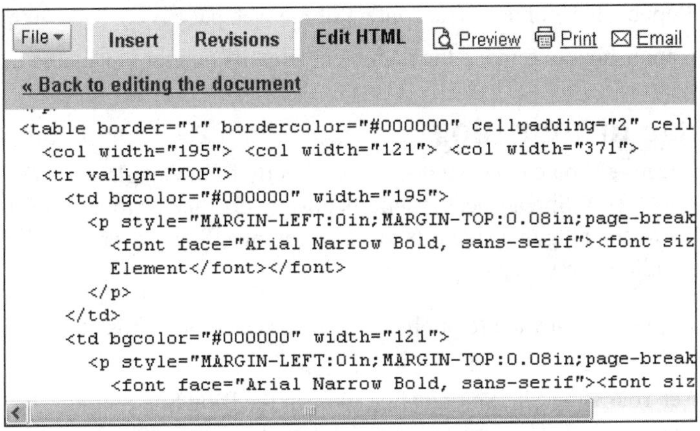

If you are familiar with HTML coding, you can edit directly from the HTML view, which is then reflected in your document view.

Preview Page   Active content such as a link isn't functional from the document view. Click Preview, which is one of the links above the document area in the program. The page opens in a separate browser window. Once you've checked out the features, close the window to return to the program window.

Generate a Web Page

To publish a document as a web page, follow these steps:

1. Select the Publish tab on the Documents Edit page to show the Publish settings.

2. Click Publish Document. A confirmation dialog opens, asking if you are sure you want to make the file available online. Click Yes. Google publishes the file as a web page and then lists the URL, just like you see here.

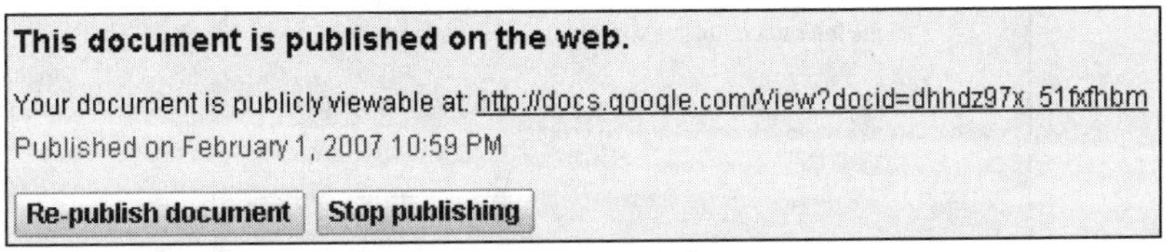

3. Send the URL to those you'd like to view the document.

You can make changes to the published material. For instance:

■ After you have made edits to a document that has been published, select the Publish tab, and click Republish document. The content of the web page is changed automatically.

■ Click Stop publishing to remove the document from its publicly-available location.

Publish a Page to Your Blog

What a convenient feature! You can post a document directly from Google Docs & Spreadsheets to your blog. Google Docs & Spreadsheets supports posting documents to most of the popular blog sites, as well as to any blog that supports the Blogger, metaWeblog, or MovableType APIs. To accomplish this, follow these steps:

1. Open the document you want to publish, and then select the Publish tab to display the settings.

2. Click the Set Your Blog Site Settings link to open the Blog Site Settings dialog box, shown in Figure 11-12. The figure shows the default settings, which are for a Hosted provider.

FIGURE 11-12   Specify settings for automatically posting content to your blog.

NOTE   *If you are using a custom server, choose the My Own Server/Custom option in the Blog Site Settings dialog box. Select the API (Application Program Interface) that powers your blog, and type the URL to the PHP file in the URL field.*

4. Insert information about your blog, including the type of service, the name and password to access the blog's administration area, and your blog's ID or title.

5. Click Test to have Google Docs & Spreadsheets test the connection to your blog.

SHORTCUT   *Be sure to take a few seconds and test the connection. It's simpler to tweak the settings as you are setting up the system than to have to troubleshoot later. You'll be glad you did.*

6. Click OK to close the dialog box and return to the Publish tab.

7. Click Post to blog. The document is published to your blog, and time stamped with the time and date of the posting.

CAUTION   *Be sure the document has been saved. Otherwise, you'll receive an error message and the posting can't be completed.*

Print and Export

If you don't want to publish a document online, you can use one of several different formats for saving your files to your hard drive. Not sure which version of a file you want to download or print? Not to worry, Google Docs & Spreadsheets has that covered, too, with a slick revision management system.

Print a Document or Spreadsheet

Printing a file is one-click easy. Open a document from the Google Docs & Spreadsheets home page. While you are working in any of the tabs, click the Print button on the window above the tabs.

Click to open your system's Print dialog box. Choose your printer and configure its settings. Click Print to print the content.

Save and Reuse Different Revisions

Google Docs & Spreadsheets stores information about your files automatically. Each time you make changes and save the file, a new version is added to the file, called a revision.

Suppose you are polishing up a cover letter to accompany your résumé and made changes to reflect the details of the position you are applying for. Now it's the next day, and you find another listing for a position you would like to apply for, but the previous version of the letter was more targeted to the position.

FIGURE 11-13 View an earlier version of a file

Recreate a Former File Version

You can use the Google Docs & Spreadsheets revision feature to recreate your former version following these steps:

1. Click the document's link on the Google Docs & Spreadsheets home page to open the file in the Edit window.

2. Click the Revisions tab to display the list of edited versions of the file.

3. Click the revision's link to open it for viewing in the Revision tab (Figure 11-13).

4. To restore an earlier revision to the active version of the document, click **Revert to this one**.

From this window, you can:

■ View a series of revisions by clicking the Older or Newer buttons, also shown in Figure 11-13.

■ Click Back to Revision History to return to the list of revisions.

■ Click Back to Editing to return to the Edit tab.

■ Click Close Document to close the Revision tab and return to the Docs & Spreadsheets home page.

NOTE *You can access the Back to Editing and Close Document links from any display in the Revisions tab.*

Compare Multiple File Revisions

From the Revisions tab, select check boxes for two revisions for comparison and click Compare Checked to load the file into the Revisions tab, as shown here.

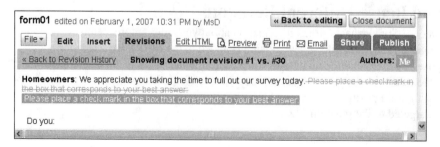

The changes made, and the collaborator involved in making the changes, are shown in highlighted text.

Export Files

Docs & Spreadsheets offers a number of ways to save your files. Depending on how you need to use the document later, you can export your document file as:

- HTML (in a zip file)
- Word DOC
- OpenOffice ODT
- PDF
- RTF
- Text

Follow these steps to export a document:

1. Open the file you want to save.
2. Click File to open its menu, and choose one of the listed file formats to open the File Download dialog box.
3. Click Open to download the file and open it automatically in the associated program; click Save to download the file to a storage location on your computer, or click Cancel to close the dialog box.

Summary

Who knew there was so much you could create and construct, share and collaborate, using Google Docs & Spreadsheets? In this chapter, you saw how to use files from your computer as online documents, and how to start new files in the program. You explored different tools Docs & Spreadsheets offers for sorting and managing your online files, from folders to stars. You saw how editing and formatting documents online is similar to working on your desktop. To make the content even more useful, you saw how documents could be shared as web pages or posted as blogs.

In the next chapter, you'll see how the spreadsheets part of Google Docs & Spreadsheets works.

Chapter 12

Handle Spreadsheets Online

How to...

- Create spreadsheets from scratch or use uploaded files
- Edit and format spreadsheets
- Use charts to display spreadsheet information
- Apply and use formulas and calculations
- Export spreadsheets in a number of different formats

A spreadsheet isn't all that different from a document. Both can be formatted in different ways, shared and viewed in different ways, and saved in different ways. The "spreadsheet" part of Google Docs & Spreadsheets lets you perform most of the common types of activities you'd do with a spreadsheet.

NOTE *Please refer to Chapter 11 "Create and Manage Documents Online" for details on features that are common to both documents and spreadsheets, such as uploading files from your computer and managing them in the Items list.*

Open a Spreadsheet

Just like with documents, you can start a new spreadsheet, or open an existing one. To start a new spreadsheet, click **New** from the Google Docs & Spreadsheets home page and choose Spreadsheet.

Upload a File from Your Computer

If you prefer to upload and use an existing spreadsheet, click Upload on the Docs & Spreadsheets home page to open another browser window. Click Browse to open a Choose File dialog box to locate and select files from your computer.

You can use files in these formats:

- CSV (comma-separated values)
- XLS (Microsoft Excel)
- ODS (OpenDocument Spreadsheets)
- TSV (tab-separated value)
- TXT (text)
- TSB (tab-separated)

Once your files are uploaded, click the name to open an existing spreadsheet in the Docs list on the Google Docs & Spreadsheets home page. Note that the icon to the left of the spreadsheet's name looks like a spreadsheet.

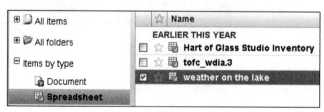

Rows   Active row   Number options   Positioning options   Columns

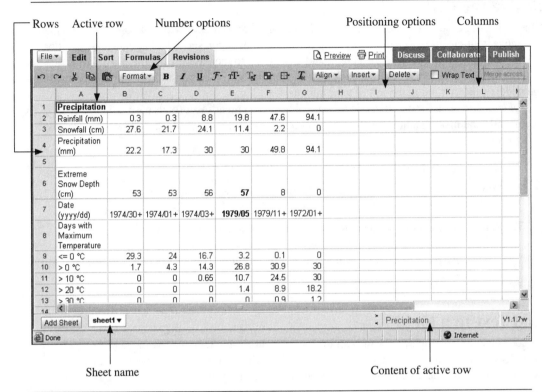

	A	B	C	D	E	F	G	H	I	J	K	L	M
1	**Precipitation**												
2	Rainfall (mm)	0.3	0.3	8.8	19.8	47.6	94.1						
3	Snowfall (cm)	27.6	21.7	24.1	11.4	2.2	0						
4	Precipitation (mm)	22.2	17.3	30	30	49.8	94.1						
5													
6	Extreme Snow Depth (cm)	53	53	56	**57**	8	0						
7	Date (yyyy/dd)	1974/30+	1974/01+	1974/03+	**1979/05**	1979/11+	1972/01+						
8	Days with Maximum Temperature												
9	<= 0 °C	29.3	24	16.7	3.2	0.1	0						
10	> 0 °C	1.7	4.3	14.3	26.8	30.9	30						
11	> 10 °C	0	0	0.65	10.7	24.5	30						
12	> 20 °C	0	0	0	1.4	8.9	18.2						
13	> 30 °C	0	0	0	0	0.9	1.2						
14													

Add Sheet   sheet1 ▼   Precipitation   V1.1.7w

Done   Internet

Sheet name   Content of active row

FIGURE 12-1   Spreadsheet layout and options

TIP   *If you have a lot of files, click Items By Type in the Items list to display only the spreadsheets.*

Tour the Spreadsheet Program

On the program window, you see the spreadsheet arranged in a grid of horizontal rows and vertical columns, like the example in Figure 12-1. Rows are always numbered, columns are always named alphabetically.

Edit the Appearance for Easy Reading

One of the great things about spreadsheets is how easily they can be configured to produce a neat and attractive appearance, while still performing calculations and displaying data using the correct formats. Google Docs & Spreadsheets offers a sizable range of features to let you produce good-looking data.

Resize the Cells

Change the dimensions of a cell by resizing the height of rows and/or width of columns. When you move your cursor over the line dividing rows or columns you see a double-ended arrow. For a row, drag upward to decrease the height, and downward to increase the height of a cell.

To change the size of a column, click and drag left to decrease the width, or right to increase the width of the column to the left of your cursor.

Of course, you use more than one row or column in a spreadsheet (otherwise it would be a document!) and making adjustments cell by cell is time-consuming. Instead, follow these steps using rows:

1. Drag to select the rows you want to resize.

2. Move the cursor over one row divider until you see the double-arrow cursor, and drag downward to increase the row to the right height (see Figure 12-2).

3. Release the mouse, and the other rows are resized to the same height.

CAUTION   *Don't spend a lot of time trying to select noncontiguous rows or columns to resize—the program doesn't allow for it.*

Add Text to a Field

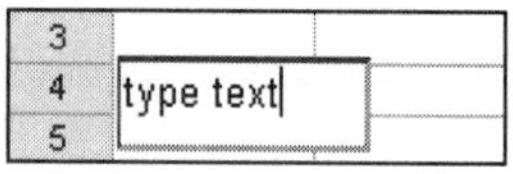

To add some text to a field, click the cell to display a cursor and then type. As you see in the example, the text entry field overlays the cell. When you click off the cell, the text is dropped into the cell's boundaries.

TIP   *To activate the existing text in a cell, double-click on the cell or click the cell and press* ENTER *or click the cell and press* F2.

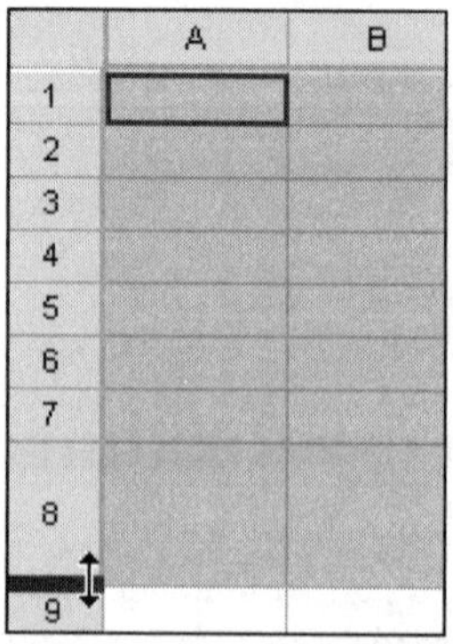

FIGURE 12-2   Row height defines height for the selection.

How to ... Modify Cell Layout for Correct Text Display

If the text is wider than the width of the cell, try one of these options:

- Select the Wrap Text check box at the upper right of the Edit window. You can apply text wrapping to the entire spreadsheet, or just selected cells.

- Type the text, and then, wherever you want to break the content, press ALT-ENTER or CONTROL-ENTER to wrap the text to the next line.

Each method produces a different look, as you can see.

D	E	F
		Mary had a little lamb, its fleece was white as snow.
	Mary had a little lamb, its fleece was white as snow	
Mary had a little		
text only	wrapped text	forced breaks

Change Text Appearance and Format

Modify the text in the spreadsheet in the same way as text in a document. That is, select the text, and then apply the edit choices for fonts, colors, faces, and so on. Text in a spreadsheet can be formatted according to its purpose, such as calculating complex data like rate exchanges.

To apply formatting, follow these steps:

1. Select the rows, columns, or cells you want to format.

2. Click Format to display the drop-down menu shown in Figure 12-3.

3. Choose the type of formatting to apply. The figure shows four named examples. The screen is updated and shows the new layout.

Add Visual Details

Along with resizing the height and width of the cells, you can also apply background colors and borders to emphasize information like headings.

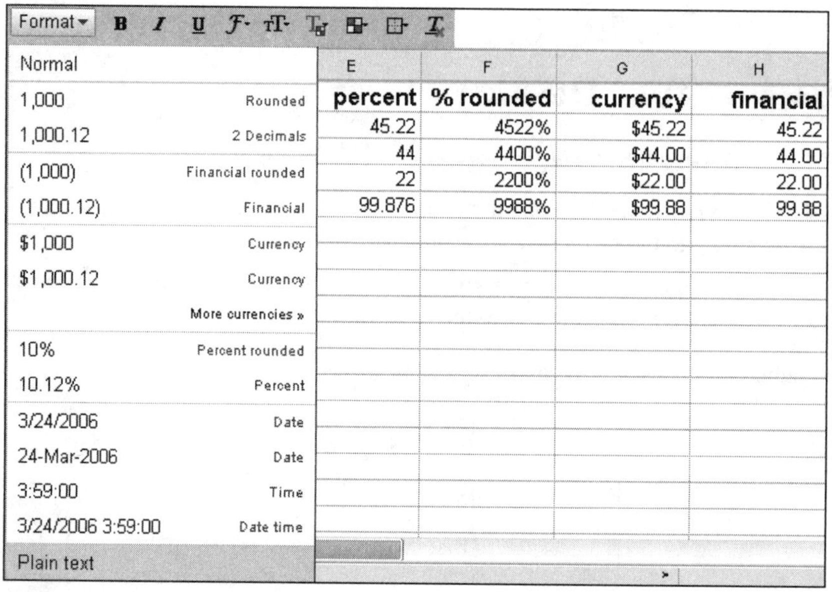

Format ▾	**B**	*I*	U	F·	ꞏTꞏ	Tᵧ	ꞏ	ꞏ	I.			
Normal					E		F		G		H	
1,000		Rounded		**percent**		**% rounded**		**currency**		**financial**		
1,000.12		2 Decimals		45.22		4522%		$45.22		45.22		
(1,000)		Financial rounded		44		4400%		$44.00		44.00		
(1,000.12)		Financial		22		2200%		$22.00		22.00		
$1,000		Currency		99.876		9988%		$99.88		99.88		
$1,000.12		Currency										
		More currencies »										
10%		Percent rounded										
10.12%		Percent										
3/24/2006		Date										
24-Mar-2006		Date										
3:59:00		Time										
3/24/2006 3:59:00		Date time										
Plain text												

FIGURE 12-3 Configure layout based on display and calculation requirements.

Insert Backgrounds

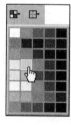

Select the content you want to change. Click Background Color on the Edit toolbar, and choose a color from the color swatches as seen here.

Apply Borders

If you want to add a border, select the cells to receive the border and then click the Borders tool to display the border options. The selected option is applied to the cells automatically.

 CAUTION *Don't select a row or column. Instead, be sure to select the group of cells only. Otherwise, there you will find that long borders are drawn across your document when the spreadsheet is posted or printed.*

Adjust Cell Alignment to Match the Contents

The alignment of the cell contents varies with its purpose. Sometimes you'll want the content of a cell to be centered, such as headings. You usually want strings of text used for calculations to be right-aligned, and you may want to add numbers or text that is left-aligned.

Choose an Alignment

To change the alignment, select the cells and then click Align to open the menu. Choose from Left, Center, or Right justifications. In addition, you can align the contents vertically using Upper, Middle, or Lower choices from the second row of the menu.

Merge Cells for Headings

There's one more type of alignment that you often see for displaying headings across a number of columns.

Here's how you do it:

1. Select the cells across the spreadsheet that you want to combine.

2. Click Merge Across.

3. The cells are now merged into one cell, and the heading can be centered across all columns. Here you see the first heading has been merged, while the second is still waiting for some attention.

A	B	C	D	E	F	G
Precipitation						
(yyyy/dd)	1974/30+	1974/01+	1974/03+	**1979/05**	1979/11+	1972/01+
Days with Maximu Tempera						

Rearrange Cells and Contents

What happens if you forget to put in a column at the start of your spreadsheet to hold numbers? You don't have to waste time moving content from cells, or copying and pasting to add the column. Instead, use menu commands and shortcuts to move, add, and delete content.

Insert Additional Columns or Rows

Click Insert and choose an option to add rows or columns surrounding the selected content. The options available vary according to what is selected on the spreadsheet. If more than one column or row is selected, the number of selected items is offered as a choice. For example, choosing seven columns offers the command to Insert 7 Columns left or right.

Delete Extra Columns or Rows

Use the Delete menu in much the same way as the Insert menu. Click Delete to display the menu and choose what you want to remove based on what you selected before opening the menu. The choices shown in Figure 12-4 are to delete a named rows or columns based on the group of selected cells.

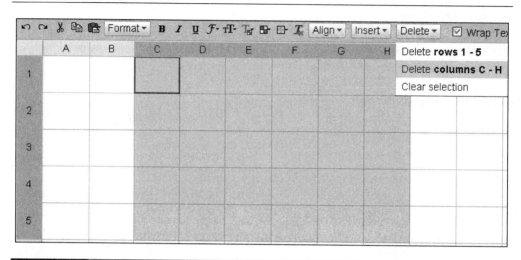

FIGURE 12-4   The Delete options are based on your selections.

 Rather than selecting and using menus, try selecting and right-clicking the content to see what pops up in the shortcut menu. For example, if you select a row, the shortcut menu offers choices for both inserting and deleting rows.

Check Your Progress

Now that you have your layout and the appearance in order, check out how the spreadsheet will look. Click Preview on the program window above the toolbar and tabs. The spreadsheet opens in another browser window as shown in Figure 12-5. Close the window when you've checked it out.

CAUTION *It's easier to have the column and row layouts finished first. Once you get involved in calculations you can lose your way if the structure is reordered.*

Sort the Contents in a Spreadsheet

You sort things all the time. Any time you hunt for a gadget on eBay and sort by auction closing time, product name, or price you are using the same kind of sorting you can perform in a Google spreadsheet.

Sometimes it is simpler to find things, see what might be missing, or keep track of detail when a list is sorted. Spreadsheets, including the Google spreadsheet, offer a way to *freeze* the display of the headings on the page so you don't loose track of what you are viewing. It's not hard to keep numbers straight when you have five or six columns, but very confusing when there are thirty or forty columns.

Precipitation					
Rainfall (mm)	0.3	0.3	8.8	19.8	47.6	94.1
Snowfall (cm)	27.6	21.7	24.1	11.4	2.2	0
Precipitation (mm)	22.2	17.3	30	30	49.8	94.1
Extreme Snow Depth (cm)	53	53	56	**57**	8	0
Date (yyyy/dd)	1974/30+	1974/01+	1974/03+	**1979/05**	1979/11+	1972/01+
Days with Maximum Temperature					
<= 0 °C	29.3	24	16.7	3.2	0.1	0
> 0 °C	1.7	4.3	14.3	26.8	30.9	30
> 10 °C	0	0	0.65	10.7	24.5	30
> 20 °C	0	0	0	1.4	8.9	18.2
> 30 °C	0	0	0	0	0.9	1.2
> 35 °C	0	0	0	0	0.05	0.1

FIGURE 12-5   Check the appearance in a preview.

Freeze Headings to Keep Track of the Contents

Here's how to keep track of what's what in your spreadsheet:

1. Click the Sort tab to display the options.
2. If you are using column headings, click Freeze Header Rows to open the menu, and choose the number of rows you want to *freeze,* which means the contents of the rows won't be included in the sorting and won't be scrolled out of view.

> TIP   *You can freeze up to five rows. In many spreadsheets, you'll want to freeze one row containing the headings.*

3. Click the first cell you want to use to begin sorting. In Figure 12-6, for example, the A2 cell is the first one included in the sort.
4. Select the A->Z (ascending sort order, used in the example) or Z-> A (descending sort order) button.
5. The rows are sorted according to the column you selected.

> NOTE   *You can select a range of cells rather than the entire spreadsheet.*

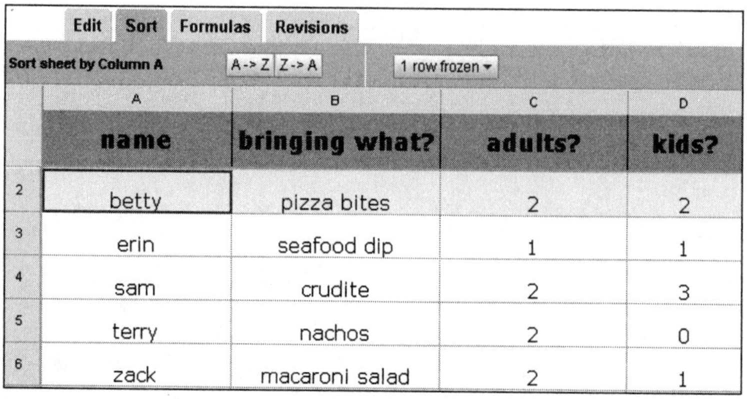
Edit
Sort
Formulas
Revisions
Sort sheet by Column A
A->Z
Z->A
1 row frozen
A
B
C
D
name
bringing what?
adults?
kids?
2
betty
pizza bites
2
2
3
erin
seafood dip
1
1
4
sam
crudite
2
3
5
terry
nachos
2
0
6
zack
macaroni salad
2
1

FIGURE 12-6 Specify the cell to start the sort.

Manage Sheets in the File

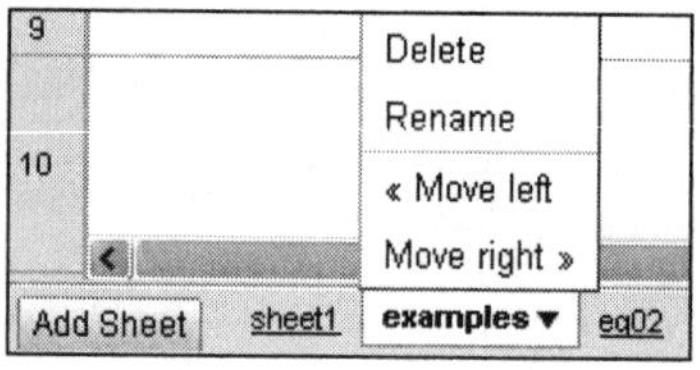
9
10
Delete
Rename
« Move left
Move right »
Add Sheet
sheet1
examples
eg02

Your spreadsheet doesn't have to contain a single page, which is the Google Docs & Spreadsheets default. You can use several sheets, as you see in the example.

Select the sheet's name, and then use these tips to manage a selected sheet in your file:

- Click the sheet's name to display the pop-up menu. Click Delete to remove the page, after confirming the deletion.
- Click the sheet's name to display the pop-up menu. Click Move Left or Move Right to move the sheet in the spreadsheet.
- Click Add Sheet to insert another blank sheet into the spreadsheet.

NOTE *When you receive an e-mail in Gmail that includes a spreadsheet attachment in either XLS or CSV format, look for links beside the attached file's name on the e-mail. Click Open as a Google Spreadsheet to view and edit the file online.*

Use Formulas to Calculate Results

Spreadsheets are used for calculating information. Sometimes you might want the information to be managed manually, such as when sorting lists. Sometimes you don't want to do the work yourself. Fortunately, you don't have to!

Add a Simple Formula

To add a formula to your spreadsheet, follow these steps:

1. Click Formula to open the Formula tab.

2. Click an empty cell to make it active. You see the number of the cell shown at the upper left of the Formulas toolbar. In Figure 12-7, the H25 cell is selected.

3. Click one of the calculation options at the right of the Formula tab. A few common calculations are listed on the tab, including Average, which is used in the example.

4. Click the first cell to include in the calculation. You see the cell name appear in the cell used for the calculation, in the example, cell B25.

5. Click the last cell to include in the calculation to include that cell name in the calculation, G25 in the example.

6. Press ENTER to finish the calculation. The formula is replaced by the results of the calculation. In the example, the wind speeds are averaged, and return a result of 12.2kph.

If you want to review your calculation, click the cell containing the result. The formula is displayed at the upper left of the Formulas tab.

Use a Complex Formula

There are far more than the six formulas listed on the Formulas tab. Click More, shown in Figure 12-7, to open the Insert a Function dialog box (Figure 12-8).

Here are some tips for using the features in the Insert a Function dialog box:

■ Choose a category from the left column, and select a function from the right column.

■ You see the variables for the function listed below the table on the dialog box.

■ Click to select the function and insert it in the cell on your spreadsheet.

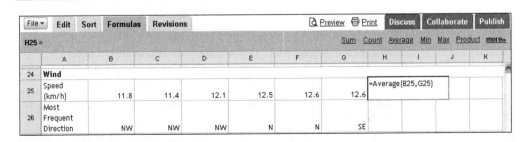

	A	B	C	D	E	F	G	H	I	J	K
24	Wind										
25	Speed (km/h)	11.8	11.4	12.1	12.5	12.6	12.6	=Average(B25,G25)			
26	Most Frequent Direction	NW	NW	NW	N	N	SE				

FIGURE 12-7   Select calculations and cell ranges

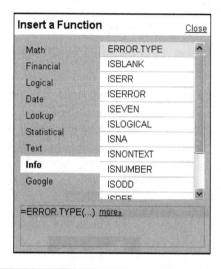

FIGURE 12-8   Choose from dozens of functions in a spreadsheet

- Click More to open a page at the Google Docs & Spreadsheets Help Center outlining the functions in detail.
- Click Close when you are finished to close the dialog box.

The function categories and examples of their use are listed in Table 12-1.

Function	Examples of Use
Math	Returns values ranging from tangents to degrees and square roots
Financial	Produces accounting values such accrued interest or asset depreciation
Logical	Generate complex calculations using If(), and(), not(), or(), and TRUE() or FALSE() functions
Date	Numbers of days, computer system date and time
Lookup	Searches for a value referenced from adjacent cells in the spreadsheet
Statistical	Returns values such as correlation coefficients and standard deviations
Text	Converts numbers to currency, capitalizes the text in a string, uses a fixed number of characters
Info	Produces values about the content of a cell, such as whether it is blank or if the contents are text or numbers
Google	GoogleFinance and GoogleLookup–specialized functions for displaying financial and other data

TABLE 12-1   Function categories in Google Spreadsheets

Did you know?

You Can Rename Your Spreadsheet's Contents

Some people simply find it difficult to equate their content with the cell addresses, such as A20 or F3. If you have a complex spreadsheet, it's often hard to keep track of areas by cell ranges. Follow these steps to divide your spreadsheet into named areas:

1. Select the cells on the spreadsheet you want to name and click Range Names on the Formulas tab to open a drop-down menu.

2. Choose Define new to open the Range Names dialog box shown below.

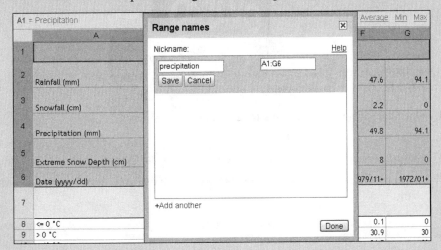

3. Type a nickname for the cell range, which is listed automatically. In the example, the range is named Precipitation and the range is A1:G6.

4. Click Save to store the information about the cell range; click Done to close the dialog box.

   Your stored ranges are listed on the Range Names drop-down menu for future selection. If you want to name more ranges, click Add Another on the Range Names dialog box to display blank nickname and cell range fields. Type the name and the cell range and click Save.

TIP

If you don't want to type the range values manually, close the dialog box and select the cells on the spreadsheet. Then, click the Range Names button on the Formulas tab and select Define New again.

NOTE   *For in-depth information on the formulas you can use, visit http://tinyurl.com/2r4slm*

Produce Charts to Display Your Data

You can display your spreadsheet data visually in Docs & Spreadsheets as different types of charts. When you publish a spreadsheet to view online it will include your charts. In addition, anyone you add as a collaborator can work with your charts. The program also lets you export an image of your chart to use offline or place into a document.

NOTE   *The charting feature is available only if you use either Firefox 1.5 and above or Internet Explorer 5.5 and above browser versions. Charts are displayed as images in other browsers, and aren't editable.*

Create a Chart

Choose one of five different types of chart displays, and several subtypes. If you wish, add column and row headings to serve as labels on the chart.

Follow these steps to create a chart:

1. Open the spreadsheet, and click the Edit tab.
2. Select the cell range to include in the chart.
3. Click the Chart button on the toolbar to display the Create Chart dialog box (see Figure 12-9).
4. Select the chart type to create. Your choices include columns, bars, lines, pie, or scatter charts.

TIP   *Choose the different chart types and subtypes to see the range of options available for data display. There are quite a few variations!*

5. Type labels for the chart in the fields. The choices vary according to the type of chart selected, and can include:

    ■ Chart Title, which displays the title of your chart, such as Inventory by Artist.

    ■ Horizontal Axis, which displays a label for the chart's horizontal axis.

    ■ Vertical Axis, which displays a label for the chart's vertical axis.

    ■ Click the Legend drop-down arrow and choose a location for the labels on the chart.

Check the data range shown in the What Data? section of the dialog box to be sure it is correct.

Click Save Chart to close the dialog box and display the chart on your spreadsheet. You can click a segment on the chart to display the values represented on the chart, as you see here.

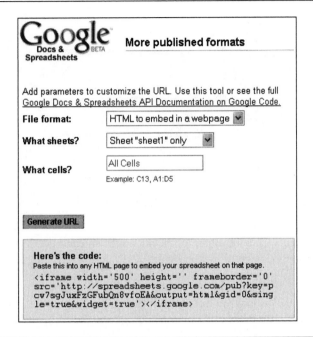

FIGURE 12-9   Configure the chart appearance in the dialog box.

TIP   *The first row and column of your selected range are listed as options for labels. In the example shown in Figure 12-9, the options are to use row 7 or column A as labels, because the selected cell range is A7:B18.*

Edit the Chart's Contents

Once you have finished a chart, you can modify its contents and appearance following these steps:

1. Click the chart image to make it active and display the Chart drop-down menu at the upper left of the chart image.

2. Select Edit Chart to open the Edit Chart dialog box, which is identical to the Create Chart dialog box. Make changes to the chart, including the type, labels, or data range.

3. Click OK to apply the changes and replace the chart on the spreadsheet.

Make Other Chart Edits

Once you have inserted a chart on your spreadsheet, you can edit other features, including:

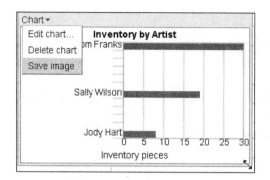

FIGURE 12-10 Relocate or resize the chart on the page as desired.

Move the Chart on the Page Click the chart to select it on the spreadsheet. Move your cursor into the gray area around the image, shown in Figure 12-10, and drag to the desired area of your spreadsheet.

Resize the Chart Move the cursor over a corner of the chart image until you see a two-ended arrow (shown in Figure 12-10). Press CTRL-SHIFT and drag from the corner to resize the chart larger or smaller.

Delete a Chart Double-click the chart you want to remove and select Delete Chart from the drop-down menu.

Export a Chart from Google Docs & Spreadsheets

You can't embed a chart directly into a Google Doc. However, you can export the chart as an image and then place it in your document. Click the chart to make it active and choose Save Image from the Chart drop-down menu. Select Save to Disk in the dialog box that displays. Click OK to download the chart as a .png image to store on your computer.

NOTE
To insert the saved chart image into a Google Doc, refer to the section "Insert Special Features" in Chapter 11.

Move and Share Content

There are some Google Docs & Spreadsheets features unique to spreadsheets. These features are used for online activity, and include:

- Inserting links in a spreadsheet
- Publishing content from a spreadsheet in HTML and other formats
- Using the Discuss option

Please refer to Chapter 11 for general information on collaborating and publishing in Google Docs & Spreadsheets.

Produce Active Links from a Spreadsheet

There are different approaches to using links in a spreadsheet, depending on how you want the viewer to see the link.

Insert the URL in a Cell

The simplest way to do this is to type the URL in the cell. When the spreadsheet cell is active, an icon displays to the left of the cell. Click the icon to open a browser window that displays the linked page.

Use Text Links in a Cell

Instead of viewing the hyperlink itself, attach the link to some text using a hyperlink formula. Select the cell you want to contain the link, and type:

=hyperlink ("*www.address*", "*Text for display*")

Here's an example:

```
=hyperlink("www.google.com","Search for it!")
```

Only the text linking to the URL displays in the cell, as you can see here. Click the text to show the pop-up icon, which is linked to the URL entered in the formula.

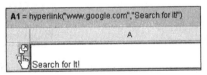

Publish Content as HTML

You can embed a spreadsheet in your blog or Web page by using the URL Generator tool.

Specify Publish Settings

Follow these steps to choose publishing settings:

1. Click Publish on the spreadsheet edit window and then click Publish Now on the tab to publish the material.

2. Choose the options from the Publish This Spreadsheet dialog box shown here. Select the check box to have the spreadsheet republished automatically when you make changes. Decide what parts you want to use, and whether or not to include all sheets in

a multipage spreadsheet or only selected sheets by choosing an option from the What Parts? drop-down menu.

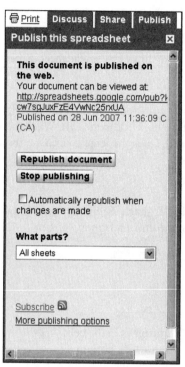

3. If the spreadsheet was published previously, click **Re-publish**.

Choose Additional Publish Features

If you want to define the output further, such as choosing different file formats, follow these steps:

1. Click More Publishing Options at the bottom of the Publish This Spreadsheet dialog box to open the More Published Formats window, shown in Figure 12-11.

2. Choose File Formats to open the drop-down menu show here.

3. To generate code that lets you place the file in a Web page, choose File Format | HTML to Embed in a Web page.

4. Select the spreadsheet content you want to embed. Choose from the entire spreadsheet, a specific sheet, or a range of cells.

FIGURE 12-11 Produce output in numerous formats.

5. Click Generate URL. The code required to view the spreadsheet information is displayed.

6. Copy and paste the code into your web page or blog. You see the content the next time you view the page online.

Chat Directly from a Spreadsheet

Google Spreadsheets offers online chat for spreadsheet users. Log in to your Chat via Gmail (refer to Chapter 5 to see how that's done). Click the Discuss tab in Google Docs & Spreadsheets to see a list of your colleagues that are currently online.

Summary

In this chapter, you saw how the spreadsheets part of Google Docs & Spreadsheets works. The program offers many features commonly used in desktop-based software, and lets you upload your existing spreadsheets or start new ones. You can configure the appearance of the spreadsheet, and rearrange content. The program offers many formulas to add functionality to your work. You can also export the content in a variety of formats for different purposes, including online use.

Coming up next, expand your presence online using Google Page Creator to build web pages.

Chapter 13

Design Websites with Google Page Creator

How to...

- Start a Page Creator site
- Insert and customize pages, text, links, and images
- Publish and unpublish content for your website
- Create and store multiple websites on Google servers

One promising program coming from Google Labs is the Page Creator, an easy-to-use web page design program. Page Creator is used online. Although there are some restrictions on the numbers of pages and types of content you can use, the available features are plenty for most of us who are interested in designing a simple site. Since it's a beta lab product, Google Page Creator isn't fully compatible with Google products, such as Blogger, and Picasa.

Start a Site

It's easy to start a new site, as long as you have a Gmail account and a current browser. Your browser needs to have JavaScript and cookies enabled.

NOTE   *You can read about testing and enabling your browser in Chapter 8.*

Sign Up for the Google Service

To add the Google Page Creator service to your Google Account, follow these steps:

1. Sign into your Google Account at https://www.google.com/accounts/Login. If you are already signed in, click More at the top of a Google page.

2. Scroll down the More Google Products page and click Labs to open the Google Labs page.

TIP   *Go directly to http://labs.google.com if you prefer.*

3. Scroll down the page, and choose Google Page Creator.

Google Page Creator automatically creates an internet address for your site, written as:

```
http://(gmail_name).googlepages.com/
```

using your Gmail account name. A home page is automatically created for you when you open Google Page Creator, shown in Figure 13-1.

Design the Site Quickly Using Program Options

Choose the page layout and visual appearance before starting a new page, for a new site, or any time you are editing an existing page. You can change both the layout and the look of the pages.

Site URL

Experimental features active

Specify site details

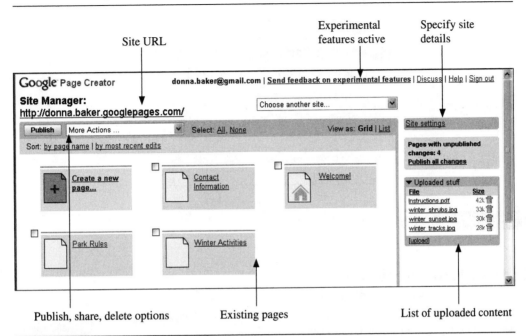

FIGURE 13-1 Google Page Creator displays the Site Manager window by default.

Publish, share, delete options

Existing pages

List of uploaded content

How to ... **Display the Page Correctly**

If you can't see the entire web page, scroll bars, or menu items check your screen resolution. The default size for Google Page Creator is 1152 X 864dpi or higher. Many of us use resolutions of 1024 X 768dpi, or even as low as 800 x 600dpi.

Instead of changing to a lower resolution screen to see the content more clearly, press F11 to hide the menus and browser interface, giving you more usable screen space. The screen displays only the page and the browser's Navigation toolbar, which may show everything you need to see.

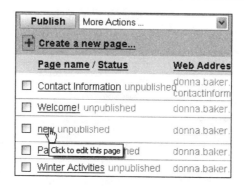

FIGURE 13-2 Site pages shown in List view

Choose a Layout for the Page

One of the first choices to make is the page layout. When the new site is started, Google Page Creator opens a dialog asking you to choose a page layout. In subsequent pages, you can make changes from the Page Editor window or in the Site Manager.

To choose a layout, follow these steps:

1. Click the page's listing in the Site Manager window (Figure 13-2) to open the Page Editor window.

NOTE *The site's page is shown in the Grid view in Figure 13-1; the layout in Figure 13-2 shows the List view: Click Grid or List to toggle the view.*

2. Click Change Layout at the upper right of the Page Editor window to display the Choose Layout window.

3. Select a layout for the page from the choices shown in Figure 13-3. Choose from:

- 1 Column Left to give you a page with a title area and a single area for content.

- 2 Columns Left to display a title area, and split the body area into content and navigation column at the left.

- 2 Columns Right to display a title area, and a split body area with the narrower column at the right.

- 3 Columns to display a title area, and the body area split into three columns of equal width.

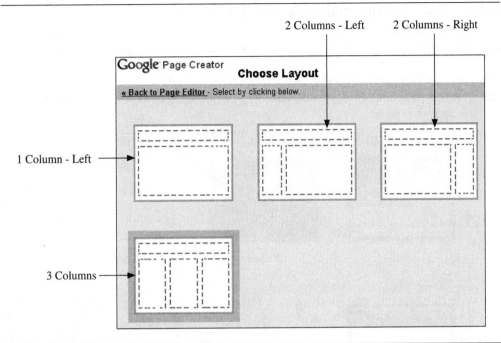

FIGURE 13-3   Choose a page layout

The layout is applied to the page and you see it in the Page Editor window, as shown here. The rectangles represent the parts of the page that you can edit.

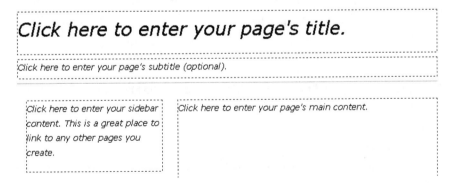

If you choose another layout having fewer columns than your original, your text may seem to disappear. It hasn't really disappeared: Return to the original layout and you see the text. Copy and paste the text to the modified location in the new layout.

NOTE

Choose a Color Scheme and Look for the Site

Your website doesn't have to remain as simple blocks of text on a white page. Google Page Creator offers a collection of different looks that you can apply to your page. Follow these steps:

1. Click Change Look at the upper right of the Page Editor window.

2. A gallery of options displays in the browser window. Scroll through the list, part of which is shown here.

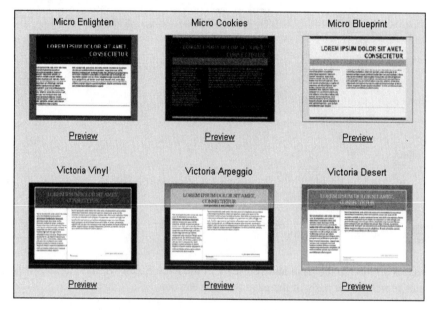

3. When you find the right look, click Select.

TIP   *At any time, click Preview to open a full-size version of a thumbnail.*

4. The appearance is applied to the page and you return to the Page Editor where you see the modified page, as in Figure 13-4.

Add Pages to the Site

Aside from the homepage, which is added automatically to a new site, it's up to you to add more pages. Follow these steps:

1. In the Site Manager, click Create a New Page.

2. An active field displays, with the default text "Your Page's Title" displayed. Type the name for the new page.

3. Click **Create and Edit**. The new page is saved and opens in the Page Editor.

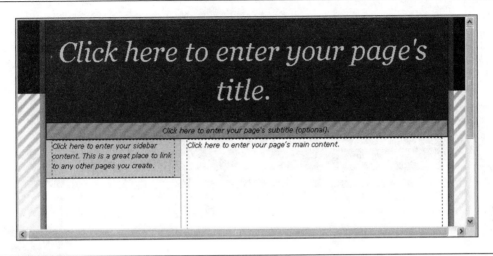

FIGURE 13-4   A look applied to a page

The new page uses the layout and look you selected; the title is shown as the page's main heading.

> **TIP**   *If you are working in the Page Editor, click Create new page at the top left corner to start another page.*

Save Your Pages

There's nothing to it! Google Page Creator automatically saves the changes you make every few minutes. When there are unsaved changes, you'll see the command for saving your progress, as well as a notation saying that there are unsaved changes at the right edge of the Page Editor toolbar. You can click the Save Now link to store the changes in your file manually.

> Unsaved 3:24pm
> [save now]

> **NOTE**   *Your googlepages site can use up to 100MB of space and up to 500 pages. An uploaded file must be less than 10MB.*

Insert and Edit Page Contents

In the Site Manager, click the name of the page you want to work with to open it in the Page Editor (Figure 13-5).

> **NOTE**   *Google Page Creator lets you add special content to pages called gadgets, which are preconfigured objects ranging from clocks to the joke of the day to horoscopes. Read how gadgets work in Chapter 8, "Create a Custom Interface."*

Return to
file list

Insert
image file

Add links

Change text
appearance

Choose heading levels

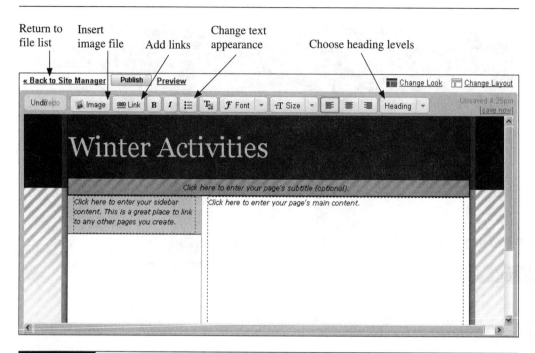

Page Editor window

How to ... Change the Program View

Is your Page Editor window different from the one shown in Figure 13-5? There is a simple
reason for that: The images and descriptions in this chapter are written using the Google
Page Creator's experimental features.

The experimental features show the toolbar across the browser window above the page
layout. If you haven't enabled the experimental features, the toolbar is shown along the
left side of the browser window. You use the same tools and the same buttons—merely a
different layout.

I find the toolbar across the top to be more efficient. Read about the experimental
features in the "Check Site Settings" section later in the chapter.

Add and Configure Text

Your page is configured when you choose a Layout. That is, a large heading style is assigned to the text at the top of the page, like the title shown in Figure 13-5, and body text is used in other areas of the page, like the columns shown in Figure 13-5. Choosing a Look for the page defines the characteristics for the text, such as the font, size, and color. In the example, the main heading is white and other text on the page is dark blue.

Select the text you want to change on the web page and then use the commands shown in Figure 13-5 to modify the default text:

- Click Bold to apply a bold face to the text for strong emphasis.

- Click Italics to apply an italic face to the text for emphasis.

- Click Bulleted List to start a bulleted list.

- Click Text Color to open a palette of color swatches and select the new color to apply to your text.

- Click the Font drop-down arrow and choose a font for the page. You can choose from one of several fonts, shown here.

NOTE   *You can only use the fonts included in the Font list. The set of fonts are those commonly used in web pages, and all display online appropriately.*

- Click the Size drop-down arrow and choose a size for the text. You can choose from Small, Normal, Large, and Huge.

TIP   *Consider using headings for changing sizes of heading text, rather than using the Size options. Use the Size settings to increase the overall size of the paragraph text, or decrease text to use as an image caption.*

- Click Left, Center, or Right buttons to set the text alignment.

- Click Heading and choose a heading size from the drop-down list. As you see here, the choices are shown as they appear on the page. What you see in the Heading list varies according to what is selected on the web page.

TIP   *If you haven't saved the file and you want to revert to an earlier setting, click Undo/Redo at the upper left of the Page Editor's toolbar.*

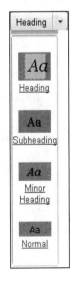

Insert Images from External Sources

The Google Page Creator offers two methods for adding images to your web page. You can either upload an image from your computer, or insert an image from a web page.

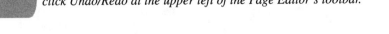

Upload and Insert an Image

To add an image from your computer to your page, follow these steps:

1. Click Image on the Page Editor toolbar. The Add an Image dialog box opens, shown in Figure 13-6.
2. Click Browse to display a Choose File dialog box. Locate and select the file or files you want to upload, and click Open.
3. Select the image to insert—you see a pale frame around the selected image.
4. Click Add Image to insert the image and close the dialog box.

TIP   *Whether you use the Add an Image method in the Page Editor window or from the Site Manager window, uploaded files are shown in the dialog box.*

Add an Online Image

The other image source you can tap into is online images. Follow these steps to locate and import an image:

1. Click Image on the Page Editor toolbar to open the Add an Image dialog box.
2. Click Web Address (URL).
3. Type the address for the image in the Image URL field, shown in Figure 13-7.
4. Click Add Image to close the dialog box and insert the image on the page.

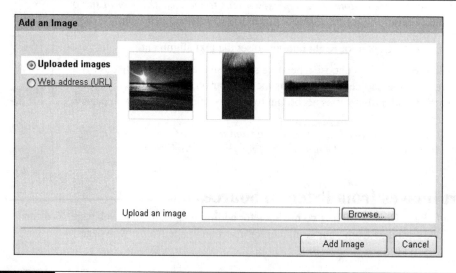

FIGURE 13-6   Options for adding images to the site

FIGURE 13-7   Locate an online image to insert on a page

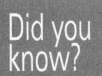 *Instead of working in the Page Editor window to upload one image at a time, use the Uploaded Stuff feature on the Site Manager window, shown in Figure 13-1. Click Upload to open a Browse window; select your file or files, and upload them all at once.*

Not All Images Are Free for the Taking

Use the image upload feature in Google Page Creator at your own risk. Your images are your own—including your own photos, illustrations, or drawings on your website is hassle-free. Images that are hosted on someone else's site aren't yours for the taking, however, and they are subject to copyright law.

If you want to use an image that belongs to someone else, e-mail the owner for permission to use the picture or drawing. You may be requested to display a notice granting you the rights to display the image or acknowledge the owner.

The same advice applies to images you find on an image bank or stock photo site. Check to see what restrictions are attached. You may have to pay a royalty fee to use the image, for example. An image displaying a copyright notice, such as:

```
Copyright © Donna L. Baker 2007, All rights reserved
```

is protected as intellectual property of the owner. Don't use the image without discussing it with the owner, and be prepared for the fact that they may refuse permission or request royalties.

Whether or not an image displays a copyright notice, the owner still holds the copyright. When in doubt, don't use the material.

FIGURE 13-8   Modify inserted images

Edit Images in Page Creator

Google Page Creator includes a nifty dialog box used for editing images that you have placed on your pages. When you insert the image on the page, the dialog box displays automatically; you can also click the image on the page to display the dialog box shown in Figure 13-8.

Basic Image Edits

Using the basic tools on the toolbar, you can:

- Click the left drop-down arrow to display options for sizing the image; Large is shown in Figure 13-8. Changing sizes is handy when your image isn't the exact size needed for your page layout.

- Click Crop to display a cropping frame on the image. Drag the resize handles to resize the cropped area, or drag the entire frame to reposition it over the image. As you see here, you can click Crop to Selection to apply the crop; or click Cancel Crop to close the cropping view and return to the regular image view and the edit dialog box. You might want to crop an image to remove background detail, making the image fit into a specific location on a page rather than changing the size.

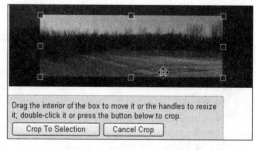

- Click the Left or Right rotate buttons to rotate the image 90 degrees counterclockwise or clockwise, respectively.

- Click Remove image to delete the image from the page.

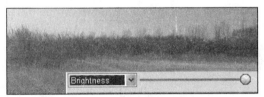

| FIGURE 13-9 | Use more editing tools |

Access More Edit Tools

On the image editing dialog box, click Show More Tools to display the drop-down menu. To apply the advanced editing features, follow these steps:

1. Click the drop-down arrow to display the choices, shown in Figure 13-9.

2. Select the command from the drop-down list.

3. Drag the slider to make the changes in the image.

Here's how to use the different commands:

Brightness   Drag the slider to the left to darken the image, or to the right to lighten it, as you see here. The example is much lighter than the original shown in Figure 13-8.

Mash-Up   Google Page Creator offers a collection of image overlays you can apply to an image. Click the right arrow to advance through the list of image choices. Drag the slider to the right to increase the opacity of the overlay.

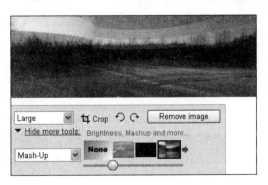

Enhance   Drag the slider to the right to adjust the contrast in the image, which makes the features stand out in contrast in the image. Images online use a lower resolution, and have less detail than those you print. You might find using the Enhance or Brightness tools help to clarify the objects in your image.

Reduce Colors   Drag the slider to the right to decrease the amount of color in the image. Dragging the slider to the far right replaces all color with shades of gray.

Sharpen   The contrast between light and dark at the edges of objects is increased, enhancing the sharpness. Try this tool if your image doesn't look as clear as it might.

Revert Edits   Return to the original image appearance before adding the special edits. Changes made using the basic editing tools (such as the size, cropping, and rotating the image) are not reversed.

TIP   *If your final image isn't as you hoped, delete the existing copy, and reinsert the image.*

Add Links for Different Uses

There are several different types of link you can use in your pages. In the Page Editor, select the text to use for the link. Click Link to open the dialog box shown in Figure 13-10.

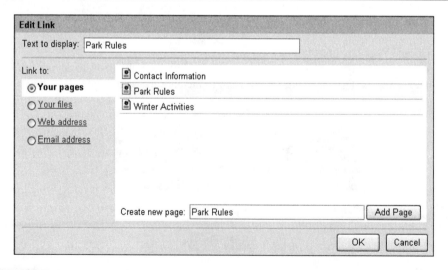

Edit Link

Text to display: Park Rules

Link to:
- ⦿ **Your pages**
- ○ Your files
- ○ Web address
- ○ Email address

📄 Contact Information
📄 Park Rules
📄 Winter Activities

Create new page: Park Rules   [Add Page]

[OK]   [Cancel]

FIGURE 13-10   Link to different types of content

Choose one of these options to create a link:

Your Pages   Select Your Pages and choose one of the existing pages in your site. The Your Pages option is shown in Figure 13-10. Click OK. Linking between pages is the basis of using a navigation system in your site.

External File   To link to a file, select Your Files to open a list of uploaded files and then choose the file you want to link from the list, like the one shown next. When a viewer clicks the link on your page, a dialog box opens asking if they would like to download or view your file.

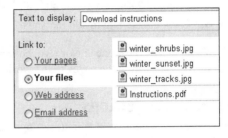

If you need to upload the file, click Browse to open the Choose File dialog box. Locate and select the file, click Open to close the dialog box and upload the file.

Web Address   If you want to link to a page on another website, click Web Address. Type the address of the page you want to link to, and then click OK.

E-Mail Address   Select Email Address and type the e-mail address to be linked. Click OK to complete the link. When your viewer clicks the link when the site is published, their default e-mail program is launched, displaying a new preaddressed e-mail message.

Manage Your Site(s)

Yes, that's "site" with an "s": You can have up to five different websites in Google Page Creator. Separate your interests, projects, and activities into separate sites. That way, when you post photos of your vacation on your family site you can send an e-mail to that group of people to let them know the pictures are ready, and won't unwittingly send e-mail notices to colleagues who are working on a team project.

NOTE   *Check out the discussion in Chapter 10 on how to extend Gmail using features such as groups.*

Add Additional Sites

To add a new site, follow these steps:

1. Click the Create Another Site link on the Site Manager.

2. Type an address for your new site in the Choose an Address field.

SHORTCUT   *There are literally hundreds of thousands of googlepages online. Be sure to use something original in the site's name to prevent wasting a lot of time finding an available name.*

3. Click Check Availability! to search the site name in googlepages.

4. Select a starting layout if you like, or add one later using the options described in the section "Choose a Layout for the Page."

5. Select a starting look or choose one later using the options described in the section "Choose a Color Scheme and Look for the Site."

6. Click Create Site to add the site to your googlepages collection.

Whether you have one site or five, be sure to check the site settings, then preview and test the site before posting the pages to the world.

Check Site Settings

Your site uses a number of default settings that you can change at any time. Click Site Settings at the upper right corner of the Site Manager to open the Settings window (Figure 13-11). When you are finished, click Back to Site Manager to return to the main Google Page Creator window.

FIGURE 13-11   Choose features for the overall site

In the Settings window, you can do all of the following tasks.

Change the Site Name   Type the name you want to display at the top of the web page after the site is published. The names of googlepages sites are fairly complex. Use a site name that's easy to read.

Review the Site URL   The URL is defined in the Site Manager, and listed on the Settings window for reference. You can't change the URL, but if you have your full complement of five sites, it helps to keep track of which site you are working with.

Optimize Images   Select the Image Upload check mark to optimize the size of uploaded images. Google Page Creator checks the files as they are uploaded, and decreases the resolution of your images if necessary for quick loading online. You don't have to remember to check and change the resolution of your images (and find the low resolution copies!) if you use the Optimize Images feature.

Participate in Experiments   Click Enable Experimental Features to display the product features currently in development. As described early in the chapter, the screen shots are taken using the Experimental features which show the Page Editor toolbar across the page, rather than down the left side of the window.

NOTE   *If you click the Enable Experimental Features button, it displays an information dialog that explains how the experimental features work and offers you the choice to continue or return to the Settings window without using the features.*

Identify Adult Content   Specify whether your site contains adult content by selecting the check box. The terms and conditions for the use of Google Page Creator include provisions for identifying your content.

Hide This Site   Select the Hide This Site check box to hide the site's pages. You can still access them as the owner, but it's a good feature to use if your site is undergoing some changes that you want to check, or aren't ready to make public.

Preview and Publish Pages

Once your pages are in order, it's time to test and publish your website. Here are some tips:

- At any time, click Preview at the top of the Page Editor window to see how a page will look online. You need to use the Preview to test some features on a site, such as the links.
- Once you've finished editing your page, click the Publish button at the top of the Site Manager or Page Editor pages.

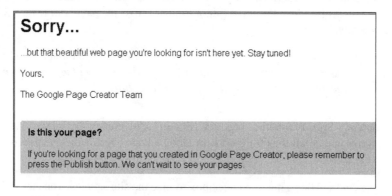

FIGURE 13-12   Notification of unpublished content

■ You can safely close your browser without losing your work if you aren't ready to publish your files. The next time you open Google Page Creator, the Site Manager shows what site content is unpublished (Figure 13-12).

■ If you open a web page that hasn't been published, the program very politely informs you of your error, as you see here.

Sorry...

...but that beautiful web page you're looking for isn't here yet. Stay tuned!

Yours,

The Google Page Creator Team

Is this your page?

If you're looking for a page that you created in Google Page Creator, please remember to press the Publish button. We can't wait to see your pages.

There are a few additional options on the Site Manager to handle your sites' pages. Follow these steps to use the commands:

1. Select the check box for the page or pages you want to modify.

2. Click the More Actions drop-down arrow at either the top or bottom of the Site Manager to open the list shown here.

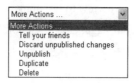

You Can Participate in a Discussion Group

Google Page Creator comes complete with a discussion group. Check it out for tips, information on using the program, and see what other users are building. The Google Page Creator discussion group is at http://tinyurl.com/eg44m.

3. Choose from the following actions:

- ■ Tell Your Friends to open an e-mail message that you can send to your associates to let them know of your new site.
- ■ Discard Unpublished Changes to delete everything from the site's pages that hasn't been published publicly.
- ■ Unpublish to remove the content of a page that was previously published.
- ■ Duplicate to create a copy of an existing page or pages you can modify for more content.
- ■ Delete to remove the selected pages from your website.

 Your unpublished page doesn't automatically disappear from the internet—it takes time for Google's search robots to scan your pages and update the content.

Summary

In this chapter, you saw how Google Page Creator helps you build up to five websites that are stored in the googlepages servers. You create new sites and manage their pages in the Site Manager. Add and configure text in the Page Editor. Insert images and other content, and use editing tools to tweak your images. Google Page Creator offers a number of features for publishing and managing your sites and pages.

In the next chapter, see how to establish an online presence using Blogger, Google's blog design and management program.

Chapter 14

Blog with Blogger

How to...

- Start a new blog
- Create and publish a blog post
- Use Dashboard to manage the blog
- Add features to blog postings
- Choose a layout and template
- Customize the appearance of your blog
- Manage the blog posts
- Use and configure AdWords to your blog

A blog is a specialized type of web page designed for easy updating and expansion. The term "blog" is short for web log. Blogs have become an important subset of the Internet and are a popular way of communicating thoughts and ideas.

In this chapter, see how the Google program Blogger is used for building your own blog site. Blogger has been a beta release since its launch in 1999, but is now a full-fledged product.

Start Your Blog

To get your blogging experience underway, open the main Blogger page at www.blogger.com/start. A Blogger blog is a service like other Google services. You can use your Google account to get started, or you can transfer an older beta Blogger site to the new program.

On the introductory page, you'll see several sections, including a sign in option, a tour, and a search feature. You'll also see an Explore feature, where you can check out the thousands of blogs listed at Blogger.

Take the Tour

Scroll down the page to the tour area, shown in Figure 14-1.

FIGURE 14-1   Take an introductory tour of Blogger and blogging.

Click Take a Quick Tour to open the first of several web pages, each describing the content and processes. Once you've read the page, click Continue to view the next topic. On the tour, read how and why blogs have become so popular. The tour also explains how blogs serve as a communication forum. You'll read an overview of templates and other features you can incorporate into your blog.

The final page of the tour states that the best way to understand blogging is to try it out, as you see here. Click Create a Blog to end the tour.

Configure Your Blog Site

The Create a Blog link is shown on the last page of the tour, and is also available from any of the tour pages, or on the main Blogger page. Starting a blog includes three steps that are shown on your browser window in a series of pages.

Create the Account

If you don't have a Google account, follow the instructions on the page to create an account and accept the terms of service. If you have a Google account, sign into your account, using the link on the page.

Once you have created or signed into your account, the second window of the creation process displays.

Name Your Blog

Naming the blog and picking an address requires a bit of creativity. Click the Help icons to the left of the form entries for the title and address shown here to open a Help window explaining how and where the information is used.

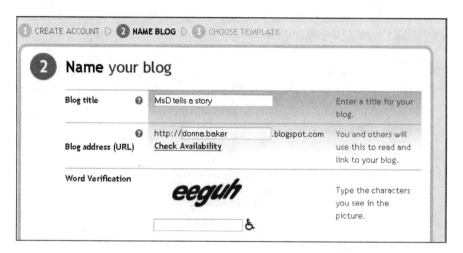

NOTE *If you want to host your blog on another server, click Advanced Blog Setup at the bottom of the screen to open further forms and information pages on configuring the blog for your server.*

Follow these steps to complete the form:

1. Type the name for your blog. Although anyone can name a blog using the same name, the blog address has to be unique. The name is shown at the top of your blog page, on the Blogger Dashboard used to manage your blog, as well as in other listings.

2. Type the name you want to use for the blog. Click Check Availability. If the name you entered isn't available, Blogger offers some suggestions, as you see here.

Did you know?

There's a Name for Those Wavy Letters You Are Asked to Type

The device used to control access to the blog address is called a *CAPTCHA*, and is shown in the example you see here. It ensures that a human is actually applying for the site, because a robot can't distinguish the wavy characters as alphanumeric characters the way humans can. CAPTCHA is an acronym for "**C**ompletely **A**utomated **P**ublic **T**uring Test to tell **C**omputers and **H**umans **A**part." The device was created and trademarked by Carnegie Mellon University.

3. Click one of the suggested names to automatically insert it in the address field. If you don't like the suggestions, keep trying until you have a name that you can use.

4. Type the verification text to confirm that you are applying for the address.

5. Click Continue to open the Choose a template page.

Select a Template

Scroll down the page and click a thumbnail to select one of several templates listed (Figure 14-2). Any of the templates can be modified later and you can also choose a different one. If you want to see a full-page sample, click Preview Template below the thumbnail to open a new window showing the layout. Click Continue when you've settled on the one you want.

NOTE *Read about choosing and configuring templates in the section "Define Your Blog's Layouts."*

The final screen explains that your blog has been created, and that you can start posting or customize its appearance. Click Start Posting to write your first post.

Your blog's address is http://[yourname].blogspot.com.

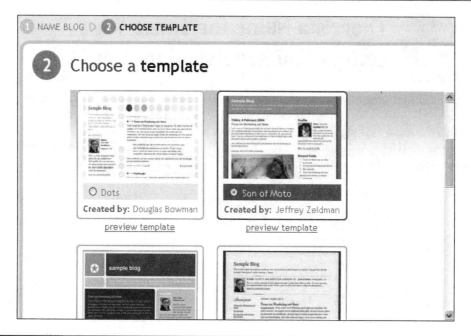

Choose a template for the blog's appearance.

Make Your First Blog Post

The new page for posting opens with a set of four tabs across the top, as shown next. You'll return to this set of pages whenever you log into your blog construction area through the Dashboard (the control window for your blog). Read about the Dashboard later in the "Use Dashboard to Manage Your Blog" section.

The Posting tab is active when your page opens. You'll see there are three sections of the page offering features for creating your post, including Create, Edit Posts, and Moderate Comments.

Create and Publish the Post Content

Creating your blog post is as simple as typing text in a document processor. Along with text, you can add items like links and images, which are described in the following section.

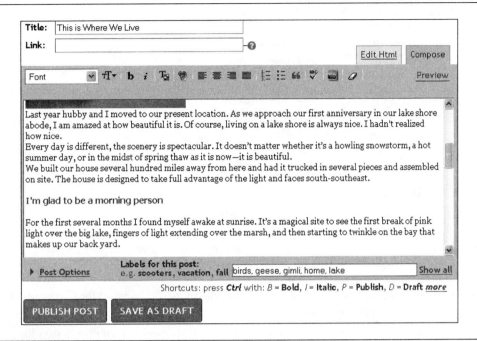

FIGURE 14-3   Add and configure the text for the post in the Create window.

Follow these steps to write and publish your basic blog post:

1. Type your title's text in the Title field. This is the heading that shows in the posting.

2. Type the text in the text area on the page. You can type the information directly, or copy and paste text from other sources into the page.

3. Once you have finished adding the text, use the tools on the Compose window to customize the appearance of the text, as you can see in the example in Figure 14-3.

4. Select the text you want to modify and then click a tool or select an option from the drop-down lists provided for the text and text color. You can:

    ■ Change the font characteristics, including choosing an alternate font from the drop-down list, choosing a larger or smaller size, adding bold or italic face, or changing the color.

    ■ Add a hyperlink to another web page.

    ■ Configure text appearances, including paragraph justification, numbered or bulleted lists, or the addition of blockquotes.

■ Perform a spell check. As you see here, when you click the Spellcheck icon, the text is scanned. Any errors are highlighted on the page; click the text to show a drop-down box listing alternate spellings.

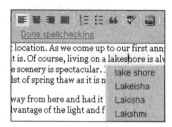

■ Insert an image on the page.

■ Remove formatting applied to selected text on the page.

Blogger doesn't include options for choosing headings as you see in Google Page Creator. Read how to build web pages in Chapter 13.

Save some time writing your posts. Along with the shortcuts shown on the Compose page, there are others you can use, including the list in Table 14-1.

5. Click Preview to open a preview window showing the content of your post in the blog page layout (Figure 14-4).

6. Click Hide Preview to return to the Compose window.

If you want to see the HTML behind the page's layout (or add some of your own), click Edit HTML; click Compose to return to the regular view.

Keystrokes	Command
CTRL-B	Bold
CTRL-I	Italic
CTRL-L	Blockquote (in HTML-mode)
CTRL-Z	Undo
CTRL-Y	Redo
CTRL/SHIFT-A	Link
CTRL/SHIFT-P	Hide/Reveal Preview
CTRL-D	Save as Draft
CTRL-S	Publish Post

TABLE 14-1   Keyboard Shortcuts to Use in Blogger.

FIGURE 14-4   View a preview of your page before posting.

7. At the bottom of the Compose window, click Post Options to open a setting for allowing or disallowing Reader Comments, Backlinks, and the time and date display, shown next.

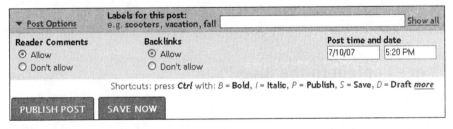

8. Add labels to the post if you like. Use the labels to categorize or search your postings later.

9. Click Publish Post to publish the post to your new blog. The time and date are included with the posting.

TIP *If you aren't ready, you can click Save Now instead and return to it later to finish. Blogger automatically saves the draft for you every few minutes.*

10. The window displays a note saying the post was published successfully. Click View Blog to display the posting in a new browser window. The page includes two links to edit the post, or to create another new post. There are more items to add to the posting, that's next.

How to ... Check the Text You Paste to a Blog Post

If you aren't familiar with XHTML or HTML you may not be interested in this tidbit. If, on the other hand, you are like me and have a need for squeaky clean code at all times, watch out for where you're getting the text you're copying and pasting into a posting. Check out this example:

```
I've spent years traveling here and traveling there. Sometimes with an urge to live
there forever (like on the shores of <st1:placetype st="on">Lake</st1:PlaceType>
<st1:placename st="on">Itza</st1:PlaceName> in <st1:country-region st="on"><st1:place
st="on">Guatemala</st1:place></st1:country-region>) and sometimes perfectly happy to
leave (like the Canadian North: It's interesting, but not for me, although I do miss
the wildness sometimes).  <p class="MsoNormal"><span style="color: rgb(51, 102, 102);
font-family: lucida grande;font-size:130%;" ><span style="font-weight: bold;">Lucky
me</span></span>
```

You can see strange bits of code such as `<st1:placetype st="on">` and `<p class="MsoNormal">` that are actually styles transported along with the text from Microsoft Word. In this case, original text in the blog posting was written in Word. There's nothing wrong with this extra code, and it certainly doesn't affect the look or function of your blog, but it doesn't belong. To fix the problem, remove the code fragments manually, or type your content in a text editor like Notepad.

Add More Content to the Blog Page

The basic blog page contains text, some of which has been modified using font and text color options. There are other features to include in the blog page, including links and images.

To return to the editing window following the path described here, click Edit Post on the window that displayed when your post was published successfully. You can also edit a post from a link on the Dashboard, described in the next section. The Edit Posts screen displays, which is identical to the Compose Screen.

Link to Other Pages or Sites

Use the linking feature in Blogger to link to other sites on your own or on other pages. The links are automatically built to open the linked content in another browser window.

Follow these steps to link to another page:

1. Open another browser window and locate the page that you want to link to. Copy the address in the URL displayed in the browser's navigation toolbar.

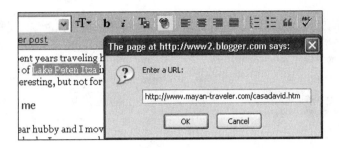

FIGURE 14-5 Paste a copied URL to form the link.

2. Select the text to use for the link on your page.

3. Click Link on the toolbar to open the dialog box shown in Figure 14-5.

4. Paste the URL into the field on the dialog box and click OK.

You can click Preview to open the formatted page in a window, but don't click your new link because it will replace the edited page in the browser window, causing you to lose your edits. Instead, wait until you are finished and have saved the edits.

Insert Images on the Blog Post

Long gone are the days when a web page might feature just one image, and more often was simply a page of text. You can upload one image at a time and specify its placement before uploading by clicking the page location to place the image. Or, as described here, pick several images and then arrange them on the post.

It's easy to add one or more images to the page, following these steps:

1. Click the location on the page where you want to add an image, and click Add Image on the toolbar to open a separate browser window, shown in Figure 14-6. You can use images from your computer, or from another location on the Web.

Images on other websites aren't yours for the taking. Click Learn More to open an information window describing fair use and how images may be copyrighted or owned by others. If you want to use an image that you have rights to use, type the URL in the field, and click Add Another Image to add a subsequent field for the URL of the next image.

2. Click Browse to open a dialog on your desktop to locate an image. Click Select to transfer the location to the Add an Image from your computer field.

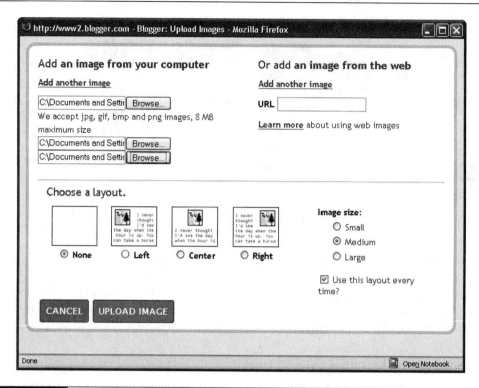

Select the images to use and specify their layout and size.

3. Click Add Another Image to activate a second Browse button. Click the button and repeat the location and selection process. Continue with as many images as you want to display on the page.

4. Choose a layout from the set of options on the page. If you aren't sure of the placement, or if you may want to use more than one placement option, select None so that you can easily position them once they are added to your blog page.

5. If you place images the same way on your pages, select the Use This Layout Every Time check box to place the images uniformly and save mouse clicks.

6. Specify a size for the images. The default size is Medium.

7. Click Upload Image. When the images have been transferred to Blogger, a message displays in the window, showing you thumbnails, as you see here. Click Done to close the browser window.

8. The image or images are added to your post in the Edit Post browser window.

Alter the Images on the Page

Imported images are placed at the top of the page. You can change the size, placement, and justification of the images once they are added to the Compose window.

Change the Image Size   Click an image to display the resize handles on the edges as you see here.

Drag a corner handle to resize the image larger or smaller proportionally and release the mouse.

Adjust the Image Placement   You can move the image vertically on the page by dragging it. If you prefer, select the image and press DELETE or CTRL-X to cut the image and place it on the clipboard. Then, move the page and position the cursor where you want to place the image. Press CTRL-V to paste it to its new location.

Modify the Image Layout   Your images use whatever horizontal layout you specified at the time of import. If you imported them using the None Placement option, make sure the image is on a line by itself, and choose a justification from the toolbar (Figure 14-7). The image can be placed at the left side, centered, or at the right of the page.

TIP   *If you don't want an image on a line by itself, you need to change the justification in the HTML view. Click Edit HTML and include* align="left", align="right" *or* align= "center" *within the* <img> *tag. If editing HTML seems like a daunting task, delete the image and upload it again.*

FIGURE 14-7   Use the justification tools to place the images horizontally on the page.

Republish the Post

If you have finished importing and organizing images, and have added all the links you need, you can click Preview to take a last look at the page. Click Publish to republish the page, complete with images and links (Figure 14-8).

You can return to a posting at any time and make edits as required.

FIGURE 14-8   Republish the page with the added images and links.

Use Dashboard to Manage Your Blog

Log in to your blog using any of the Google account dialog boxes on programs such as Gmail, at www.google.com/accounts, or at www2.blogger.com/home. The Dashboard page opens, shown in Figure 14-9.

TIP *To log into your blog you can use the basic URL at www.blogger.com. This URL will automatically redirect you to your blog.*

From the Dashboard, you can

- Change the details of your account or edit your profile.
- Create a new blog or find help on using Blogger.
- Click New Post to open the Create window and design a new posting.
- Manage your posts, including editing existing posts, discussed in the previous section. You can also configure settings for your blog, and modify the layout.

Modify Your Profile

Like other programs in the Google repertoire, you can manage your Google account settings from Blogger. Click My Account to modify your account settings, or click the Language dropdown arrow to select an alternate language for the program.

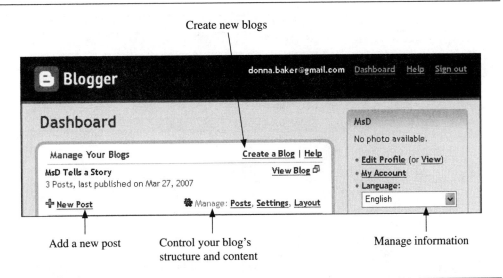

FIGURE 14-9   Control the features and content of your blog from the Dashboard.

Blogger offers a profile feature so that your blog readers can find out more about you. To configure your profile, click Edit Profile to open the Edit User Profile window.

Add as much or as little personal information as you like. The only required information is your username and display name, which you chose when you created the blog. You can include everything from your e-mail address to your birth date, from your photograph to your hobbies. Choose from a long list, a portion of which is shown here.

Click Save Profile at the bottom of the window to store the profile information. Click Dashboard at the top of the browser window to return to the Dashboard interface.

There are many ways you can configure the settings you use in Blogger, either for an individual blog or globally for any number of blogs you have created. On the Dashboard, click one of the Manage links to open the appropriate window to configure your blog.

There are three aspects to managing your blog. You can configure the settings, define the layout, and manage your site.

Configure the Blog Basics

Click the Settings tab to display the configuration tabs. The Basic tab is shown by default (Figure 14-10).

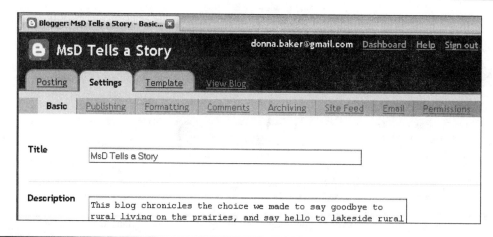

FIGURE 14-10 Configure settings for your blog in the collection of tabs.

Setting	Description
Title	Your blog title is listed as you created it; you can change its title
Description	As you see in Figure 14-10, you can type a description for the blog of up to 500 characters.
Add Your Blog to Our Listings?	Choose Yes or No to add your blog to the Blogger listings. The blog is public by default; choose No to make it private.
Show Quick Editing on Your Blog?	By default, quick edits are active so you can edit posts with a single click, as described in the section "Add Custom Content to the Blog Page."
Show E-mail Post Links?	Choose Yes to let visitors e-mail your posts to others. The option is set to No by default.

TABLE 14-2   Choose Features for the Selected Blog.

Configure Settings for Your Blogs

There are both blog-specific and global settings to choose on the Basic tab. You can have many blogs, provided you have the time to keep up with all of them! For each blog, look for these settings and options, listed in Table 14-2.

The page also includes Global Settings, applied to all your blogs. There are a couple of choices here.

Choose Compose Mode for All Your Blogs   You'll want to leave this setting as Yes, because it allows you to create your blogs visually, using toolbar buttons and commands.

Show Transliteration Button for Your Posts   Choose Yes if you want to add a button to the toolbar to convert text from English to Hindi script.

If you decide you no longer need your blog, scroll to the bottom of the page to the Delete Your Blog area. Click Delete This Blog, but be sure you are deleting the right blog! When you have finished configuring the settings, click Save Settings.

Specify Publishing Details

Click the Publishing tab to open the page. On this tab, you see details of how your blog is published that were specified when you created the blog. You can switch to your own domain from the blogspot.com domain, which is the default for the Blogger program. Also, you see your blog's name in the Blog*Spot address field shown here.

Blog*Spot Address   http:// talesofmsd .blogspot.com
Subject to availability.

If you decide to change the blog's name, you'll have to experiment to find another available name, just as you did when the site was created.

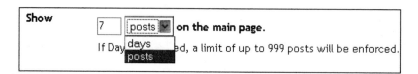

FIGURE 14-11   Define whether to use days or posts as a guide for content on the main page.

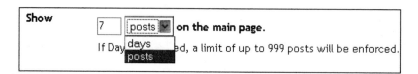

NOTE   *One option that may or may not be visible in your version of Blogger is the option to Send Pings, which is active by default. Pings are notifications made to weblogs.com. Each time you make a new posting or update an existing post, a notification is sent and distributed to those services that track blogs.*

Indicate Format Features

So far, all the blog images have shown the default formatting. However, there are quite a few options you can choose to enhance and change the way the blog's content is displayed. Click the Formatting tab, and choose from these configuration options.

Number of Posts   Choose the number of posts or days to show on the main page (Figure 14-11). By default, the blog will show seven posts on your main page. If you are a very prolific blogger, or dates are important (such as a countdown to a major family or business event) choose the date option instead.

Times and Dates   Choose from several options for configuring the dates shown and used in your blog as seen here.

Date Header Format	Wednesday, March 28, 2007 ▾ –❷
Archive Index Date Format	March 2007 ▾ –❷
Timestamp Format	3/28/2007 01:35:09 PM ▾
Time Zone	[UTC -06:00] Central Daylight Time

Specify the format of the date shown in the header, the way that the index date is shown, or the timestamp format used to show the time of a blog post. Specify your time zone and the language used for the blog.

How to ...   Offer Links with the Link Field

The Link field is a handy feature to offer your blog viewers if you often make postings that reference other postings. If you choose to show the Link field, it is displayed on the Compose window below the Title field, shown earlier in Figure 14-3.

Using the Link feature requires copying and pasting several lines of code into your template's code view. You can read about using links between posts in the Blogger help at http://tinyurl.com/3e3ums.

Visual Features   There are four features you can choose for configuring the appearance of content on the blog post, including the following:

- You can substitute a manual line break in the Compose window with a `<br />` HTML tag, or substitute two manual line breaks with two `<br />` tags. The default is to convert the line breaks, which produces the appearance of a new paragraph on your post, shown in Figure 14-12.

- You can choose Yes or No to display the Title field, which is shown by default.

- You can choose Yes or No to show the Link field, which is shown by default.

- You can choose Yes or No for enabling float alignments. In XHTML, a `<div>` tag can be placed around an object allowing you to specify how the object is displayed horizontally on the page. The default is No.

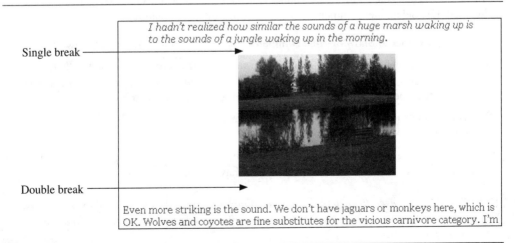

FIGURE 14-12   Use breaks to divide content on your blog post.

Manage Viewer Comments

Comments are replies that viewers make to your posts. Some can be very entertaining, but unfortunately there are a lot of spam comments as well, many of which simply list dozens of URLs to other real or fictitious locations, like the example shown next.

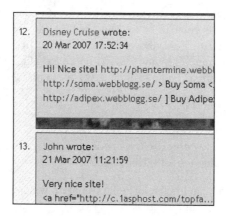

If you want your viewers to add comments, you can provide a template for the appearance of their comments that is included in your blog's code view. Read how to use a template at http://tinyurl.com/2vue6h.

For most people, using the comment defaults provided by Blogger is sufficient. To write a comment, click the Comments link at the bottom of the posting to open the Comment Input window. You'll see any existing comments listed at the left; type in the Leave Your Comment field to add a new comment (Figure 14-13).

Of course, you can change the way comments behave and appear. Return to the Dashboard, and click Settings. Select the Comments tab and choose from these features:

- Specify whether to Show or Hide comments. By default comments can be viewed.
- Decide who can comment. Click the Who Can Comment? drop-down list and then choose from Only Registered Users (anyone with a Blogger or Google account), Anyone, or Only Members of This Blog to restrict commenting to a selected group.
- Set a default for whether new posts have commenting or not. By default, comments are allowed.
- Choose whether to show or hide Backlinks, which display another hyperlink on your page. Also, specify whether new posts should have Backlinks or not.

Backlinks are used to keep track of other blogs that are linked to your posts. If someone references a post on your blog, the backlink offers a way for readers to find out how other posters have referenced your blog post.

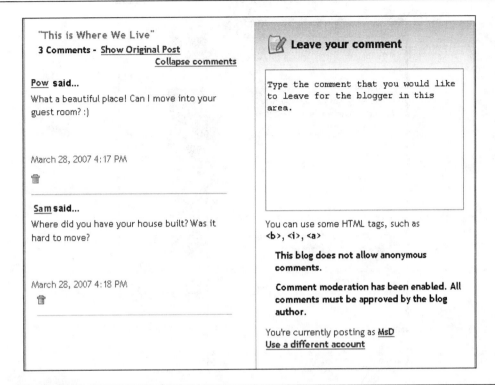

FIGURE 14-13 Review existing comments and add new ones in the window.

- Choose a Comments Timestamp Format from the drop-down list.
- Select Yes or No to show your comments in a pop-up window, like the example seen in Figure 14-14. By default, pop-ups are set to No.

 Many people have pop-up windows disabled on their computers and won't see your comments or the window for inserting a new comment.

One final group of Comment tools helps you block comment spam. Look for these settings:

- Enable Comment Moderation to have comments held in your Blogger site until you review them. Type your e-mail address to receive copies of these comments, which you can then accept or reject.
- Choose Yes or No for the Show Word Verification for Comments option, which requires the user to type text seen on the screen in order to submit their comment.

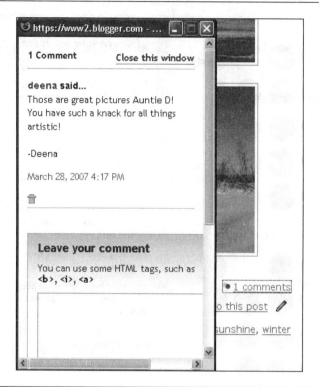

FIGURE 14-14   Comments can be read and written in a pop-up window.

- Choose Yes or No for the Show Profile Images on Comments setting to display an image of someone who has commented; the default is Yes.

- Type an e-mail address in the Comment Notification Address field to have comments sent to you by e-mail so you can monitor them for spam.

Archive Older Postings

Click the Archiving tab on the Settings window to display the options. There are only two options for *archiving,* or storing your older postings. The default frequency for Blogger is Monthly. Click the Archive Frequency drop-down arrow and choose to archive Daily, Weekly, or Never if you prefer.

The second archiving feature deals with Post Pages, which are enabled by default. Each of your blog postings is given a complete URL, known as a *permalink,* rather than being included in a single archive page. The post page includes comments.

TIP   *Be sure to leave the Post Pages feature active if you reference pages on your blog often. That way, your readers can easily locate the information you are referring to.*

The page names are composed of the site, date, and page title. For example, http://talesofmsd.blogspot.com/2007/03/this-is-where-we-live.html refers to the post made in March entitled "This is Where we Live."

To see the permalink for a page, click its name in the archive listing on your blog page and read the address in the Navigation bar at the top of the browser window.

Specify Site Feeds

A feed is way of distributing content from your postings to other websites and tools. Feeds are *syndicated*, meaning that the published blog post automatically generates machine-readable content that is picked up by syndication tools such as newsreaders or aggregators.

A visitor to your site can click the Subscribe To: Posts (Atom) link at the bottom of your posts. Read more about syndication and newsreaders in Chapter 5.

Click the Site Feed link from the Settings tab of the Dashboard to display the options. The default shows the Basic Mode. Click the Allow Blog Feed drop-down arrow and choose an option for the amount of your content inserted into the blog feed. You can choose Full, which syndicates the entire content, Short to syndicate the first 255 characters or first paragraph, or None to not include content aside from the link information.

You can also move into an Advanced Mode to define feeds for the posts, comments, and the number of comments as separate items.

TIP *If you are operating a commercial blog, consider using a Feed Item Footer. The footer is text that is attached to each post in your Site Feed. The content can include contact or advertising information, AdSense for Feeds, or other advertising. Type the text in the Feed Item Footer, or paste code for an advertising feed program.*

Manage E-mail

There are two types of e-mail to configure in Blogger. You can specify that an e-mail message is sent to you every time a post is published on your blog, or configure an address to automatically send posts to your blog via e-mail. Click the E-mail link on the Dashboard's Settings tab to display the options.

Suppose you are working on a team project and have three or four members, all of whom are posting to the blog. To prevent duplication and save time, consider the BlogSend feature. Type an e-mail address in the BlogSend Address field that is used to forward a copy of your blog to you whenever you have published a post.

The Mail-to-Blogger Address feature is a handy way to keep your posts up to date. If you are traveling, you might have time to work on your e-mail every few days, but it's harder to make the effort to log into a blog account, too. Send postings to your blog automatically.

The address used to send e-mail directly to your blog includes a longer address string (Figure 14-15). It's important to maintain the privacy of the address to prevent anyone from posting to your blog.

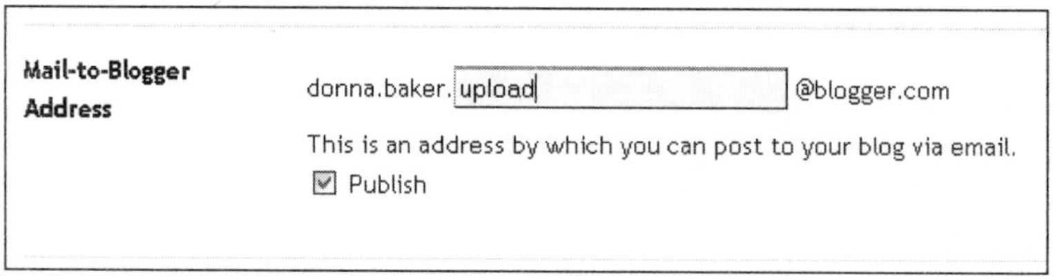

> Mail-to-Blogger
> Address
>
> donna.baker. upload   @blogger.com
>
> This is an address by which you can post to your blog via email.
> ☑ Publish

FIGURE 14-15 Expand your basic address to include a confidential component for blogging from your e-mail.

Mail-to-Blogger does not support images or other attachments. Blogger mobile supports images from camera phones. Read about Blogger Mobile at http://tinyurl .com/zvdyh.

Select Publish to automatically publish the posts. If you deselect the check box, your posts are saved in your Blogger account, but you have to log into Blogger to publish them.

When you use the Mail-to-Blogger feature, the subject of the e-mail is the title, and the body of the e-mail is the actual post.

Many e-mail programs attach advertising or other content at the end of the message. To make sure that doesn't show up on your blog, when you finish the post type #. When Blogger transfers the content to your blog, it stops when it sees the # sign.

Set Permissions for Authoring and Reading

The Permissions tab includes two settings that are tailor-made for different types of work (or play). You can either add more authors, or specify a list of readers for your blog.

If you are attending a conference with some colleagues and want to keep your coworkers apprised of the goings on, add additional authors to the blog. You can do this by following these steps:

1. Click Add Authors to open a text field.

2. Type the e-mail address of the person or persons you want to add.

3. Click Invite to send e-mail invitations and close the Invite field.

4. On the Permissions tab, you now see an open invitation, like the one shown in Figure 14-16.

There are many instances in which you might not want the contents of your blog read by the public at large. For example, you might be at the aforementioned conference, but have insights for your colleagues that you don't want your competitors to get wind of. On the fun side of things, you might be off on your honeymoon, and want a select group of friends and family to be able to read your posts.

Invite others to author posts to the blog.

To restrict access to the blog by specifying blog readers, follow these steps:

1. Click Only People I Choose in the Who can View this Blog? choice (shown in Figure 14-16).

2. Click Add Readers to open a text field.

3. Type the e-mail addresses of those you want to read the blog and click Invite to close the text field and return to the Permissions tab.

4. Those you have invited are shown in the Blog Readers section of the tab.

Define Your Blog's Layouts

When you start a blog you are required to choose one of a small list of templates. Your page is laid out in a single way, with only Archive and About Me elements displayed on the blog. You are given a specific set of colors to use. That's fine when you are a newbie, but over time you'll likely want to customize the appearance of your blog.

The Template tab offers four categories of features you can use for configuring your blog, shown here. These include adding page elements, choosing fonts and colors, editing the HTML, and picking a template.

Pick a Template

It's easiest to pick a template first, and then look at color schemes and page elements. Click Pick New Template on the Template tab to open a window containing templates similar to those you chose from when you originally built your blog site. Many of the templates have color and font variations like the example shown here. Click the buttons below each template to see the alternate templates.

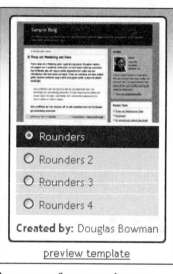

Once you have made your choice, click Save Template to apply it to your blog.

 *You can find dozens of templates and other page elements at blogger-templates.blogspot.com/*

Add and Adjust Page Elements

Click the Page Elements link to open the tab. Page elements are features that are added to the page to provide more tools and resources for you and your readers. The default page layout elements include the Blog Archive list and the About Me features.

If you change from one template to another, the page elements are maintained, although their layout may be different on the page. Click the different fields on the page layout to open choices for configuring the contents (Figure 14-17).

Keep these tips in mind as you configure the layout on the page:

Add Specific Content You can add specific types of content to different areas of the page according to the selected template. For example, the template shown in Figure 14-17 shows the margin elements such as the archive and labels at the right, and the blog posts at the left. The example used earlier in the chapter uses a reverse layout with the posts at the right and page elements at the left.

Insert Additional Elements You don't have to add any more elements to the page if you prefer the clean look of the basic templates. If you want to add more content (such as the Labels element shown in Figure 14-17), click Add a Page Element to open the Choose a New Page

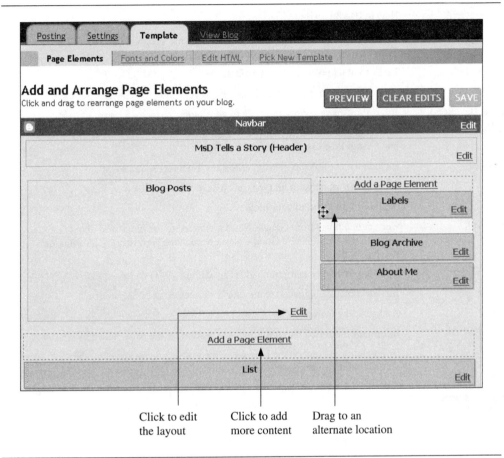

Posting | Settings | **Template** | View Blog

Page Elements | Fonts and Colors | Edit HTML | Pick New Template

Add and Arrange Page Elements
Click and drag to rearrange page elements on your blog.

PREVIEW | CLEAR EDITS | SAVE

Navbar   Edit

MsD Tells a Story (Header)   Edit

Blog Posts   Add a Page Element

                                        Labels   Edit

                                        Blog Archive   Edit

                                        About Me   Edit

                                 ➤ Edit

Add a Page Element

List   Edit

Click to edit   Click to add   Drag to an
the layout   more content   alternate location

FIGURE 14-17   Specify the elements and features on your blog page.

Element window. You can add many features, listed in Table 14-3. Click Add To Blog to include the new element.

Edit Page Elements   Each element on the page can be edited. Click Edit to open a pop-up window that offers choices depending on your selection. Figure 14-18 shows the Edit window for the blog posts. You see a list of items that can be selected or deselected to display on the page.

At the bottom of the window, you can drag some of the elements to reorder the display on the page, also shown in Figure 14-18.

Page Element	How to Use It
AdSense	Display ads on your blog page using the AdSense program (see the sidebar "How To: Insert AdSense Ads on Your Blog")
Blog Archive	Links to older posts, added by default
Feed	Add content from an Atom or RSS feed to your blog
HTML/JavaScript	Insert third-party scripts and code to your blog
Labels	Show the labels used in your posts (Labels are mentioned in the section "Edit and Search Post Lists")
Link List	Include lists of links to your favorite sites, references, and so on
List	Include lists of items of all types, such as movies or books
Logo	Add a Blogger logo to your blog
Newsreel	Current headlines from Google News are added to the blog (read about Google News in the section "Use Google News to Manage Newsworthy Information" in Chapter 5).
Page Header	The blog title and description, added by default
Picture	Include a picture uploaded from your computer or an online source
Poll	Add a survey feature
Profile	Information inserted into the About Me section on the page, added by default
Text	Insert additional text on the blog page like a welcome message or other description of your blog
Video Bar	Lets visitors view YouTube and Google Video clips directly from the blog page

TABLE 14-3   You Can Include Different Features on Your Blog Pages.

Choose Fonts and Colors

Click the Fonts and Colors link to display the palettes. The color palettes include the set of colors from your template, as well as another set of colors that match your blog, handy for those who have difficulties with color choices. If you prefer, choose another color from the More colors palette.

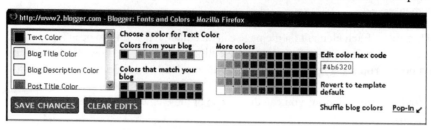

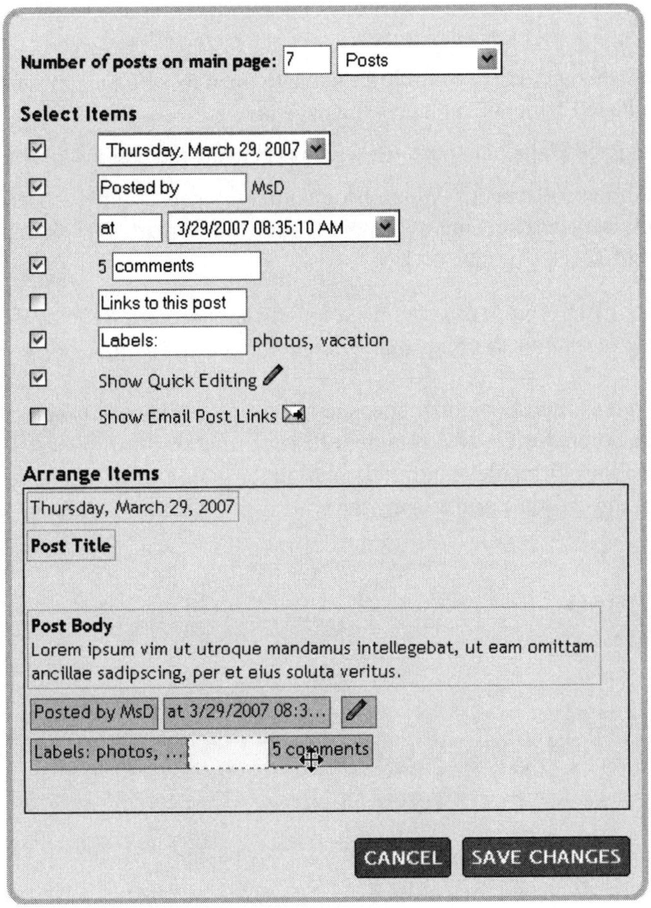

FIGURE 14-18 Configure the layout of the page elements, such as blog posts.

How to ... Insert AdSense Ads on Your Blog

You can use AdSense advertising to help make money for your website, as described in Chapter 7. Blogger lets you use the same technology to insert Google AdSense ads on your blog.

Here's how you do it:

1. From the Dashboard, click your blog's name to open its settings tabs and then click Template | Page Elements to display the page layout.

2. Click Add a Page Element to open the window showing the options listed in Table 14-3.

3. Click the AdSense element's Add to Blog button to open a window. Here you can create a new AdSense account by simply typing your e-mail address in the E-mail Address field. Click Continue.

> **TIP** *Click Sign In to sign into your existing account. Refer to Chapter 7 to learn how to create and configure a new account.*

4. The Configure AdSense window opens next. As you see here, you can choose the Format and Colors for the ads from their respective drop-down boxes. The colors are based on the color palette currently chosen for your blog. The Preview shows a sample of the chosen Format using the chosen color scheme.

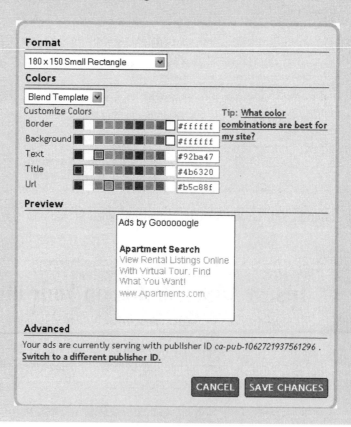

5. When you have made your selections, click Save Changes to close the window, returning you to the Page Elements page.

6. Reposition your AdSense element as desired on the page.

7. Click Preview to open another browser window, showing the page and the ads (Figure 14-19).

8. Close the Preview browser window to return to the Page Elements window. Once you are finished, click Save to include the AdSense feature in your blog.

9. Check the e-mail inbox for the address specified in your AdSense application and follow the instructions in the e-mail.

10. When your blog has been approved, your ads will start to show on your blog posts.

NOTE *Unlike ads inserted on your web page using AdSense, you can only insert one ad unit in Blogger.*

TIP *If you need a color to match another element, such as your logo, open your file in your image editing or illustration program and sample the color you want to match. Find the color hex code in your program's color palette and type it in the Edit Color Hex Code field.*

Scroll down the list at the left of the palette to display the font elements on your page, and click an element you want to change. The palette changes to a set of font features, including the family, size, and style (Figure 14-20).

When you have finished modifying the colors and fonts, click Save Changes to incorporate the changes into your template.

NOTE *The Fonts and Colors palettes can be popped out of the page. By default, the palettes are nested above your blog page so you can view your color changes. Click Pop-Out to separate the palettes from the window.*

FIGURE 14-19   Review the placement, layout, and color scheme for the ads.

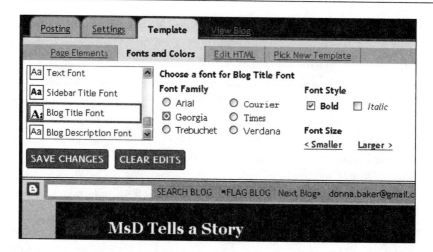

FIGURE 14-20   Specify the characteristics for the text on your blog.

Edit the HTML

If you aren't content with the features on the blog template, and are comfortable using HTML and CSS, click Edit the HTML to display the page, shown in Figure 14-21.

On the Edit the HTML page, you can

- Download a copy of the blog's template.
- Upload your own template.
- Edit the content in the template.
- Find and replace code in the blog template (such as the background image pointed out in Figure 14-21).
- Open the templates that are included for *widgets*, the features added to the blog.

If you make changes to the template, be sure to preview and save the changes. Of course, if you don't like the results, you can always reapply the template.

Hand coding isn't for the faint of heart. Click Learn More to open a Help window at http://tinyurl.com/295vg5 that explains how the templates are coded.

Manage Posts

The final group of tasks is used for managing your posts. Click Manage: Posts on the Dashboard, or click the Posting tab in the tabs to display three panes, including Create, Edit Posts, and Moderate Comments.

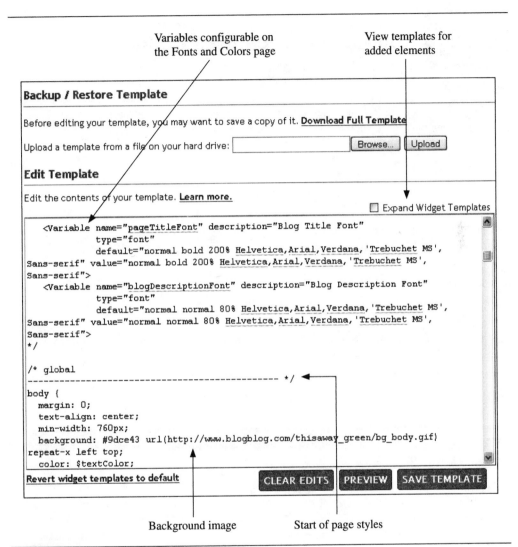

Variables configurable on
the Fonts and Colors page

View templates for
added elements

Backup / Restore Template

Before editing your template, you may want to save a copy of it. **Download Full Template**

Upload a template from a file on your hard drive: [   ]   [Browse...] [Upload]

Edit Template

Edit the contents of your template. **Learn more.**

☐ Expand Widget Templates

```
    <Variable name="pageTitleFont" description="Blog Title Font"
          type="font"
          default="normal bold 200% Helvetica,Arial,Verdana,'Trebuchet MS',
Sans-serif" value="normal bold 200% Helvetica,Arial,Verdana,'Trebuchet MS',
Sans-serif">
    <Variable name="blogDescriptionFont" description="Blog Description Font"
          type="font"
          default="normal normal 80% Helvetica,Arial,Verdana,'Trebuchet MS',
Sans-serif" value="normal normal 80% Helvetica,Arial,Verdana,'Trebuchet MS',
Sans-serif">
*/

/* global
-------------------------------------------------- */
body {
  margin: 0;
  text-align: center;
  min-width: 760px;
  background: #9dce43 url(http://www.blogblog.com/thisaway_green/bg_body.gif)
repeat-x left top;
  color: $textColor;
```

Revert widget templates to default

[CLEAR EDITS] [PREVIEW] [SAVE TEMPLATE]

Background image

Start of page styles

FIGURE 14-21   Edit the template manually.

Create a New Post

Click the Create tab to open the same input page as shown in Figure 14-3, and described in the
section "Create and Publish the Post Content."

Edit and Search Post Lists

Your Blogger posts aren't static items. That is, you can edit, review, or delete any of your posts at
any time on the Edit Posts tab, shown in Figure 14-22.

You Can Edit Features Right from a Blog Page

On a blog page, click the tool icon below an element on the page to open settings for editing and configuring the object, such as the Archive or About Me objects.

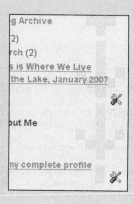

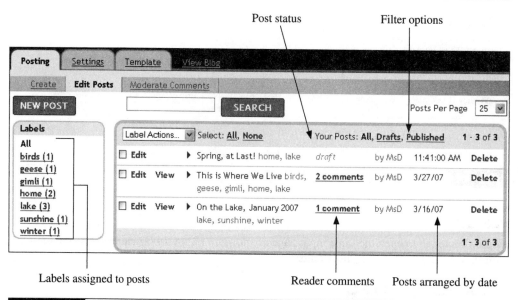

Post status   Filter options

Labels assigned to posts   Reader comments   Posts arranged by date

FIGURE 14-22   Work with your blog's posts.

Here are some maintenance and organizing tasks you can use:

- Edit, view, or delete an existing post.
- Open a draft to complete its editing, or delete it.
- Sort posts by All (default), Drafts, or Published status.
- Add, change, or remove labels that can be used for sorting or locating content in your posts.
- Type a term in the Search field and click Search to locate content in a post.

Moderate Comments

Comments added to your posts that you want to review before allowing them are listed in the Moderate Comments tab. In order to use the feature, you must have Enable Comment Moderation selected in the Comments pane of the Settings tab. Read how to do that in the section "Manage Viewer Comments."

Summary

This chapter showed you how to work with Blogger. You saw the necessary steps to create a blog and make a posting. Editing posts and working with other content such as images and links was covered. You walked through the Blogger Dashboard, an interface that offers access to the configuration features of the program. You saw how to modify a profile, how to adjust and customize the way your blog appears, and how readers can interact with your posts. You learned numerous ways to customize the appearance and content of your blog, and how to maintain the postings and site.

Coming up next—it's all up to you! You may choose to move full speed ahead into Google products and services, or use a combination of your existing desktop methods with some Google tools. Either way, you are sure to find products that make your work, online explorations, and communications simpler and more effective using Google tools.

Index

Description field, 78
Description setting, 401
descriptions, My Maps, 82–84
Desktop, 264–267
Destinations feature, 75
Detail area, 108
directions, driving, 73–74
Directions link, 76
Directions tab, 116–119
Directions view, 76
Directory, 57–59
directory listings, 112–116
Discuss option, 360
discussion groups, 383. *See also*
  Google Groups
Docs & Spreadsheets home page, 324, 342
Docs list, 318, 319, 320, 321, 324, 325, 346
documents. *See* Google Docs & Spreadsheets
Documents Edit page, 339
Domain drop-down list, 22
downloads
    AdSense reports, 231
    Gmail Contacts Lists, 283
    Google Earth, 96–97
    Google Talk, 164–165
Drafts category, 293
drifting, 103
Drive link, 75
driving directions, 73–74

E

Edit Color Hex Code field, 415
Edit HTML tab, 416
Edit My Membership page, 142
Edit page, 411
Edit Picture screen, Picasa, 185–196
    adjusting preview, 186–187
    correcting image flaws, 187–190
    Effects tab, 192–195
    overview, 185–186
    saving and exporting edited images, 195
    Tuning tools, 190–192

Edit Post browser window, 397
Edit Posts screen, 394
Edit Posts tab, 417–419
Edit tab, 342, 358
Edit This Personalized Page form, 149
Edit toolbar, 325, 326, 327
Edit User Profile window, 400
Edit window, 342, 349, 411
editing
    Blogger, 418
    Google Docs & Spreadsheets, 325–329,
      359–360
    image editing tools, 376–377
Editing section, 321
Editing window, 325
Effects tab, 186, 192–195
Element window, 411
Elevation Exaggeration value, 108
Elevation key, 91
e-mail. *See also* Gmail
    custom AdSense reports, 234–239
    Google Docs & Spreadsheets files,
      322–323
    sending Picasa photos by, 200
Enable Experimental Features button, 381
entertainment, searches for, 41–45
events, Google Calendar, 301–304,
  309–314
Excel format (XLS), 26, 318, 354
Exchangeable Image File (EXIF) format, 180
Exclude operator (–), 25
EXIF (Exchangeable Image File) format, 180
Exit Slideshow tool, 184
Explore feature, 386
Explore Groups section, 132
exporting
    charts from Google Docs &
      Spreadsheets, 360
    files from Google Docs &
      Spreadsheets, 343
    from Gmail Contacts List, 282–283
    images, Picasa, 195